WORKSHOPS IN COMPUTING

Series edited by C. J. van Rijsbergen

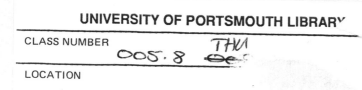

Also in this series

continued on back page...

B. Thuraisingham, R. Sandhu and T.C. Ting (Eds.)

Security for Object-Oriented Systems

Proceedings of the OOPSLA–93
Conference Workshop on Security for
Object-Oriented Systems, Washington DC,
USA, 26 September 1993

Published in collaboration with the
British Computer Society

BCS

Springer-Verlag
London Berlin Heidelberg New York
Paris Tokyo Hong Kong
Barcelona Budapest

B. Thuraisingham, PhD
The MITRE Corporation
Burlington Road, Bedford
MA 01730, USA

R. Sandhu, PhD
ISSE Department, George Mason University
Fairfax, VA 22030, USA

T.C. Ting, PhD
School of Engineering,
University of Connecticut,
Storrs, CT 06268, USA

ISBN 3–540–19877–6 Springer-Verlag Berlin Heidelberg New York
ISBN 0–387–19877–6 Springer-Verlag New York Berlin Heidelberg

British Library Cataloguing in Publication Data
A catalogue record for this book is available from the British Library

Typesetting: Camera ready by contributors
Printed by Athenæum Press Ltd., Newcastle upon Tyne
34/3830-543210 Printed on acid-free paper

Contents

Part IV: Multilevel Applications, Systems, and Issues

Security for Object-Oriented Systems: An Editorial Overview

Bhavani Thuraisingham
The MITRE Corporation
Bedford, MA 01730

Ravi Sandhu
George Mason University
Fairfax, VA 22030

T. C. Ting
University of Connecticut
Storrs, CT 06269

1. Introduction

Object-oriented systems are gaining increasing popularity due to their inherent ability to represent conceptual entities as objects, which is similar to the way humans view the world. This power of representation has led to the development of new generation applications such as Multimedia information processing, Artificial Intelligence, CAD/CAM, and Process control systems. In addition to the power of representation, object-oriented approaches are also being used to design software components and to interconnect heterogeneous database systems.

However, the increasing popularity of object-oriented systems should not obscure the need to maintain security of operation. That is, it is important that such systems operate securely in order to overcome any malicious corruption of data as well as to prohibit unauthorized access to and use of classified data. For applications such as C4I (command, control, communications, and intelligence), it is also important to provide multilevel security. Consequently, multilevel secure object-oriented systems are needed in order to ensure that users cleared to different security levels access and share a database with data at different security levels in such a way that they obtain only the data classified at or below their level. Recently several research efforts have been reported on incorporating multilevel security into object-oriented systems. In addition, much work has also been done on incorporating discretionary security into object-oriented systems. With discretionary security, users are granted access to the objects based on their identification. Many commercial products enforce some discretionary access control measures.

In order to promote the exchange of ideas on security for object-oriented systems between the security community and object-oriented community, we organized the OOPSLA 93 Conference Workshop on Security for Object-oriented Systems. This was the first workshop on security to be part of an ACM (Association of Computing Machinery) OOPSLA (Object-Oriented Programming Systems, Languages, and Applications) Conference. Participants at this workshop were from France, Germany, Greece, Italy, United Kingdom, and the United States. It consisted of four sessions with each session having four papers. The papers were published in the workshop proceedings and distributed at the workshop. Following the paper presentations, there was a discussion session. In section 2, we summarize the papers presented at the workshop and the discussions that took place. Enhanced versions of these papers are published in this book.

One of the main concerns that resulted from this workshop was the role of the object-oriented approach in designing and developing secure systems. That is, is the object-oriented approach better for secure systems than the traditional non object-oriented approach? Some issues on this topic are discussed in section 3. An overview of the papers published in this book is given in section 4. Related references and activities are listed in section 5. Acknowledgements are listed in section 6.

2. Summary of the Workshop

The first session was on applications and systems and consisted of four papers. The first paper by George Pangalos is entitled: *Integrating Object-Oriented Technology and Security in Medical Database Systems*. It was presented by George. It describes the application of object-oriented technology in the healthcare system and shows how this technology could help provide better security for such systems. George also described the various medical information systems that have been developed in Europe. The second paper by Barry Bird is entitled; *The Security Facilities of PCTE*. It was presented by Barry. It describes an existing object management system called PCTE which has several security features. It was stated that PCTE has been standardized by the European Computer Manufactures Association. Mandatory access control, discretionary access control, and administrative features were described by Barry. The third paper by Karin Vosseberg, Peter Brossler, and J.L. Keedy is entitled: *A Base for Secure Object-Oriented Environments*. It was presented by Karin. It describes a base protection mechanism for an object-oriented environment upon which different security models can be constructed. In particular, the support of the specification of access based on the right to invoke interface routines is discussed. The fourth paper by James (Jim) Talvitie is entitled: *Object Model for Security System*. It was presented by Jim. It describes a set of roles to be played by the object classes of an object-oriented security system. As stated in the paper, many of the ideas have been influenced by POSIX and DCE.

The second session was on multilevel secure systems and consisted of four papers. The first paper by N. Boulahia-Cuppens, F. Cuppens, A. Gabillon, and K. Yazdanian is entitled: *Techniques to Handle Multilevel Objects in Secure Object-Oriented Databases*. It was presented by Gabillon. It describes how multilevel entities could be supported in an object-oriented database. Two alternatives are proposed and mappings to single-level entities are discussed. The second paper by Sarbari Gupta is entitled: *Object-Oriented Security in the Trusted Mach Operating Systems*. It was presented by Sabari. It describes the object-oriented features of the Trusted Mach (trademark of Trusted Information Systems) operating system. The essential features of the design are the message-oriented client-server model and heavy usage of layering, modularity, abstraction, and information hiding. The third paper by Elisa Bertino, Sushil Jajodia, and Pierangela Samarati is entitled: *Enforcing Mandatory Access Controls in Object-Oriented Databases*. It was presented by Pierangela. This paper focusses on how multilevel entities could be modelled as single-level entities. It also describes issues on object updates and secure garbage collection. The fourth paper by Ciaran Bryce is entitled: *Information Flow Control in Object-Oriented Programs*. It was presented by Ciaran. It describes security for parallel object-oriented languages. It also examines how coarse-grained policies may be expressed in the security model framework.

The third session was on authorization and access control and consisted of four papers. The first paper by Eduardo Fernandez, Maria Larrondo-Petrie, and Ehud Gudes is entitled: *A Method-based Authorization Model for Object-Oriented Databases*. It was presented by Eduardo. It describes an authorization model for object-oriented databases where access constraints are defined in terms of methods. A notion called implied authorization is applied along the data hierarchy and a set of policies for generalization, aggregation, and relationship are developed. The second paper by Steven Demurjian and T.C. Ting is entitled: *Shouldn't the Object-Oriented Paradigm Influence and Guide the Approach for Security*. It was presented by T.C. It agues whether one should really look at security for object-oriented systems or whether the object-oriented paradigm should influence security. It favors the latter and continues to give reasons for it. The third paper by Ciaran Bryce is entitled: *An Access Control Model for Parallel Object-Oriented Languages*. It was presented by Ciaran. It describes an access control model for parallel object-oriented languages. In particular, the constraints that are needed for security are described and subsequently a protection model is given. The fourth paper by Elisa Bertino and Pierangela Samarati is entitled: *Research Issues in Discretionary Authorizations for Object-Oriented Databases*. It was presented by Pierangela. It discusses the developments in discretionary security for object-oriented systems and describes a set of research issues. In particular issues on administration, propagation, and various types of authorizations are given.

The fourth session was on multilevel applications, systems, and issues and consisted of four papers. The first paper by Myong Kang, Oliver Costich, and Judith Froscher is entitled: *Using Object-Modeling Techniques to Design MLS Data Models*. It was presented by Oliver. It describes the approach to database development and shows how Rumbaugh et al's OMT methodology could be used to generate multilevel relational database schema. The second paper by William (Bill) Herndon is entitled: *Can we do without Monotonically Non-decreasing Levels in Class Hierarchies?* It was presented by Bill. It states that many of the secure object-oriented data models assume that the security classifications applied to classes are monotonically nondecreasing. It argues that this assumption is not really necessary and gives examples to support the arguments. The third paper by

Roshan Thomas and Ravi Sandhu is entitled: *Concurrency, Synchronization, and Scheduling to Support High-Assurance Write-up in Multilevel Object-based Computing*. It was presented by Roshan. It describes concurrency, synchronization, and scheduling issues that arise with the support of high assurance write-up actions in multilevel object-based environments. An approach is presented which closes channels by executing the methods in the send and receiver objects concurrently when write-up action is requested. The fourth paper by Vicki Jones and Marianne Winslett is entitled: *Secure Database Interoperation via Role Translation*. It was presented by Vicki. It describes an approach for translating roles between role lattices. It also states that such an approach would facilitate the interoperation between secure databases.

In the discussion that took place following the paper presentations, several issues were discussed. In particular, a discussion of the role of security in object-oriented systems standards (such as OMG's CORBA, ANSI X3/H7's work, and ODMG) and issues on integrating security and object-oriented technologies were discussed. One possible approach would be to identify the various object-oriented technology areas, such as object-oriented operating systems, object-oriented database systems, distributed object management systems, object-oriented programming languages, and object-oriented design and analysis methodologies, and determine how security could influence or benefit from these technologies. It seems that much of the work has been on incorporating security into object-oriented database systems. The workshop also had presentations on secure object-oriented programming languages and object-oriented design and analysis methods for secure applications which showed much promise. Some efforts on secure object-oriented operating systems and secure distributed object management systems were discussed. Finally, one of the main concerns that resulted from this workshop was whether the object-oriented approach was better for designing secure systems.

3. Can the Object-Oriented Approach Facilitate Security?

The question as to whether the object-oriented approach was between for secure systems was discussed by Ravi Sandu and T.C. Ting at the panel chaired by Bhavani Thuraisingham on integrating security and object-oriented technologies at the OOPSLA 93 Conference. Some of the essential points of their presentations are given below.

As stated by Sandhu, a symbiotic integration of security and object-oriented technologies is critical for the maturing, and widespread acceptance, of object-oriented database systems. Security is clearly an essential requirement in large-scale multi-user information systems. At the same time, the real security concerns of an enterprise can be properly addressed only at a semantic level such as offered by object-oriented systems.

Security means different things to different people. It has become generally accepted that there are three major security objectives, as follows.

5

1. Secrecy is concerned with improper disclosure of information.
2. Integrity is concerned with improper modification of
    information or processes.
3. Availability is concerned with improper denial of access to
    information or services from the system.

Recently, it has also become apparent that there is a fourth security objective which is quite distinct from the above.

4. Protection of intellectual property rights is concerned with the
    improper usage of information assets.

Object-oriented systems offer substantial advantages in all four aspects of security. The most obvious benefit is in the area of integrity. Objects offer a protected interface, consisting of the methods applicable to the particular class of which the object is an instance. In the more sophisticated models it is possible to ensure that sequences of operations on an object must satisfy application-dependent semantic properties.

In the secrecy arena, object-oriented systems suggest a paradigm of controlling information flow by regulating the flow of messages between objects. Research in this area indicates that it is essential to distinguish between method invocations which can change the state of an object, and those that cannot. It also becomes necessary to introduce asynchronism in computations which are otherwise logically sequential.

The availability and intellectual property areas have not received much study in the object-oriented (or for that matter, any other) context. The initial work that has been done does indicate similar benefits in these two areas as have been demonstrated in the integrity and confidentiality arenas.

A truly semantic data model cannot omit the increasingly important security requirements of enterprise-wide information systems. At the same time, security services must be made available at the semantic level where individual users see them as a benefit to their job functions rather than as an hindrance. A symbiosis between security and object-oriented technologies therefore is an appealing prospect.

Ting also shares similar views on the role of the object-oriented approach. He has stated that one of the difficulties in specifying data security requirements for an application is the complexity. The characteristics of application-dependent security policies or requirements have not been clearly understood. These requirements must be defined within the context of the application domain and they must be modeled and defined as an integral part of the application's data semantics and specifications. Data access controls in an application system must be designed so that its users will be permitted to read, write, manipulate, and transmit relevant data in order to fulfill their assigned responsibilities in the application. The user's assigned roles in the application determine the types of access functions to the relevant data permitted to the user. The user's authorized access privileges are directly related to his or her roles assigned by the application's manager. This type of access controls is defined based on the user's "need-to-know", and it is often referred to in the literature as discretionary access control. The assignment of user roles is the responsibility of the application's manager and it is not governed by a predetermined clearance level as in the government data security system which protects classified data.

Object-oriented data models and systems offer great potential for modeling sophisticated application data security requirements. Object-oriented data models can be extended to implement user-role based data access controls. It is a great challenge to the data security and database research and development communities to understand application data security semantics and to develop data modeling methods and tools which can support the development of security sensitive information systems.

Other proponents of the object-oriented approach to designing secure applications are Peter Sell (of the DoD) and Bhavani Thuraisingham. Their work adapts Rumbaugh et al.'s OMT (Object Modeling Technique) to design multilevel secure database applications. They have developed a methodology called MOMT (Multilevel OMT) for this purpose. The multilevel object model of MOMT represents the structural aspects of the application. The model also attempts to control certain types of unauthorized inferences. The multilevel dynamic model of MOMT represents the control aspects of the application. Since one cannot avoid the interactions between the entities at different security levels, the intent of the dynamic model is to capture these interactions and identify potential problematic situations in the automated system. The multilevel functional model of MOMT represents the transformational aspects of the application. One can think of the functional model as representing the functions that must act on the objects. The system design phase of MOMT designs the multilevel database, the integrity constraints, the transactions, and the modules of the automated system. The details of the automated system are determined during the object design phase.

Although the object-oriented approach shows much promise for security, if a system is designed in such a way that the encapsulation principle can be bypassed, then the approach does not offer an advantage to a non object-oriented approach. Another issue with the object-oriented approach is the assurance that one can get from the system. That is, is it possible, to develop high assurance systems using the object-oriented approach? These are issues that need further investigation before one can claim the superiority of the object-oriented approach for designing secure systems.

4. Overview of the Book

Many of the papers presented at the workshop have been enhanced and published in this book. The topics are: security in medical database systems, security facilities of PCTE, a base for secure object-oriented environments, object model for a security system, multilevel objects in secure object-oriented databases, object-oriented security in Trusted Mach operating system, enforcing mandatory access in object-oriented database systems, information flow control in object-oriented programs, a model-based authorization for object-oriented databases, research issues in discretionary security for object-oriented systems, on the object-oriented paradigm to influence and guide security, access control model for parallel object-oriented languages, using object modeling technique to design multilevel secure data models, concurrency, synchronization, and scheduling to support high assurance write-up, on eliminating the property of monotonically nondecreasing levels in class hierarchy, and secure database interoperation via role translation. The papers published in this book are grouped in the same way in which they were presented at the workshop. They cover a variety of topics in security for object-oriented systems from applications, access control and authorization models to multilevel systems and issues. This book should serve as a useful reference to those interested in security for object-oriented systems.

5. Related References and Activities

Several papers have been published on security for object-oriented systems since the mid-80's. Many articles on discretionary security for object-oriented systems have appeared in the descriptions of various commercial products as well as research prototypes. Since the work of Thomas Keefe, Wei-Tek Tsai, and Bhavani Thuraisingham on multilevel security for object-oriented database systems in 1988, several articles on this topic have been published in various journals and conferences including the Journal of Object-Oriented Programming, Computers and Security, Proceedings of the ACM OOPSLA Conference, Proceedings of the IEEE Symposium on Security and Privacy, and the Proceedings of the IFIP 11.3 Working Conference on Database Security. A panel on security for object-oriented systems was chaired by Ravi Sandhu at the 1990 National Computer Security Conference. Also, a workshop on this topic was organized by Teresa Lunt (of SRI) in 1990 at Karlsruhe, Germany. In addition to the workshop at the OOPSLA 93 Conference, the most recent activity was the panel on integrating security and object-oriented technologies at the OOPSLA 93 Conference.

Research activities on security for object-oriented systems have been reported not only in the U.S.A. and Europe, but also in Canada and South Africa. We expect that interest in this subject will continue to increase in various parts of the world. New journals and conferences in object-oriented systems have identified security as one of the topics of interest. As object-oriented technology and security technology continue to grow, work on integrating the two technologies will receive increasing attention.

6. Acknowledgments

Thanks are due to many people who made the workshop a success. In particular, we thank the contributors of the papers and the participants. We also thank the ACM OOPSLA 93 Program Committee and Dr. Mamdouh Ibrahim, the chair of the workshops program, for their support for this workshop. Last, but certainly not least, we are grateful for the support of Springer Verlag, London for publishing the papers and Rosy Kemp (of Springer) for her coordination of this effort.

Part I: Applications and Systems

Integrating Object Oriented Technology and Security in Medical Database Systems

G. Pangalos
Computer Science and Statistics Dept., 264 Tyler hall,
University of Rhode Island, Kingston, RI 02881, USA. E-mail:
pangalos@cs.uri.edu. (Visiting from: Computers Div., Faculty
of Technology - Gen. dept, Aristotelian University of
Thessaloniki, Thessaloniki 540 06, Greece, E-mail:
GIP@eng.auth.gr)

Abstract

The application of object oriented (OO) technology in the health care sector is of particular interest today, both because of the nature of the field and its social and financial importance. Database security in particular plays an important role in the overall security of medical information systems since not only involves fundamental ethical principles (e.g. privacy and confidentiality), but also essential prerequisites for effective medical care. The development of appropriate secure medical database design and implementation methodologies is therefore an important research problem and a necessary prerequisite for the successful development of such systems. Object oriented techniques can play a decisive role in developing better security systems in this area. There are however a number of problems related to the nature and complexity of the applications and the ill-defined structures involved that have to be addressed first in order to successfully integrate OO technology and security in medical database systems. Some of the potential and limitations of integrating OO technology and security in medical database systems and the European approach to this problem are discussed in this paper and a number of specific implementations are briefly described.

This work was supported in part by the Commission of the European Communities, AIM program, SEISMED (A2033) Project.

1. Introduction

The problems related to the application of object oriented (OO) technology and its integration with security in the health care sector are of particular importance. This is both because of the important role of informatics in helping to provide better health care services and the financial importance of this sector today (health care has often been classified as one of the 10 major "industries", in financial terms, world wide (41)). The importance of the sector is reflected today in Europe by the emphasis given in medical informatics by both the industry and the universities and also by the commitment of the EEC in the area (which includes programs like AIM, the Informatics Security task force (INFOSEC) activities, the Green Paper on Security, the White Paper on Data Protection, etc., see section 4).

Security is a major problem when dealing with computer based medical information systems which is directly related to the quality of medical care. It does not only involve fundamental ethical principles, like privacy and confidentiality, but also essential prerequisites for effective medical care (2,6,7). Current thinking in information systems security is that the issues center on confidentiality (information is only disclosed to those users who are authorized to have access to it), integrity (information is modified only by those users who have the right to do so), and availability (information and other IT resources can be accessed by authorized users when needed). Medical systems are 'risky' systems with respect to at least these issues (1,2,41). Introducing security into a medical system is however a balancing process between providing the desirable level of protection of privacy on the one hand and maintaining an adequate level of availability and performance, so that health care professionals have easy access to medical data, on the other. The later is particularly important, for example, in cases of emergency. The level of security that should be included in a medical information system involves therefore some judgment about the dangers associated with the system, the required level of availability and the resource implications of various means of avoiding or minimizing those dangers.

Database security plays an important role in the overall security of medical information systems and networks. This is both because of the role and the nature of database technology (handles and communicates stores of valuable and sensitive data), and its widespread use today (1,2,10,41). We can classify the requirements for medical database security into four basic categories: (I) the authorization policies, which govern the disclosure and modification of information in the database; (ii) the data consistency policies, which govern the consistency and correctness of information in the database (involving issues like the integrity constraints, the database recovery policies, the concurrency policies, etc.); (iii) the availability policies, which govern the availability of the information in the database; (iv) the identification, authentication and audit policies, which govern the identification and authentication procedures to be followed and the auditing policies for the database.

Despite its importance, however, research in database security is still comparatively limited, if taken into account our growing dependence on database systems (over 90% of computer systems in use today contain some kind of database system (10)). Progress seems to be even slower in the integration of object oriented technology and security in this area, despite the fact that many of the paradigms in database security papers are from the health care environment (37,41,45).

Object oriented technology provides a new, powerful tool for analyzing and implementing information systems, capable of handling the complex data types often required in health care, which is expected to be used extensively in health care systems. It will therefore be necessary to move at some stage from the existing, data oriented, security methods and techniques to new ones, geared to the new environment. That is to give priority to the procedural/usage rather than the data security level. Given however the complexity of health care systems and the ill-defined structures involved (41), it is still a subject of discussion whether the time has already come for moving from the existing established security procedures and techniques to the new environment, at least as far as real life applications are concerned. In what follows we will limit the discussion on the problems related to medical database security and the potential of integrating OO technology and security in this area.

2. Database Security

2.1. Definition - General Framework

Database security is concerned with the ability of the system to enforce a security policy governing the disclosure, modification or destruction of information. Within (health care) organizations humans typically use a database as a technical tool for storing, processing and communicating information. At any time an amount of data has been stored in it, a large amount of messages has already been sent and the corresponding data can be called for duplication and further transmission on demand from potential receivers. The database relays the messages by persistently memorizing the corresponding data following the three phase procedure (2):

accept messages ==> store / process data ==> assemble, duplicate and communicate data on demand

The quality of mediation is dependably assured by special protocols enforcing completion of transactions and integrity constraints on stored data. Mediation is shared among many users and is required to be efficient in time and space (2).

2.2 Database Security Policies

Given the above general framework and definition of medical database security, if more technically, we can regard a database as a channel in the sense of communication theory. Then a database security policy states (2):

i. which type of sub channels between (groups of) users can be established

ii. requirements of the availability of certain facilities of the sub channels

iii. requirements on the (partial) separation and noninterference of sub channels.

Seen from this point of view, we can identify three prominent proposals for database security policies (see also (1,2,41,45)):

a. The Multilevel (or mandatory or military) security approach.

It dates back to the traditional non-computerized practice. The need for such a policy arises when a computer database system contains information with a variety of classifications and has some users which are not cleared for the highest classification of the information contained in the system. The approach is based on the following assumption (constructs): there are users, data items and a lattice of security levels (1,41).

b. The discretional or (commercial) security approach.

It evolves from good commercial practice. Discretional access controls in today's database systems are designed to enforce a specific access control policy (1,41). The approach is based on the following assumption (constructs): there are users, (well informed) transactions, and (constraint) data items (1,2,41).

c. The personal knowledge approach.

Was developed with an emphasis to favor support of privacy before any other design goal. Technically it combines techniques of relational databases, object oriented programming and capability based information systems (2,41).

2.3 Requirements for DB Security

The following general principles related to database security have been widely accepted today (10,11,14):

a. The database system security considerations must take into account all system S/W and H/W that touches information flowing into, and out of, the database. For example, an easily penetrated operating system would render a superbly protected DBMS useless.

b. Data integrity is a key requirement. The database system must preserve the integrity of the data stored in it. The user must be able to trust the system to give back the same data that is put in the system and to permit data to be modified only by authorized users. The data should not be destroyed or altered either accidentally, as in a system crash, or maliciously, as in some unauthorized person modifying the data. At the very least, the user should know if the data was corrupted.

c. Data should be available when needed. This implies system fault tolerance and redundancy in data, software and hardware. Inference and aggregation must be studied and controlled.

d. Audit should be detailed enough to be useful and sufficient enough so as not to severely burden system performance.

e. The aim should be at providing adequate level of secrecy (prevent disclosure) and yet preserving integrity by using appropriate concurrence and integrity controls (e.g. referential integrity).

f. The prototypes should be of general purpose, commercial quality and, according to most proposers, relational systems. The relational system has been chosen because it is (10) currently the model of preference in the commercial world.

Various sets of security evaluation criteria have also been proposed to date, to help ensure that database systems satisfy the security requirements set (10,11,12). The exact set of such criteria to be applied in each case obviously depends on the particular environment the system is operating in. For a medical database system, for example, detailed security evaluation criteria and interpretations like the ones described in (11,12,13,14,15) could be used as guidelines. Some of the factors used, for example, by the NCSC in building their series of secure database prototypes are shown in figure 1 (10,12).

---

i. *"C2" prototypes:*
discretionary access control, object reuse, identification and authentication, audit, security testing, data integrity, performance, security features user's guide, trusted facility manual, test documentation, design documentation

ii. *"B" prototypes:*
labels, label integrity, exportation to: multilevel hosts; single level hosts, exportation of labeled information, mandatory access control

---

Figure 1.
Some of the factors used by NCSC in building secure database prototypes.

2.4 Database and Operating System Security

Database security is usually regarded as junior to operating systems security because it often has to depend on a trusted operating system. Research on secure operating systems is important to secure batabase systems for two main reasons. First, most database systems sit on OSs and depend on this systems for services. If the OS is not secure it is usually useless to built a secure batabase system. Second, secure OS research is important since many concepts of this research are applicable to secure database system research (for example most of the concepts in figure 1 above). Operating systems research to date has resulted in several usable, quite secure OSs. For example, a number of OSs that have been evaluated to have a certain amount of security by the NCSC (USA) have been listed in their evaluated products list (10). It can therefore be said that an adequate number of trusted OSs are, or will soon be, available as hosts to trusted database systems. Research is however open and active in this area (1,2,10). Example sets of such criteria for secure OSs can be found in (11,14).

This however can change. Database security could to our opinion be to a large degree independent from OS security if for example access to the (OO or traditional) database system's data is controlled by encryption, governed by the DBMS (user/DB administrator). This will make it a lot more difficult to by-pass the database management system in accessing the data. A database structure in which (selected parts of the) database data are encrypted can therefore provide a model for information systems that is attractive, since control can be enforced by hardware as it is for example in traditional communications (computer network) systems, thereby avoiding the uncertainties that surround the security of operating systems (41,48).

3. Object Oriented Technology and Security of Medical Databases

Existing security methods give usually priority to the protection of the data stored in (medical) database systems. OO technology is changing substantially the methods and techniques in the field, since the emphasis shifts to the methods and procedures associated to the various objects. This will inevitably affect the traditional security policies. For example, it could shift gradually the emphasis from the mandatory to the discretional (e.g.. roles-based (45)) or personal knowledge type of approaches.

The integration of OO technology and security in real life medical database systems remains however a disputed issue today, at least in Europe, where a significant amount of research work on security is currently under way (see below) on medical information systems security (The SEISMED project (41) which is financed by the EEC is a good example of inter-European research on the subject). Arguments can be raised on this issue in both directions. It can be claimed on the one hand that, since it is accepted that the OO approach is going to provide the main vehicle for the analysis, design and implementation of future information systems, security of health care systems has to be geared to the new directions the soonest possible. The emphasis when analyzing the security problem of health care institutions must be put therefore on implementing security mechanisms in terms of objects, methods, procedures, etc., and less on the data itself.

It can also be claimed however that, since security design must be an integral part of the overall system's design process, no effective OO security policies can be applied, at least in real life applications, until those overall problems, which are related to the nature and complexity of health care applications and the ill-defined structures involved, are satisfactorily solved and the techniques are stabilized. The fact that no complete OO medical database system that works on a real life health care environment is currently available (at least in Europe), probably means that given the nature and the problems related to the health care delivery, the integration of OO technology and security in real life applications in this field should not be attempted yet.

No matter when, however, it is evident that the traditional basic procedure currently applied in many cases, e.g.. by European hospitals:
perform risk analysis ---> assign sensitivity levels to the health care data ---> decide on the security measures and countermeasures to be taken
which puts more emphasis on the level of sensitivity of data and less on their use, should be at least enriched at this stage with OO oriented considerations (e.g. put more emphasis on the use of the data, the methods and procedures).

4. Current European Research in the Area - The SEISMED Project

The SEISMED (Secure Environment for Information Systems in MEDicine) project is one of the research programs financed by the European Commission (EEC) in the framework of the AIM (Advanced Informatics in Medicine) program. The AIM program invests currently approximately 90 million ECU (approx. 130 million dollars) in the area of medical informatics. SEISMED is one of the major projects of AIM and the only one in the area of security. Its duration is 3 years (1992-94). The overall objective of SEISMED is the in depth investigation of the problem of security in medical information systems. The research work under way covers all aspects of the problem (technical, procedural, legal, etc.). The results of the research will be applied in four reference centers (hospitals) throughout Europe. The research work is undertaken through a number of work packages which cover areas like: Quality assurance, Security survey, High level security policy, Risk analysis, Security in system design, Security in existing operational systems, Encryption, Network security, Database security, Legal framework and code of ethics, Reference center management, etc. Our participation and that of our laboratory in this project is focused on the problems of database security and the problems of secure database design in existing and future systems. The SEISMED research consortium consists of the following institutions: *France: National Research Center (CNRS); Switzerland: University Hospital of Geneva; Germany: University of Hildersheim; Holland: University Hospital Laiden: BAZIS co.; England: The Royal London Hospital, University South West; Belgium: Catholic University of Lueven; Ireland: University College Dublin; Greece: University of Thessaloniki, University of the Aegean.*

The current initiatives at European level in the area of security also include the activities of the INFOSEC (INFOrmation SECurity) task force. This unit which operates in the framework of the EEC (DG XIII) has as objective to undertake actions in information security. Two recent initiatives of this unit are the development of the so-called Green Book on the Security of the Information Systems (Draft 3, June 1993) and the coordination of the implementation of a number of research projects in the area. A number of such projects are already under implementation by a number of European consortia (a new call for projects is also expected to be issued by October). Through these projects the researchers and companies interested in security can work together at European level. It is also expected that the above mentioned Green Book on security will be formally accepted by the EEC soon. This book will thus become a text for reference on security for Europe in the future. The White Paper on data protection is another significant effort, which is directly related to the security issue. This document, which is also prepared by the EEC (DG XIII) is also expected to be adopted formally in the near future. Other publications, like the information security evaluation criteria (INFOSEC) and the information security evaluation methodology (INFOSEM), that provide an alternative to the ones already published by the DoD in USA have also been available recently, which describe a systematic way for evaluating the security of a computer based information system (11,12,14,15).

5.   Secure   Medical   Database   Development Methodologies

From the perspective of a user who needs a secure medical database system, there are two possible basic approaches for its development, depending on the scope of the target database system and on the expected degree of trust: exploiting and enhancing the security functions of a DBMS, or, the use of a "secured" DBMS. In both cases either traditional or object oriented systems can be used. The discussion that follows concentrates mainly on non object oriented systems.

5.1. Exploiting and Enchanting the Security Functions of a DBMS

The first approach is to use a general purpose DBMS that optionally provides some security functions, such as user authentication, access control, auditing etc.. These functions can be exploited by including them into the applications that perform security-crucial functions (29). In these cases the design and implementation problem becomes that of introducing the appropriate security checks in the applications and of designing the data schemas according to security requirements. Some examples of general purpose DBMSs that provide security mechanisms are: INGRES (17), where security and integrity constraints can be specified in the system query language QUEL; QBE (18), that supports field-level access control by means of rules stored in access tables; System R

(19), where access rules and integrity constraints are stored in access tables; IMS (20), that provides control of transaction access to data on a value-independent basis and control of end-user access to transactions; etc..

Security of general purpose systems can also be enhanced by retrofitting security features, that is, by adding new security functions through the introduction of add-on security packages or security special-purpose hardware (21). For example, a number of software packages exist that can be added to the DBMS for access control purposes, these include: ACF2 (22), which was designed as an extension to the IBM OS/VS_MVS operating system; SECURE (23), which authorizes access to data in the TSO environment by replacing the OS, VS,or MVS password facilities with its own modules etc.. A promising approach to security retrofitting seems to be the so-called integrity-lock one (24) that combines cryptography and front-end architecture issues, thus exhibiting high security qualities without requiring dramatic changes to an existing system.

5.2. The use of "Secured" DBMSs

Exploiting or enhancing the security functions of a general purpose DBMS is, however, an appropriate approach only in cases when security is not the most crucial concern for the database. In fact, the degree of trust that can be achieved in data handling is limited in that security checks are optional and in that the DBMS software that performs the security-related functions does not undergo a certification process according to some evaluation criteria (11,14). When security of the database system is a prominent feature, for example in cases where the target database system is demanded to operate in a critical environment (as for example a hospital information system), a "secured" DBMS is needed.

"Secured" means that some security mechanisms are automatically invoked upon each data access operation. These mechanisms are often required to perform quite complex checks, depending on the kinds of threats the system is required to face, and must have been formally proved to work correctly. Formal proves need a security policy for the database to have been stated and modeled through a database security model.

Formal models of the security policies have guided the design and implementation of several secured databases (25). The benefits of this approach have been widely recognized (25,26). The availability of such a model directly focused onto one (or more) security problems (e.g. information flow, access control, integrity, statistical inference etc.) allows to execute design checks and to prove correctness properties of the future systems. For example, models of revocation control for database authorization mechanisms (such as (27,28)) prove the correctness of the privileges revocation strategies in the system.

In general a formal database security model identifies the set of entities and operations which are security relevant for the future system and has an associated set of axioms expressing the security policies. Then some algorithms are run against the model structures for proving the correct behavior of the system that will interpret the model. Security models for databases are still an open subject of thorough research. Multilevel military systems are for example the systems where many attempts have been made in the past for solving the certification problem and for tackling a number of sophisticated security problems. Often their design and implementation has been based on a formal model of the so-called multilevel security policy and on an architectural approach based on security kernels, or, on trusted computer base concepts, etc. (1,2).

Finally, as far as the available architectures for secure databases are concerned, the basic approaches to secure DBMS architectures proposed todate, include (39,41):
i. The Integrity-lock architecture. It consists of three major components: the 'untrusted front end (UTFE)' which handles query parsing, output formatting, and computations etc. ; the 'trusted front end (TFE)' which handles user authentication, tuple formatting etc.; and the 'untrusted logical access manager (LAM)' (previously known as the DBMS) which handles searchings from the database, selections of requested tuples etc.
ii. The Hinke-Schaefer architecture, where all of the data security separation and protection is provided by the operating system.
iii. The Dual-Kernel architecture. There are multiple variations on a dual kernel SDBMS. The key aspect of any dual kernel SDBMS is that it has a security kernel in the DBMS handling data access mediation, and the SDBMS kernel is in communication (via some trusted communication path) with the operating system trusted computing base (TCB).

Several general purpose non - OO DBMSs in wide use today, as for example INGRES, were designed and implemented according to such a specific architectural philosophies that exploit, for example,: the results of security kernels, database machines, specialized architecture and hardware for high performance secure databases (associative memories and back-up processors etc.), etc. (29).

6. Some Specific European Proposals for Medical Database Security Policies

A number of specific proposals for medical database security are presented briefly below, based on a number of reports on medical database security systems published (2,4,8,41,42,43,44). Despite the fact that non of them has been based on the integration of object oriented technology and security, they provide a clear picture of the strategies and methods adopted on the problem of health care security by the European hospital todate.

1. The BAZIS system. The BAZIS system (Central Development and Support Group Hospital Information System in Laiden, NL), aims at all aspects of security: high availability, accuracy, logical consistency, privacy, confidentiality etc. It supports a strict separation of the roles of the physicians etc. and the programmers etc. by providing duplicate H/W for 'production' and 'development', by running the 'production' system without any programming tools (e.g. compilers, debuggers etc.), and by administering access rights by the Medical Records Department (and not by the computer department). The various roles of the medical and administrative staff are described by an access matrix that distinguishes 10 user groups and 13 types of data (2,42,44).

BAZIS emphasizes that organizational structures, decisions and procedures must closely harmonize with the design of the information system. It also convincingly demonstrates that regarding security as a primary design goal has a considerable impact on the system structure. It points out that the integration of subsystems is not only indispensable to availability and consistency, but it also offers means to support the privacy issue though seemingly in contrast to the principle of the separation of duty. For example, as soon as the personnel department updates the computerized personal file of an employee who leaves the institution, the personal file subsystem can trigger the medical records subsystem to revoke all access rights.

2. The University Hospital Heidelberg system. The university hospital Heidelberg system considers the person oriented patient database as the most important component for the integration of the various special purpose subsystems. Besides storing and retrieving data, this database system is used as the common communication system within the hospital. A strategy which is however clearly opposed to the requirement of separating the different roles. Therefore the designers tried to remedy the conflict by adding a further security tool to the standard security methods provided by the commercial database system used (ADABAS/NATURAL): user were granted access to the so-called 'applications' (a set of procedures with possibly restricted range of parameters) with respect to views (2,43).

3. The MSS system. The MSS system, developed at Uppsala University Data Center, rejects the monolithic system approach as incompatible with the structure and the dynamics of medical services systems. Instead they propose a federative approach: each basic organizational unit of the 'enterprise' defines itself its specific procedures and its specific database; communications between units is defined and regulated separately by special 'communication contracts'. Thus the main burden of ensuring both functionality and security of 'enterprise-wide' applications is shifted to the underlying computer network facilities and appropriate standards for the components (2,44).

22

4. The BAIK system. The BAIK system (2) is divided into two strictly separated subsystems. The first one manages the complete medical records of patients on behalf of the treating physician who holds all access rights. The second one maintains a findings oriented register where medical data coming from all co-operating physicians is collected for purposes of statistics, research etc. Before the first subsystem communicates data to the second, these data is made anonymous by substituting the identifying information about an individual by an appropriate anonym, and the data is classified according to the available thesaurus of the register. Afterwards only the treating physician is able to directly re-identify data of his patients within the second subsystem.

The BAIK system has achieved a clean separation of treatment of individual patient and research, education etc.. The problem remains however that it is not possible to automatically join all data of a particular individual within the register, because the register lacks information on how to decide identity among acronyms. Although this feature clearly supports the confidentiality and privacy issue, it substantially diminishes the usefulness of the register(2,8,43).

All proposals above, and especially the BAZIS and the Heidelberg ones, can be (roughly) classified as variants of the discretionary security approach. They all also advocate to physically separate subsystems that perform special tasks. The reintegration of the information is proposed however on different layers of the overall computer system: BAIK and BAZIS manage information as part of the specific database application, The Heildeberg proposal uses a centralized database as a generic integration tool for various more or less independent subsystems; finally, MSS favors to integrate on the network layer.

7. Conclusions

The integration of object oriented technology and security in medical database systems offers significant advantages when compared with traditional security methods and technics. The nature of health care delivery, the complexity of health care systems and the ill-defined structures involved poses however some difficult problems for this integration, at least for this stage. The problem of medical database security has been discussed in this paper and the potential and limitations of the various security approaches to it have been presented briefly. A number of current European projects and initiatives have also been discussed briefly, which help demonstrate the approaches on the problem adopted at European level.

References

1. Lunt T., Security in database systems, Computers and security journal, Vol

7,No.1, 1992.

2. Biskup J., Medical database security, in data protection and confidentiality in health informatics, EEC/DGXII ed.,IOS press, 1991.

3. Landwehr C., ed., Database security II: Status and prospects, North-Holland, 1989.

4. Spooner D., Landwehr C., eds., Database security III, North-Holland, 1990.

5. Proceedings ESORICS (European Symposium on Research in Computer Security), Toulouse, France, 1990.

6. Jajodia S., Landwehr C., eds., Database security IV, North-Holland, 1991.

7. EEC/DGXII, ed., Data protection and confidentiality in health informatics, IOS press, 1991.

8. Biscup J., Analysis of the privacy model for the information system DORIS, in (3).

9. Cannataci A., Data protection issues in database management and expert systems, in (7).

10. Campbell J, A research and development program for trusted distribute DBMSs, in Database security IV, Jaodia (ed), North Holland, 1991.

11. DoD, Department of Defence Trusted computer system evaluation criteria, DoD 5200.28-STD, 1985

12. National Computer Security Centre, Draft trusted DBMS interpretation of the DoD trusted computer system evaluation criteria, USA, 1989

13. National Computer Security Centre, Trusted network interpretation of the trusted computer system evaluation criteria, NCSC-TG-005, USA, 1987.

14. Information Technology Evaluation Criteria (ITSEC), Version 1.2, EEC Document, Brussels, June 1991.

15. Information Technology Security Evaluation Manual (ITSEM), Draft V0.2, EEC Draft Document, April 1992.

16. Landwehr C. E., Minutes of IFIP-TC11 1986 meeting, Montecarlo, December 1986.

17. Stonabraker M., The design and implementation of INGRES, ACM TODS, Vol. 1, No. 3, 1976.

18. Zloof M., Query by example: a database language, IBM systems Journal, Vol. 16, No. 4, 1977.

19. Astrahan M., System R: Relational approach to database management, ACM TODS, Vol. 1, No. 2, June 1976.

20. McGee W., The information Management System IMS/VS. Part V: Transaction processing facilities, IBM systems journal, Vol. 16, No. 2, 1977.

21. Landwehr C., The best available technologies for computer security, IEEE Computer, Vol. 16, No. 7, 1983.

22. ACF2: The access control facility - General information manual, 1983.

23. Secure product description, Bull and Babbage publ., 1979.

24. Duffy K. and Sullivan J., Integrity lock prototype, in the Proceedings 4th IFIP international security conference, Montecarlo, 1986.

25. Cerniglia C. and Millen J., Computer security models, MTR project, Report No. 9531, 1984.

26. Landwehr C., Formal models for computer security, ACM computer surveys,

Vol. 13, No. 3, 1981.

27. Griffiths P. and Wade B., An authorisation mechanism for a relational database system, ACM TODS, Vol. 1, No. 3, 1976.

28. Fagin R., On an authorisation mechanism, ACN TODS, Vol. 3, No. 3, 1976.

29. Fugini M., Secure database development methodologies, in (3)

30. Dwyer P., Multilevel security in database management systems, Computers and security, Vol. 6, No. 3, 1987.

31. Akl S., Views for multilevel database database security, IEEE Trans. on S/W Eng., Vol. 13, No. 2, 1987.

32. Hartson H., Database security - system architectures, Information systems, Vol. 6, N0.1, 1981.

33. Leveson J., Safety analysis using Petri nets, IEEE Trans. on S/W Eng., Vol. 13, No. 3, 1987.

34. Bussolati U., A database approach to modelling and managing of security information, Proc. 7th Int. Conf. on VLDB, Cannes, 1981.

35. Bussolati U., Data security management in distributed databases, Information systems, Vol. 7, No. 3, 1982.

36. Date C., An introduction to database systems, Vol. 2, second ed., Addison-Wesley, 1986.

37. Ting T., Application information security semantics: A case of mental health delivery, in (4).

38. Hinke T., DBMS trusted computing base taxonomy, in (4).

39. Graubart R., A comparison of three secure DBMS architectures, in (4).

40. Hosmer H., Designing multilevel secure distributed databases, in (3).

41. Pangalos G., Security in medical database systems, EEC, SEISMED project report, No. INT/S.3/92, 1992.

42. J.V. Marel, A.B. Bakker, User accessrights in an intergrated hospital information system, IFIP-IMIA, North-Holland, 1988.

43. J. BisKup, A general framework for database security, Proc. EROSICS, Toulouse, France, 1990, pp. 35-41.

44. J. Biskup, Medical database security, Proc. GI-20, Jahrestagung II, Stutgart, October 1990, Springer-Verlag, 1990, pp. 212-221.

45. T.C. Ting, S.A. Demurjian, M.Y. Hu, A specification methodology for user-role based security in an object-oriented design model, Proc. 6th IFIP WG11.3 on database security, 1993.

46. C. Pfleeger, Security in computing, Prentice hall, 1991.

47. S. Katsikas, D. Gritzalis, High level security policies, SEISMED report, June 1993.

48. S. Oliver, S., Building a secure database using self-protecting objects, computer security journal, vol. 11, no. 3, pp. 259-71.

The Security Facilities of PCTE

Barry Bird
Software Engineering Group, EDS, Pembroke House
Camberley, U.K.

1. Introduction

This paper presents an existing Object Management System (OMS), PCTE, which
has an extensive set of security facilities. PCTE is a well-developed repository
service designed to support integration of CASE tools and is standardised by the
European Computer Manufacturers Association as ECMA-149 [1], ECMA-158 [2]
and ECMA-162 [3]. It is now also a draft international standard ISO/IEC DIS
13719. From a security point of view PCTE is particularly interesting because of
the range and breadth of security facilities it provides, well integrated with the many
functions of PCTE.

The PCTE OMS supports attributes and associations of objects which are strongly
typed. New object types may be defined which inherit these attributes and
associations from one or more parent object types. PCTE can therefore be
characterised as statically object-oriented. Object types may also be defined to have
contents, as files, pipes or devices with basic Posix-like I/O operations.

PCTE also controls the environment in which programs or processes accessing the
repository execute, and models the subjects, or principals, on behalf of whom these
processes run. It therefore exercises sufficient control over repository access in order
to be able in principle to provide a high degree of assurance. The sheer size and
complexity of PCTE, however, does militate against achieving a very high assurance
level.

A PCTE Installation consists of a network of workstations which is treated as one
unit for authentication purposes. For access purposes, the location of objects is
largely transparent. How authentication of access to objects remote to the accessing
workstation is implemented is not defined by PCTE.

PCTE also defines the security administration operations necessary in order to define
and maintain the user's desired security policy, and these operations are also governed
by the same security policy.

2. Mandatory Access Control

2.1 Classes and Labels

Two kinds of mandatory security are defined: confidentiality and integrity. The purpose of confidentiality is to prevent unauthorised disclosure of information ("secrecy"). Conversely the purpose of integrity is to prevent the unauthorised modification ("contamination") of information. The rules for integrity are often the opposite of those for confidentiality.

Mandatory security is defined in terms of one or more "towers" of confidentiality and integrity classes. Each tower defines successive levels of domination of one class over another. Each object has a confidentiality and an integrity label. These labels are derived from the defined confidentiality and integrity classes by AND and OR connectives. Nesting using brackets is permitted without restriction making possible very complex labels. Domination rules are defined for the general case of a label.

Processes are modelled by PCTE and themselves have labels. Accesses to the PCTE repository are only possible from these processes, so that mandatory access control is defined in terms of domination rules between the labels of the calling process and the object being accessed. Simple confidentiality is maintained by controlling read access directly to the user (whose agent is the process), that the confidentiality label of the object being read is dominated by the label of the reading process, and confidentiality confinement is maintained by controlling the flow of information between objects, such that the confidentiality label of the object written to dominates the label of the writing process. Simple confidentiality must also be preserved on writing to objects. Conversely simple integrity is maintained by controlling write access directly from the user, and integrity confinement maintained by controlling the flow of information between objects, such that the integrity label of the object being read dominates the label of the reading process.

2.2 Multi-level secure devices

PCTE not only defines the accessing processes but also the volumes and storage devices on which the Object Base is partitioned and located. It also models the workstations on which the processes run, and the "controlling" relationship between a device and a workstation. Since one may expect object and process with a variety of mandatory labels to coexist, PCTE defines volumes, devices and workstations to be multi-level secure devices and the domination rules for objects to be able to reside on volumes, processes to run in workstations and similar relationships involving devices.

2.3 Floating security labels

It often happens that processes start life at a low confidentiality level, and when higher confidentiality data has to be read, raising their confidentiality label appropriately. Conversely, a high confidentiality process may need to update a lower confidentiality object instance, which must first have its label upgraded if the access is to satisfy the confidentiality constraints. In order to avoid this inconvenience caused by the mandatory security rules, PCTE processes may invoke a "floating labels" facility whereby, if an access would normally fail, the label of the process or the object is automatically upgraded in confidentiality (downgraded in integrity) subject to certain limitations due to the user's clearance, the user's privilege to change labels, and the multi-level security of volumes and workstations.

2.4 Self-referentiality and Covert channels

An important feature of PCTE, known as "self referentiality", is that almost all aspects of the internal state of PCTE with its multifarious functions are represented in terms of objects and their associations in the Object Base. Part of the PCTE specification consists of schema definitions of the object, link, attribute and enumeral types used in this representation. Further schema definitions can be added in order to support user applications. Largely as a consequence of this self referentiality, PCTE recognises that some accesses, mainly associated with system administration functions, will violate the normal mandatory security constraints. These covert channels are only one bit wide and do not constitute a significant gap in security. The standard gives the opportunity for any implementor to make it possible to audit all such breaches.

Self referentiality extends to representing all mandatory classes and their dominance relationships as objects and associations in the PCTE Object Base. Mandatory and Discretionary security is therefore modelled as objects, links and attributes in the PCTE predefined schema (figure 1). In this diagram, boxes represent object types. When a box is nested inside another box, the inner box represents a child type of the object type of the outer box. Lines between boxes represent link types, or relationship types, between object types. An arrowhead indicates the "many" end of a relationship. Attribute types are not shown.

Dominance relationships between confidentiality classes are modelled by "dominates_in_confidentiality" links to dominated classes, with reverse "confidentiality_dominator" links. Similarly for integrity classes.

The model will be explained further as the description of facilities unfolds.

The mandatory access checks required for all operations are defined in the PCTE API. The nature of these checks has been determined by a consideration of the accesses made to all objects involved in each operation.

28

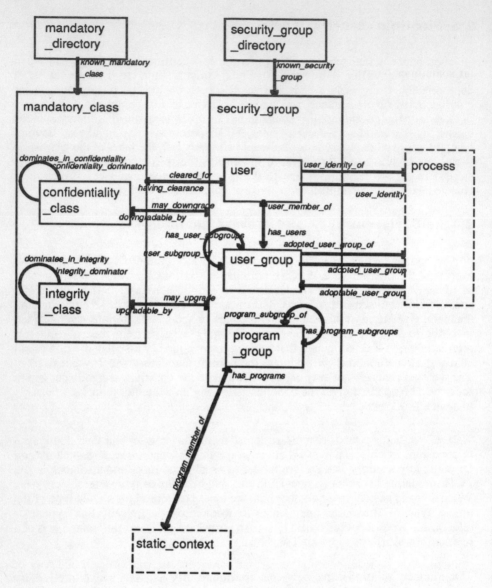

Figure 1. PCTE Security Schema (Security SDS)

2.5 Integrity

Verification and validation of software is a difficult and imprecise subject. Quality assurance demands that the correct amendment and verification procedures are always followed. This is particularly true for safety critical systems, for example. These procedures rely on developers with the correct level of trust performing the actions that their roles require.

It sometimes happens that there is a "trusted kernel" of a system which must be developed to a higher degree of trust than the rest of the system.

Mandatory integrity facilities can be used to label components according to the degree of trust which exists in the procedures by which they were produced. Objects of high integrity may only be updated by users and programs which are cleared to update this class of object. The rules of mandatory integrity prevent objects of low integrity being used as sources of data in this kind of update.

Mandatory integrity can be used for example in controlling system builds in order to to ensure that no objects, such as include files, are used in the build process unless they have been produced by procedures which have the right degree of trust. Mandatory integrity can be used to isolate a build process from accepting contributions from any source other than those defined in advance, or else to record the reduction in integrity if such conributions are allowed e.g. by floating labels. This will not, on the other hand, prevent components with a higher level of trustedness (a "secure kernel") from being included. In this way greater assurance in the integrity of a built system or subsystem can be achieved .

3. Discretionary Access Control

3.1 Security Groups

PCTE also exhibits discretionary security facilities. Discretionary security is defined in terms of "security groups" which are specialized into users, user groups and program groups. These groups are not exclusively used for discretionary security. There is some interaction between mandatory security and discretionary security. Users have confidentiality and integrity clearances. Security groups may have confidentiality downgrade and integrity upgrade privileges. These are discussed later.

A user must be a member of one or more user groups, and user groups may be subgroups of other user groups (which are their "supergroups"), and thus construct an acyclic graph of user groups with one predefined user group, called ALL_USERS, at the apex. ALL_USERS is the ultimate supergroup of all user groups.

All processes in PCTE are executions of executable programs, called "static contexts" and both are modelled in the Object Base as instances of descendant types of the basic "object" type (in fact, "static context" is the immediate child type of "file"). Static contexts may be members of one or more program groups. Again, program groups may be subgroups of other program groups, building up a separate acyclic graph. There is, however, no ultimate program supergroup ("ALL_PROGRAMS") because it was considered that was no need to be able to grant access to all programs in the same way that may be needed for the world of all users. In any case, a program need not be a member of any program group, so "ALL_PROGRAMS" would not actually encompass a PCTE universe of programs.

3.2 Discretionary Context of a Process

When a program runs as a process, a set of security groups, called the effective groups of the process, is established on the basis of which discretionary access control is determined. The effective groups consist of:

- the user on behalf of whom the process is running
- the user's adopted user group
- all the program groups to which the executing static context belongs
- the supergroups of the adopted user group and their supergroups etc.
- the supergroups of all the above program groups and their supergroups etc.

One of the user groups of which the user is a member must be selected as the "adopted user group". In fact, the adopted user group can only be chosen from among the "adoptable user groups" of the process, which is in general a subset of all the user's user groups. Such a user group may lose its adoptability when a new child process starts. A child process inherits the user, adopted user group and some of the adoptable user groups of its parent process. The parent process may flag one or more of its adoptable user groups as "not inheritable", thereby reducing the child process's adoptable groups. The child process's user may regain his user groups for adoptability purposes by re-logging in (if this is permitted).

An alternative approach was considered where there would be no graph of groups, subgroups or supergroups, but each user may belong to any number of user groups. The process would be able to choose to include any subset of these user groups in the effective groups. This was felt to be deficient in not having the concept of obligatory subsets whereby the inclusion of one group automatically brought with it other members of a collection of groups, thereby losing control of which combinations of groups a process may use.

Since ALL_USERS is the ultimate supergroup of all user groups and there must be an adopted user group, it is automatically included in any process's effective groups. Therefore access permissions granted to ALL_USERS will apply to any running process.

PCTE supports interpretable processes. In this case, there are two static contexts: the interpretable static context, and the interpreter. The program groups which contribute to the effective groups of the process are those of the interpreter, as it is this program to which trust must be conferred. An interpretable program e.g. a shell script, may perform privileged operations, but it is actually the interpreter which must verify the correctness and validity of the operation requested by the script.

3.3 Access Control Lists

Each object has Access Control Lists (ACL) which define the permitted access modes for a variable number of security groups. An ACL consists of one or more ACL entries where each ACL entry records the access mode permissions for a given security group. A PCTE implementation is free to define the limit on the length of the ACLs of objects it manages, but it must be at least 64 ACL entries.

There are in fact two ACLs for each object, controlling atomic and composite access.

PCTE has a well-developed composite object model, where "atomic" objects are grouped together by a particular category of link, called a composition link. Many PCTE functions (locking, moving, stabilisation, deletion, link navigation) have two variations, one with an "atomic" scope and one with a "composite" scope. Thus the option exists to lock explicitly an atomic object, or alternatively to lock the object including all its component objects. This concept extends to ACLs: each object has an atomic and a composite ACL. Which of these ACLs is used to determine access rights depends on the scope of the operation: atomic or composite scope respectively.

Access permissions in an ACL entry have three mode values for each access mode: DENIED as well as GRANTED and UNDEFINED.

Access right evaluation for a group g on object o with scope (atomic or composite) s and access mode m is given by

```
EVALUATE_GROUP(g, o, s, m)
                = {GRANTED, UNDEFINED, DENIED}
```

The access right of a process p to object o, scope s for access mode m is given by:

```
EVALUTE_PROCESS(p, o, s, m) = TRUE

iff there exists an effective group g for p where
 EVALUATE_GROUP(g, o, s, m) = GRANTED
    and for all other groups g'
 EVALUATE_GROUP(g', o, s, m) = GRANTED or UNDEFINED.
```

The existence of a DENIED mode value means that specific groups can be prevented from gaining access. For example, a specific user can be prevented from gaining READ_ATTRIBUTES access even though READ_ATTRIBUTES access is permitted to the group to which the user belongs.

3.4 Access Control for Composite Objects

In fact, for composite ACLs, a fourth mode value exists: PARTIALLY_DENIED.
This arises from the mode values of the component's atomic ACLs. The rules for the
relationship between the composite access mode values of an object o and the atomic
access mode values for a given mode m of the components c are as follows:

```
EVALUATE_GROUP (g, o, COMPOSITE, m) = GRANTED iff
            EVALUATE_GROUP (g, c, ATOMIC, m) = GRANTED
for all c and
            EVALUATE_GROUP (g, o, ATOMIC, m) = GRANTED

 EVALUATE_GROUP (g, o, COMPOSITE, m) = DENIED iff
            EVALUATE_GROUP (g, c, ATOMIC, m) = DENIED
for all c and
            EVALUATE_GROUP (g, o, ATOMIC, m) = DENIED

 EVALUATE_GROUP (g, o, COMPOSITE, m) =
                          PARTIALLY_DENIED iff
        EVALUATE_GROUP (g, a, ATOMIC, m) = DENIED and
        EVALUATE_GROUP (g, a', ATOMIC, m) not = DENIED
            where a and a' is o or some c

    EVALUATE_GROUP (g, o, COMPOSITE, m) = UNDEFINED
in all other cases
```

It seems reasonable to distinguish PARTIALLY_DENIED from DENIED to
indicate that the mode permission for the whole composite has not been
intentionally set.

These rules mean that the composite access right to an object is not the same as the
sum of the rights of the components. Suppose there is a composite object A with
component B with ACLs with two entries for groups X and Y for a mode m:

	X	Y
atomic ACL for A	GRANTED	UNDEFINED
atomic ACL for B	UNDEFINED	GRANTED
composite ACL for A	UNDEFINED	UNDEFINED

Therefore a process with effective groups X and Y will have atomic access rights on
A and B, but no composite access right on the composite object A.

When establishing ACLs for composite objects, there are two methods by which composite ACLs could be updated in conformity with the defined relationships between the ACL of the composite object and the ACLs of the components:

- The composite ACL is derived automatically from the ACL of the components: when the ACL of a component is changed, the ACL of the whole composite object changes in conformity with the above constraints.
- The composite ACL is updated explicitly when the ACLs of the components are such that the constraints above would not be violated.

The first rule is convenient to use (although it may cause problems with implementation), but can cause unintentional changes, because changes to the composite ACL occur as side-effects of other actions, for example, adding a new component with an ACL not in conformity with the ACLs of previously existing components.

The solution adopted was that for all modes except OWNER, which controls the modification of compoiste ACLs, the first update rule was chosen. In the case of OWNER, the second rule applies. The reason for the latter choice was that the OWNER permission is a critical privilege and should only be set intentionally. This means that OWNER permission GRANTED (or DENIED) for a composite object can only be set when all the components if any have OWNER GRANTED (or DENIED) and the CONTROL_ DISCRETIONARY permission (the atomic counterpart of OWNER) is GRANTED (or DENIED) on the object for the group.

If a new component is added to a composite object which has OWNER permission GRANTED to a particular security group, and this new component does not have OWNER GRANTED for this group, either the addition (actually the creation of a composition link) could fail, or the OWNER mode is propagated to the component (subject to some constraints). It was felt on balance that it would be undesirably inconvenient if the component's OWNER permissions must first be made to conform. The new component can be regarded as passing into the ownership of the composite object's owner. Therefore OWNER permission propagation occurs. However, this only applies if the new component has the relevant OWNER permission UNDEFINED. A DENIED OWNER right would not be over-ridden, and the component addition would fail.

3.5 Discretionary Access Modes

The nature of the access modes is specific to PCTE, the form that its repository takes and the facilities it provides. There are 21 different access modes, covering separately reading, writing and appending attributes, links and contents of objects, plus in addition special kinds of privileged access, including permission to change mandatory labels and ACLs.

The access modes are:

- NAVIGATE: controls navigation along an outgoing link of an object (link navigation is the primary means of accessing objects in PCTE's ERA Object Base).
- READ_ATTRIBUTES: controls reading the attribute values of an object.
- READ_CONTENTS: controls reading the contents of an object.
- READ_LINKS: controls reading the attributes of the outgoing links of an object, or to scan sets of links of an object.
- APPEND_CONTENTS: controls appending to the contents of an object.
- APPEND_LINKS: controls creating new outgoing links, other than implicit links, from an object.
- APPEND_IMPLICIT: controls creating new outgoing implicit links of an object.
- WRITE_ATTRIBUTES: controls changing the attribute values of an object. It does not control changing of the attribute values of the outgoing links.
- WRITE_LINKS: controls deleting outgoing links, other than implicit links, of an object and to change values of link attributes.
- WRITE_IMPLICIT: controls deleting outgoing implicit links of an object (for this category of link, there are no attributes to change).
- WRITE_CONTENTS: controls writing to the contents of an object.
- DELETE: controls deleting a (composite) object (i.e. to remove the last composition or existence link pointing to the object). This permission only has effect in a composite ACL.
- EXECUTE: controls executing a program (a "static context").
- EXPLOIT_DEVICE: controls mounting a volume on a device or unmounting a volume from the device.
- EXPLOIT_SCHEMA: controls using a Schema Definition Set (SDS) in a process' working schema or reading the typing information in the SDS.
- EXPLOIT_CONSUMER_IDENTITY: controls using a consumer group as consumer identity for the accounting mechanism.
- STABILIZE: controls stabilizing an object, which happens when a stabilizing link is created to the object, or else a compositely stabilizing link to an object of which this object is a component.
- CONTROL_DISCRETIONARY: controls changing the atomic ACL of an object (except CONTROL_MANDATORY). This discretionary access mode occurs only in atomic ACLs.
- CONTROL_MANDATORY: controls changing the mandatory labels of an object and to change the CONTROL_MANDATORY rights of other groups.
- CONTROL_OBJECT: a somewhat miscellaneous access mode. It controls converting the type of an object to a descendant type, moving it to another volume, modifying the version history relationships of an object, and changing the values of the "last_access" and "last_modification" time attributes.

- OWNER: the OWNER right for at least one discretionary group on an object controls modifying the composite ACL of that object (except that composite ACLs are implicitly modified when the atomic ACLs of components are changed). This access mode occurs only in object ACLs. If, however, no OWNER permission exists for a composite object, an OWNER right may be granted if all components and the "root" object have CONTROL_DISCRETIONARY right granted.

3.6 Use of the user group acyclic graph

The obvious application of the user group structure, consisting as it does of supergroups and subgroups, is to model an organisation structure, with as many levels of supergroups and supergroups of supergroups as is necessary. It is generally observed that individuals tend to move around an organisation, so that, although they are modelled as users, the roles that they perform should always be separated and modelled by user groups. Any objects private and confidential to an individual should be accessible to the user rather than one of his current user groups, but the objects used, produced, modified or developed in his work should be accessible to the user group.

If however the organisation is modelled in the obvious way, representing a manager role as a supergroup and the subordinate roles as subgroups, the expected result is not obtained. Since the use of a user group adds its supergroup to the effective groups of a process, any of the manager's subordinates obtains access to the objects to which the manager has access. The converse is not true. When the manager's user group is the adopted group its subgroups are not included in the process's effective groups and the manager does not have access to his subordinates' objects.

The answer is that the organisation must be modelled "upside down" by the supergroup/subgroup relationships. The manager role should be modelled by a subgroup of the user groups which represent the subordinate roles, and which are therefore supergroups of the manager's user group. The more senior the manager role, the further down the user group graph (taken as having ALL_USERS at the top) will his user group appear. Such a user group has the maximum privacy and the maximum (and automatic) accessibility to other's objects. Conversely, ALL_USERS, the supergroup of all supergroups, and representing the "man in the street", will have minimum access rights to objects belonging to members of development teams, projects and whatever other organisational units may be represented. This is illustrated in Figure 2. Arrows connecting user groups represent supergroup/subgroup relationships with the subgroup at the arrowhead end.

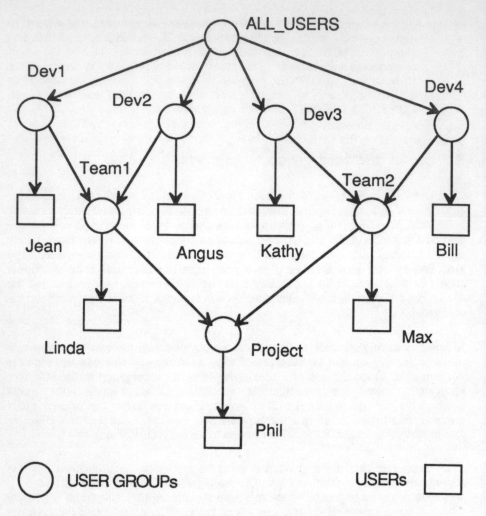

Figure 2. Organisation modelled as Discretionary Groups

If more detailed requirements exist, such as that subordinate roles can update their objects, but supervisory roles may only read such objects, more complex structures must be established with separate groups controlling read and update access.

A common requirement in software development is to pass developed items from one team to another for example for system integration. This again is most simply achieved by modelling the integration team as a subgroup of the teams.

More complex organisations, such as matrix management, can also be represented by using multiple subgroups. If it is required to "publish" objects within a team or project, common supergroups can be added. Publication then involves adding an ACL entry to the object permitting read access to the common supergroup.

3.7 Type-related discretionary access control

PCTE provides access control of a kind on instances of object, link and attribute types dependent on the type, rather than the instance. This however, is unspecific to the accessor and is not in conformity with discretionary access control on instances.

Access control related to types is connected to the schema view mechanism in PCTE: the schema definition sets. Five Definition Modes are defined: these are CREATE, DELETE, READ, WRITE and NAVIGATE. Only a subset of these modes apply to any given kind of type:

- object types: CREATE
- link types: CREATE, DELETE and NAVIGATE
- attribute types: READ and WRITE

For any process, a sequence of SDSs is defined as a Working Schema, which determines type visibility for the process. A given type may occur (with different usage mode values) in more than one of these SDSs. The resultant permission for the type in the Working Schema is obtained by taking the union of the usage modes of the SDSs. This means that the effective mode values are only GRANTED and UNDEFINED.

4. Security Administration

4.1 Mandatory Security

Facilities exist to establish and maintain mandatory security policies. New confidentiality and integrity classes may be defined, including any dominance relationships. Confidentiality and integrity towers must be built "ground up". Once defined, a mandatory class cannot be deleted. This restriction is necessary in order to provide a sufficient level of assurance. Once a mandatory class exists a label for an object may be created. There is no connection between a class and uses of that class in objects' labels. If that class were to be removed it is not possible to determine whether objects exist for which dominance relationships can no longer be determined because their labels contain undefined classes.

Operations exist to change the labels of an object. When an object is created it acquires the labels of the creating process. The confidentiality label of an object may be upgraded providing that the process has CONTROL_MANDATORY permission. It is also necessary sometimes to downgrade the confidentiality of object, perhaps because it was accidentally set too high, or because circumstances have changed. This can be achieved by the same operation, providing that one of the effective groups has a downgrade privilege. The converse holds for integrity labels. Operations also exist for the setting of the mandatory ranges of a multi-level secure device (volume, device or workstation). This again is only possible with CONTROL-_MANDATORY permission.

The existence of a downgrade and upgrade privilege means that this facility also has to be maintained. Operations again exist, and apply to any kind of security group. Downgrade privileges are represented by "may_downgrade" links from security group objects to confidentiality class objects, with reverse "downgradable_by" links, and similarly for integrity. It is important that the security labels and ACLs of the security group and confidentiality class objects are set correctly so that only authorised persons, such as a security officer, can enable downgrade privilege.

The labels of a process may also be changed: upgrading for confidentiality, downgrading for integrity. This is limited by the user's confidentiality and integrity clearances. Changing a process's label in the other direction can only be achieved by re-logging in. In this situation, the confidentiality label of the process is set to the minimum value, and integrity to the maximum.

Again user clearances need to be maintained, and user clearances are defined for each mandatory tower. They are represented by "cleared_for" links from a user object to the corresponding mandatory class with a reverse "having_clearance" link. Only one link may exist between a user and any class in a mandatory tower. Again care must be taken that the security labels and ACLs of the user and mandatory class objects are set so that these clearances can be set or changed only by authorised persons.

Operations exist to control the mandatory label floating facility for each process for confidentiality and for integrity. Separate options exist to float object labels and the process's label. Even if object label floating is switched on, the consistent application of the CONTROL_MANDATORY access right means that floating is forbidden unless the process has that access right on the object.

4.2 Discretionary Security

As for mandatory classes, security groups may be defined at any time by any process having APPEND_LINKS access rights on the security group directory. This right must be reserved for a security officer-like role. The existence of a security group is modelled by a "known_security_group" link from the "security_group_directory" to the object modelling the security group. Unlike mandatory classes, security groups may be removed, in accordance with the lower stringency of discretionary access control. Discretionary access control is so defined that not all ACL entries have to be considered in order to determine access rights so that redundant entries usually cause no problems. That is not always the case however, and it has been found necessary to include a facility to re-introduce security groups. The ACL entry may include the only permission to perform a necessary action such as changing the ACL, or even deleting the object. In accord with the highly irregular nature of this facility it can only be performed by a program which belongs to the predefined program group PCTE_SECURITY.

The user group acyclic graph can be changed by the addition and removal of supergroup/subgroup relationships, and by the addition and removal of users as members of user groups. Link types exist to model these relationships. There are two important constraints in the modification of the graph:

- it must remain acyclic;
- ALL_USERS must remain the ultimate supergroup of all user groups.

In fact, this last constraint cannot be entirely observed. Whenever a new user group is initialized, it has no subgroup/supergroup relationships at all. The important consideration is that no process may set up its effective groups such that ALL_USERS is not included. Therefore, when a new user group is being introduced, or an old one is being removed, the addition and removal of relationships, which can only be done one relationshp at a time, must be done in such an order that an effective-groups version of the rule is observed. Thus, no user can become a member of a user group unless that user group has ALL_USERS in its transitive supergroup relationships. Likewise a supergroup/subgroup relationship cannot be removed if it means that user groups which have users as members no longer have ALL_USERS as a (transitive) supergroup.

Similar operations exist for changing the program group acyclic graph. Programs can be members of program groups. Program groups can be subgroups of higher-level program groups. Again, the graph must remain acyclic, but there is no contraint analogous to that for ALL_USERS.

The ACL of an object may be changed, but this requires CONTROL_DISCRETIONARY permission for changing atomic ACLs, and OWNER permission for changing composite ACLs. When a composite ACL is changed explicitly in this way, all the components are changed to conform.

An ACL may be retrieved by any process having permission to read the attributes of the object instance. It is expected that when a composite ACL is retrieved, the implementation will actually compute it from the atomic ACLs of the components.

5. Auditing

Most PCTE operations and events belong to one of 14 types of auditable event:

- write
- read

40

- copy
- access_contents
- exploit (processes and volumes)
- change_access_control_list
- change_label
- use_predefined_group
- set_user_identity
- write_confidentiality_violation
- read_confidentiality_violation
- write_integrity_violation
- read_integrity_violation
- covert_channel

Auditing can be selectively switched on. There is however a bare minimum which cannot be switched off. Events which are always audited are events under the headings of security administration, audit event selection and moving objects from one volume to another.

Auditing is flexible: there are five kinds of audit criteria: return code-dependent, user dependent, object dependent, confidentiality label-dependent and integrity label-dependent criteria. The criteria consist of event type and return code, user, object or label.

These criteria enable events to be fairly precisely selected for auditing. For example, if it is desired to audit attempts by user X to write to specific sensitive objects, two audit criteria, one for write events for user X and one for write events for the specific object(s) are introduced. A simple record selection program may then scan the audit file to find such events, if they exist.

There are two ways of deactivating the auditing mechanism:
- removing audit criteria;
- switching auditing off. The audit criteria are saved, so that they become operative again when auditing is switched back on.

Neither of these methods affects the auditing of events which are always audited.

Audit information is written to an audit file. However, if an audit file cannot be written to, for whatever reason, any process performing an auditable operation is stalled. This problem is ameliorated by there being one audit file per workstation, so that auditing is at least resilient to workstation disconnection.

6. Conclusion

The nature of the PCTE security facilities is to a large extent (excluding the details of the access modes) orthogonal to the general repository features of PCTE itself and provide a reference point for other object-oriented databases. They show what can be achieved in integrating mandatory and discretionary security and in the provision of a basis for a wide variety of security policy options.

A consequence of its power and flexibility means that in the design and day-to-day use of a security policy, there are many options available. It is important that the need for the supply of the right set of user tools and for guidance in their use be realised.

Usage of mandatory access control is made easier by the use of the floating labels facility. It is believed that this facility is necessary to prevent the mandatory access controls becoming too onerous to use.

The large number of discretionary access modes enable access permissions to be tuned as desired. The 21 modes can be grouped into a small number of higher-level modes according to the precise requirements of the user's security policy. Suitable interactive tools can be used to minimise the complexity seen at the user interface.

PCTE provides support for a large number of options of user authentication, although not defining any specific method. The EDS implementation includes a password-based authentication tool, which may be replaced by a user-written tool if special authentication techniques are required. Access is provided to the OMS not only on the basis of users, but also user roles, by adoption of one of several user groups to which a user may belong. Adoption of user roles must be built into the authentication tool.

PCTE also provides support for security administration by providing operations necessary in order to define and maintain the user's desired security policy. Use of these operations themselves also needs to be defined in that security policy.

Access to particularly sensitive data which should be restricted to trusted tools can be supported by the use of user-defined "program groups". PCTE enables users to define their own privileged facilities under the exclusive control of trusted programs. In fact, PCTE itself defines several program groups for application to trusted tools, covering such functions as authentication, system management, updates to schemas, changes to version histories, update of replicas, and audit administration.

In the second edition of the ECMA PCTE standard, two security facilities have now been made optional: mandatory security (with or without floating labels) and auditing. This optionality is likely to have the unfortunate effect of reducing the number of implementations supporting the full range of security facilities specified for PCTE.

There can be little doubt that security access controls add to the overhead in accessing objects. Implementations need to adopt special measures to reduce these overheads to a minimum while still maintaining a reasonable level of assurance. The EDS implementation, for one, is specifically designed to optimise discretionary and mandatory access controls.

The specification PCTE security facilities is the result of a review and assessment process over several years by many security experts. However, it is true to say that little practical experience of its use yet exists. Now that an international standard exists, implementations are beginning to appear and it is hoped that this deficiency will soon be remedied.

7. References

1. Standard ECMA-149 Portable Common Tool Environment (PCTE) Abstract Specification, Edition 2, ECMA, Geneva, June 1993.

2. Standard ECMA-158 Portable Common Tool Environment (PCTE) C Programming Language Binding, Edition 2, ECMA, Geneva, June 1993.

3. Standard ECMA-162 Portable Common Tool Environment (PCTE) Ada Programming Language Binding, Edition 2, ECMA, Geneva, June 1993.

A Base for Secure Object Oriented Environments

Karin Vosseberg and Peter Brössler

University of Bremen
Department of Mathematics and Computer Science
D-28334 Bremen, Germany
Email: {karla, pb}@informatik.uni-bremen.de

J. Leslie Keedy

University of Ulm
Department of Computer Structures
D-89069 Ulm, Germany
Email: keedy@informatik.uni-ulm.de

Abstract

In object oriented environments a small but powerful base protection mechanism is needed which supports the specification of access based on the right to invoke an object interface routine. This base protection mechanism can be used to build up different security policies. The MONADS computer architecture is an efficient realisation of the base protection mechanism. The paper presents a solution for an implementation of different security policies in the MONADS environment.

1   Introduction

An important aspect of computer security is confidentiality and integrity of data. Access to data should only be possible for authorised users. In object oriented systems data are encapsulated by the associated operations. The direct object state is hidden from the outer world since access to it is only permitted through the well-defined object interface.

A much finer granularity of access control can be achieved for objects defined according to the information hiding principle than for pure data files. Access rights can be organised in terms of an object's interface routines instead of basic read, write, or execute rights. Illegal access and manipulation are prevented by the object mechanism. Greater flexibility can be achieved by the adaptation of security models to specific application environments [1].

We believe that for secure systems a small but powerful base mechanism is needed upon which different security models can be constructed. In an object oriented environment this base protection mechanism can support the specification

44

of access based on the right to invoke interface routines. For each such invocation the access rights relation between subjects and objects has to be verified. This approach presupposes a protection matrix similar to Lampson's [2]. On top of such a base protection mechanism it is possible to build up different independent security policies, e.g. discretionary access control or mandatory access control.

In the following sections we describe the essentials of the base protection mechanism and discuss how it can be used to construct different security policies. We then sketch a successful efficient realisation of the base protection mechanism in the form of the MONADS computer architecture. Finally the implementations of different security models in the MONADS system are outlined.

2 Requirements for the Base Protection Mechanism

We proceed on the assumption that the unit of protection, i.e. an *object* in terms of Lampson's protection matrix, is a large-grain object, with a well-defined semantic interface, such as an object containing a set of bank accounts (Figure 1), i.e. equivalent to a file of bank accounts in a conventional banking system.
According to [3] a large-grain object
- can only be accessed by invoking its interface routines
- may contain internal data structures which can only be manipulated by the interface routines
- can be composed of medium-grain and fine-grain objects.
We further assume that a large-grain object
- has a system-wide unique identifier for the lifetime of the whole system
- can be shared among users.

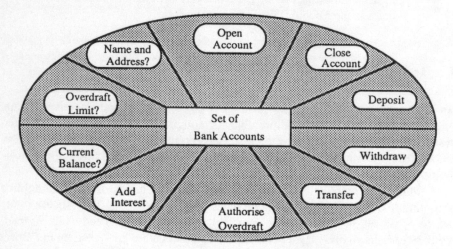

Figure 1: Interface of a Bank Accounts Object

Subjects are active entities and must be always correctly identifiable by the system. Usually subjects are users who have successfully passed an authentication step. The exact form of authentication (password, challenge response functions, smart cards, etc.) should be definable on a per user or user group base. Subjects may also be other objects or processes.

The resulting access rights relationship is a form of Lampson's protection matrix, in which the actual *access rights* denote the invocable procedures of an object for the relevant subject. In practice this protection matrix can be implemented using either the capability approach or the access list approach. Capabilities are stored by the holder of the access right whereas access lists are stored within objects. Each invocation of an object's interface routine must be verified by the base protection mechanism using the access rights relationship.

The access rights relationship is merely a snapshot of the currently allowed object invocations. It does not contain encoded information on how a subject can obtain additional access rights. The strategies for the distribution of access rights depend on the security policy. What is needed in the base protection mechanism to realise this is a means of granting and revoking access rights.

In the following we describe the possible realisation of different security policies based on this simple but powerful protection mechanism.

3 Realisation of Different Security Policies

Different security policies can be characterized by various attributes, for instance
- ownership of objects
- possibility to define and change the access rights relationship between objects and subjects
- classification of objects and subjects
- roles of subjects.

McLean divides security models into two classes of security policies: discretionary access control and mandatory access control [4].

Discretionary access control requires a user to remain the owner of the objects created by him or her and to be responsible for the protection of these objects. A user can grant an access right to another user if he or she has the appropriate right to do so and if he or she considers the other users need for the access right as truly necessary and legal. The given access right reflects the relationship between one subject and one object.

An implementation of discretionary access control above the base protection mechanism is straightforward to achieve. A user receives the access rights for all interface routines of an object when he or she creates it. The user decides which interface routines may be called by other users and grants appropriate access rights to these users. In terms of the base protection mechanism he or she sets up a new column in the protection matrix for the newly created object. Each time an interface routine of the object is invoked the base mechanism verifies that the caller indeed has the appropriate access right for this object.

In an environment with *mandatory access control* the system is the owner of secure objects and is responsible for the protection of these objects. The underlying security model contains rules which define who may possess what access rights. The access right relationships between objects and subjects are defined in the rule set before any secure object is created, while with discretionary access control the object is first created and then the access right relationship is defined. The rules of mandatory access control have to be enforced by the protection mechanism. They may be checked either when access to an object is attempted or when access rights are transferred from one user to another. In the latter case it should also be possible to invalidate access rights if the rules are changed. There may also be rules regarding the right to change the current rule set. If rules are represented as objects the rule system can be used to govern the meta-level of rule modifications as well.

Mandatory access control is often expressed in terms of particular security evaluation criteria. For example [5] describes requirements for multilevel security models of mandatory access control (starting with class B1). The rules when a subject may be granted access rights for an object are specified in more detail. Objects must be associated with security levels which are ordered hierarchical. The access rights for objects are determined by their security level (classification). Subjects must be also characterised by security levels (clearances). The rules describe the circumstances under which a member of a given security level may be granted access to an object at a given security level. A realisation of this model upon the base protection mechanism requires the classification of objects and subjects. These classifications are then used in the rules governing the granting and passing of access rights.

In some other approaches the line between discretionary access control and mandatory access control models is not drawn that sharp. For instance discretionary access control can be combined with user-role based security [6].

4   The MONADS System

The MONADS computer architecture has been designed to support both software engineering principles such as modularisation, information hiding, and persistent programming, and also security and protection of objects. To demonstrate an efficient and realistic implementation of this, a series of projects were undertaken, culminating in the development of the MONADS-PC computer [7].

In contrast with conventional computer architectures, the MONADS system does not distinguish between a transient computational "virtual memory" and a persistent "file system". All objects are stored in a single, persistent, globally shared virtual memory. This allows a single set of mechanisms to be used for management, access, synchronisation, and protection of all objects regardless of type and life-time [8]. In a network of MONADS-PCs the uniform virtual memory is extended to a distributed shared memory allowing location-transparent access to all objects [9, 10].

The virtual memory space of the MONADS-PC is decomposed into a set of logically contiguous *address spaces*. Each such address space is uniquely identified by the first 32 bits of a 60 bit address and may be up to 256M-bytes in length. Disk space allocation for address spaces is based on 4K-byte pages [11].

Objects. There is a one-to-one relationship between (large-grain) objects and address spaces. For this reason the unique address space number can be used as the unique object identifier. Address space numbers are never reused; this ensures that after deletion of an object retained object identifiers cannot be used to access a newly created object.

Objects have a procedural interface and can be used only by invoking the interface routines. The architecture enforces the information-hiding principle in that the internal data structures of an object can be accessed only via the object's own interface and internal routines. All major user and system components (e.g. application programs, operating systems modules, subroutine libraries, and "files") are implemented as objects.

Subjects. When a user is introduced to the system a new process is created. In contrast with conventional systems this process persists in the virtual memory until the accreditation of this user ceases. A process is represented by a *process stack* which is stored in an address space. The address space number of a process stack serves as a unique and unforgeable identification of a user.

When a user logs out from the system his or her process is not destroyed as in conventional systems such as Unix. Instead the logout routine invokes the basic protection mechanism (the Kernel), which then suspends the process. When the user logs in again the Kernel reactivates the process identified by the "username" and returns to the logout routine at the instruction following the previous logout invocation. At this point the logout routine can carry out checks to authenticate the identity of the logging-in user (see Figure 2). This allows the use of very flexible user-specific authentication procedures because the logout and subsequent login can be performed by any user-programmed module. It is thus possible for a user to provide arbitrary authentication checks, which can be much more complicated than simple password mechanisms. For example the authentication procedure may use time locks for bank employees, challenge response functions which create dynamically new passwords for a given output string, a special sequence of commands, or a questions-answer play etc. Using this approach different users may have different authentication procedure.

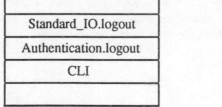
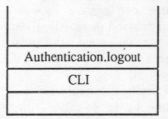

(suspended) persistent process stack   (reactivated) persistent process stack
after logout   after login

Figure 2: Authentication of Persistent Processes

What exactly is a subject in the MONADS environment? In this context we have three different kinds of subjects. A subject in the meaning of a user is the persistent process stack which carries out all object invocations for the user. A kernel interface routine returns the persistent process number of the currently active process which is the unique user identification. Persistent Processes do not hold any access rights for objects by themselves. Subjects which possess access rights for objects are in the MONADS system normal objects. How objects relate to access rights is described in the following paragraph. Subjects in the notion of the Lampson's matrix are persistent process stacks which invoke an object. The access rights of an invoker results from the access rights possessed by the currently invoked object and can be further restricted by using the persistent process number.

Access rights. No object can be invoked unless the invoker possesses and presents the appropriate right to do so. The rights are encoded in so-called *capabilities*.[1] A capability has three fields relevant to this discussion (see Figure 3). The address space number is the unique object identifier of the object to be invoked. The status field contains information such as the kind of the object, the ownership, and the right to copy the capability. The access rights field indicates which of the interface routines associated with the target module may be called by the presenter of the capability. When a new object is created the creator receives an *owner capability* with all access rights enabled. The deletion of an owner capability results in the deletion of the object. Capabilities can be freely stored in any object and can be passed between users and between objects subject to the necessary access right. The MONADS-PC architecture prevents arbitrary modification of capabilities. However copies of capabilities can be made, with reduced access rights where appropriate.

address space number	status	access rights

Figure 3: The Structure of a Capability

The possession of a capability implies the right to call the specified interface routines of an object. Revocation of capabilities can be achieved by either renaming the object (and thereby invalidating all existing capabilities for this object) or by restricting the access rights of specific capabilities using the address rights field as an index into a table containing the actual access rights which is stored as part of the object.

Normally capabilities are stored along with symbolic names and possibly further information in so-called "directories", similar to conventional file system directories. Such a directory is itself a user-programmable object which allows associative retrieval of other capabilities. The interface routines of a directory

---

[1] The MONADS system provides a two level security mechanism based on segment-capabilities and module-capabilities. In this context we only refer to module-capabilities which provides security at the user level of objects.

module will normally provide services similar to those of conventional directories. A simplified version of the directory interface is shown in Figure 4. These services are typically invoked by presenting an appropriate capability for the directory itself and providing a symbolic name as a parameter. By storing capabilities for directories within other directories arbitrary complex directory structures can be created.

```
class Directory

type order = [alphabetic, by_creation, by_user]

proc insert_entry (name: string; cap: capability; message: string)
proc delete_entry (name: string)
enq get_entry (name: string) returns [capability, time, string]
...
proc list_entries (output_device: capability; required_order: order)

end_class Directory
```

Figure 4: A Simplified Interface Definition for Directory Modules

There are two ways of providing a user (process) with a capability. The first is at the time a new process is created. The new process is passed an initial capability, typically for a directory containing further capabilities. The standard user environment is usually set up this way. The second way requires the granter of a capability to share an object with the receiver. The former inserts the capability into the shared object and the latter can then retrieve it from there. The shared object will usually be a directory. This approach is also the basic form of electronic mail between users. Instead of a full text or graphic documents, capabilities with rights to use a certain object are sent.

Discretionary Access Control. Discretionary access control is realised as follows: Each user has a private directory structure. The creator of an object retains the owner capability in one of his or her directories, and capabilities are passed from one user to another by *secure communication* using directories which additionally maintain the unforgeable identification of the user who inserted the capability.

A capability for a central *mail recipient directory* is made available for each user who is allowed to communicate with other users, when the user is created. He or she inserts a capability with appropriate access rights for his or her own *mailbox directory* in the mail recipient directory. The mailbox owner can be identified by the persistent process number which is part of the entry in the mail recipient directory. Figure 5 shows an example of the directory structure for secure communication between users. The users Ann and Tom have inserted capabilities for their mailbox directories in the mail recipient directory. If Tom wants to grant access rights for an object to Ann, he inserts a capability in her mailbox directory.

50

The sender of capabilities can be verified by the persistent process number of the mailbox entry[2].

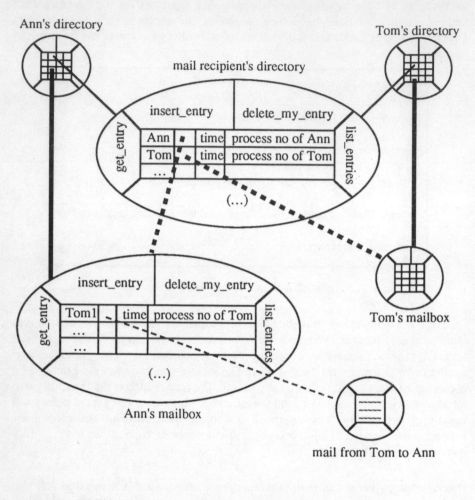

Ann's directory

mail recipient's directory

Tom's directory

get_entry	insert_entry			delete_my_entry	list_entries
	Ann	∎	time	process no of Ann	
	Tom		time	process no of Tom	
	...				

(...)

Tom's mailbox

get_entry	insert_entry			delete_my_entry	list_entries
	Tom1	∎	time	process no of Tom	
	...				
	...				

(...)

Ann's mailbox

mail from Tom to Ann

——— capability with access rights: insert_entry, delete_my_entry
∎ ∎ ∎ capability with access rights: insert_entry, delete_my_entry, get_entry, list_entries
▬▬▬ capability with all access rights
- - - - capability with access rights for accessing mail

Figure 5: Directory Structure for Secure Communication between Users

Mandatory Access Control. In an environment with mandatory access control secure objects have to be maintained by the system. If capabilities for secure objects can be stored in private directories the secure communication mechanism between

---

[2] See [12] for a full description of secure communication between users.

users via mailbox directories has to enforce the rules of the underlying security model, but it is difficult to control indirect communication by normal shared objects. Therefor in the MONADS system users are not allowed to retain capabilities for secure objects directly in their private directory structures.

A system object maintains the owner capabilities of secure objects and enforces the rules of the security model. It checks whether a user is allowed to possess access rights for the required object and has additional interface routines to allow changes to the rules of the security model. The system object can be implemented either like a command processor which invokes the object's interface routines after checking the access rights, or like a directory which returns a capability with the appropriate access rights for the object.

The command processor implementation makes it unnecessary to grant a capability directly to the user. Granting access rights for an object to the user and the invocation of the object interface routine are handled together. The rules of the underlying security model are checked with each object invocation. This approach has some disadvantages. For instance a special mechanism for passing an object as a parameter to another object is required. In the implementation of objects a call of an interface routine of a secure object has to be transformed to a call of the secure command processor and cannot be managed as a normal inter-object call. Existing programs cannot be reused for secure applications.

If access rights for objects are maintained in directories with the standard directory interface and with additional interface routines for changing the rules, then the standard command language interpreter can be used for managing user requirements of an object invocation. Granting access rights for objects to users and the invocation of an interface routine are distinct. The rules of the underlying security model are checked when the access right is transferred to the subject. Objects can be passed as parameters to other objects in the usual way. The user is not allowed to retain the capability in his or her private directory structure or to transfer the capability to another user. To enforce this the directory returns a capability in which the "no copy"-bit in the status field of the capability is set. The "no copy"-bit prevents copying a capability, but the capability may be passed as a parameter for another object. There is also no possibility for the user to copy the whole object and then transfer a capability for the new object to another user. In order to copy an address space of an object the owner capability is needed. If the rules of the security model are changed all capabilities which have been granted to users have to be revoked.

The system object for maintaining the access rights of secure objects can be organised in different ways:
- A central system object maintains all secure objects in a similar way to a reference monitor. There is one place in the system where the security model is implemented and the rules of the security model can be maintained in a straightforward way. But this central system object can easily become a bottle-neck in the system.
- All secure objects are classified and the maintaining of access rights is distributed to several system objects relating to different object classifications. An object classification can be seen as an object security level, all objects of one

52

project, or all objects offering the same interface. The complexity of system objects which maintain only the rules expressing the access rights for the objects of one classification is smaller than of the central system object. Figure 6 shows an example for a rule-based directory of an object classification. If in this example a subject of a given security level calls the *get_entry* routine of the directory the rules are checked and a capability subject to the appropriate access rights for the required object is returned. The returned capability is invalid when the security level of subjects does not match the rules of the secure objects in this directory. The rights for administration of an object classification and the associated security rules can be granted to different users in an easy way using the same protection mechanism.

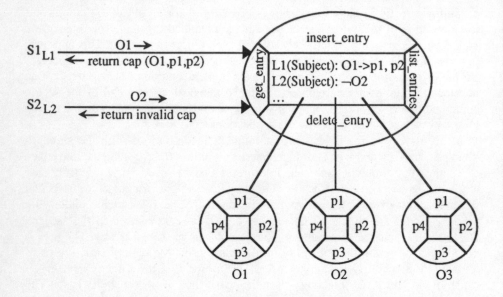

Figure 6: A Rule-Based Directory of an Object Classification

– The rules of the security model may be divided into object-specific rules. Each secure object is related to a system object which maintains only the security rules for granting the access rights of this object. The system object can for instance be a shadow object with the identical interface routines plus additional routines for changing the security rules. Each interface routine of the shadow object checks the rules and then invokes the interface routine of the secure object with a capability subject to the appropriate access right or refuses the call (Figure 7). Understanding the rules for one object becomes easier but the distribution of rules increases the complexity of system administration. This approach is only useful for a limited number of objects.

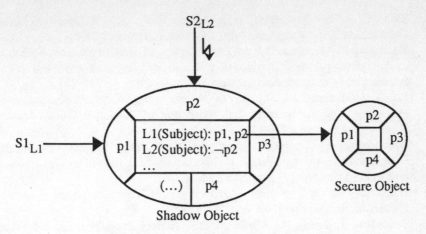

Figure 7: A Shadow Object

5 Conclusion

We have presented a technique for implementing different security policies in an object-oriented environment on top of a simple base protection mechanism. In our approach there is no need for a range of different protection mechanisms for each security policy.

Existing capability-based systems offer different ways of enforcing security policies. The security policy can be checked on each invocation, as in the SCAP system [13]. Alternatively the check can be performed when a capability is transferred. The ICAP system [14] follows this approach. A third way has been proposed for the KeyKos system [15], where capabilities within a *compartment* can be used without further checks and invocations of objects in other compartments have to be checked by a central reference monitor. All these approaches are possible in MONADS and can be chosen according to the application's needs.

Current work in the MONADS project is directed towards solving the confinement problem [16] in an object-oriented environment.

References

1. Evered M, Keedy JL. A Model for Protection in Persistent Object-Oriented Systems. In Rosenberg J, Keedy JL (eds.). Security and Persistence. Springer-Verlag, London, 1990, pp 67-82
2. Lampson BW. Protection. ACM Operating System Reviews 1974; 8,1:18-24
3. Chin RS, Chanson ST. Distributed Object-Based Programming Systems. ACM Computing Surveys 1991; 23, 1:91-124
4. McLean J. The Specification and Modelling of Computer Security. IEEE Computer 1990; 23,1:9-16
5. Department of Defence. Trusted Computer System Evaluation Criteria. 1985

6. Ting TC. A User-Role Based Data Security Approach. In Landwehr C (ed.). Database Security: Status and Prospects. North-Holland, 1988

7. Rosenberg J, Abramson DA. MONADS-PC: A Capability Based Workstation to Support Software Engineering. In Proceedings of the 18th Hawaii International Conference on Systems Sciences. 1985, pp 222-231

8. Keedy JL, Rosenberg J. Support for Objects in the MONADS Architecture. In Proceedings of the International Workshop of Persistent Object Systems. Newcastle, 1989, pp 202-213

9. Abramson DA, Keedy JL. Implementing a Large Virtual Memory in a Distributed Computing System. In Proceedings of the 18th Hawaii Conference on System Sciences, 1985, pp 515-522

10. Henskens FA. A Capability-Based Persistent Distributed Shared Memory. PhD thesis, University of Newcastle, 1991

11. Rosenberg J, Keedy JL, Abramson DA. Addressing Mechanisms for Large Virtual Memories. The Computer Journal 1992; 35,4:369-375

12. Keedy JL, Vosseberg K. Persistent Protected Modules and Persistent Processes as the Basis for a More Secure Operating System. In Proceedings of the 25th Hawaii International Conference on System Sciences, Kauai, 1992, pp. 747-756

13. Karger PA. Improving Security and Performance for Capability Systems. PhD thesis, University of Cambridge Computer Laboratory, 1988

14. Gong L. On Security in Capability-Based Systems. ACM Operating Systems Review 1989; 23,2:56-60

15. Landau CR Security in a Secure Capability-Based System. ACM Operating Systems Review 1989; 23,4:2-4

16. Lampson BW. A Note on the Confinement Problem. Communications of the ACM 1973; 16,10:613-615

An Object-Oriented Application Security Framework

Dr. James Alan Talvitie
American Management Systems, Inc.
Arlington, Virginia, USA

Abstract

This paper outlines an object model for security authorization framework to be implemented in Smalltalk. The system is based upon POSIX-like access control matrices, but extended to incorporate "role-based" authorization. In certain aspects it is also influenced by a DCE model and by conversations with T.C. Ting on role-based security. The framework is intended to support business applications coded in Smalltalk using relational databases.

1. Introduction

This paper outlines an object model for a security authorization framework for business oriented applications to be developed in Smalltalk using relational databases. It expands on a paper delivered to the 1993 OOPSLA conference workshop on security in object oriented systems [2].

The authorization model is based upon POSIX-like access control matrices, but extended to incorporate "role-based" authorization designed to handle problems outlined by Ting [3]. In certain aspects it is also influenced by DCE notions [1].

2. Terminology

An *object*, for purposes of this discussion, is something transient. In Smalltalk terms, it is something "in the image."

An *entity* is an identifiable something about which information is captured in persistent storage, i.e. in the database. For the most part our work is with relational databases in which talk of "persistent objects" is at best confusing, and so we prefer the more common term "entity" for the items assigned identifiers in an RDBMS.

A *representation* is an object which represents an entity. Representations capture certain data about database entities. They do not necessarily capture all there is to know about an entity. Representations in general are responsible for updates to entities.

The relationship between an entity *kind* and a representation *class* is many-to-many. Since a representation represents only certain aspects of an entity, the instances of a representation class can represent common aspects of different kinds of entities. For examples,

*   A Taxpayer representation might be created both for an organization entity, IBM, and a person entity, Fred, since both IBM and Fred pay taxes.

*   A SecuritySubject representation might be created both for a process and a person.

*   A Student representation might be created for both, Fido, a dog entity in a dog training academy, and a Fido's owner, Fred.

Likewise since a representation represents only certain aspects of an entity, the same kind of entity may be represented by instances of many distinct representation classes. For examples:

*   The same persistent person entity, Fred, might be represented as a Student and as an Alumnus.

*   The same persistent person entity, Fred, might be represented both as a SecuritySubject and as a DepartmentChairman.

*   The same persistent academic class, *PHIL201-Section-100,* might have several representations, e.g. one incorporating the features needed to teach and grade its students, and one incorporating the features needed to determine the required characteristics of any room in which it may be taught. In the second role it functions as a RoomUse. Not all room uses are academic classes.

One may think of a representation of an entity as a logical picture of that entity playing a certain *role*. The persistent entity has a kind (person, academic class, organization) and the object representations picture it playing a role (Student, Alumnus, AcademicClass, RoomUse, Taxpayer).

A *protected object* is any object access to which is controlled by the security system. Representations in general are protected objects. Security over database entities is primarily handled through protecting access to the methods of their transient object representations. Note that not all protected objects need be representations of entities. Windows, menu items, buttons, etc. might also be protected objects.

Each access to a protected object executes some *action*. An "action" might be identical to a method selector or might be a classification of method selectors which are equivalent for security purposes. "Granting access" does not simply mean granting the right to obtain information, but granting the right to execute one or more methods of a protected object. The methods could do anything whatsoever.

A *security subject* is anything to which access to a protected object is granted or withheld. The primary examples are end users. A representation of a security subject is loaded into the Smalltalk image as a result of a login process in which the subject's identity is authenticated. The same persistent entity which is represented as a security subject may also be represented by instances of other object classes. Being a system user is only one of the roles it may play in the system.

3. Access matrices and situations

An access matrix is sometimes explained as a two-dimensional table with security subjects as row headings, protected objects as column headings, and with each cell filled with the access types which may be executed in behalf of the security subject by the protected object. The problem of security authorization is how to effectively represent and check such an access matrix. The table below is an example of an access matrix.

	PHIL201 Section 100	PHIL601 Section 200	ENG301 Section 300	Payment Voucher #3212345
Fred	drop	register	drop	
George	assign class grades, assign TA, grade tests			
Sam	assign room	assign room		
Sally	grade tests	register		
Martha	assign instructor	assign instructor		approve

This picture is however too simple. It assumes that the actions allowable for a given subject/object pair are a function of the identities of the object and the subject alone. For example once we know the identity of the subject Fred and the protected object *PHIL101-Section-100*, the above matrix tells us that the *PHIL101-Section-100's drop* method may be executed.

In reality the allowed actions are dependent not only upon the *identities* of the subject and the object, but also upon their momentary *states* and *relationships* to one another and to other entities. For examples:

• The payee on *PaymentVoucher #3212345* cannot approve it. Martha may be the payee at one time and not the payee at another time.

- The right to assign the teaching assistants to *PHIL201-Section-100* belongs to its instructor. George may be the instructor at one moment, but be relieved of those duties at another.

- The right to assign the instructor to *PHIL601-Section-200* belongs to the departmental chair of the department responsible for the general subject area of the topic of the course of which *PHIL601-Section-200* is a section. If the subject area is assigned to a different department, or the departmental chairman changes, or the course topic is re-categorized, then the possessor of the right to assign the instructor will also change.

- Certain subjects may approve *PaymentVoucher #3212345*, but only for less than a $1000. If the amount of the voucher changes the required approvals will change as well. Martha may be able to approve up to $1000 but not over $1000.

All of these examples come to the same thing. The identities of the subject and the object can remain the same, while contents of any cell may change. Security relations are not therefore properly representable with a two-dimensional matrix. An adequate access matrix must contain another dimension. The third dimension must account for variability of the allowed actions according to the momentary relations and states of the subject and the object at the time access rights are determined.

3.1. Situations

Let us define a "situation" as a possibility that some things have a particular state and set of relations to one another. For examples:

- *Martha being the Philosophy Department chair and PHIL201-Section-100 being a section of PHIL201 and the topic of PHIL201 being Ethics and Ethics being a branch of Philosophy and the Philosophy Department being responsible for Philosophy and Mary being the instructor of PHIL201-Section-100 and George being the Teaching Assistant for PHIL201 and Fred being an undergraduate in the College of Arts and Sciences* is a situation. This situation is not only possible, but we shall assume, actually occurs.

- *Martha being the Psychology Department chair and PHIL201-Section-3 being a section of PHIL201 and the topic of PHIL201 being Ethics and Ethics being in the general area of Psychology and the Philosophy Department being responsible for Psychology* is another situation. However since Ethics is not a branch of Psychology and the Philosophy Department is not responsible for Psychology and Martha isn't the Psychology Department chair, this situation, although possible, does not occur.

We can then represent an access matrix as a three-dimensional matrix, with situations as the third dimension. Any cell contains the actions which may be taken *by* a subject *on* a object *in* a situation.

3.2. Logical components of a situation

A situation can be represented as the conjunction of as series of *component* situations. For example the situation:

> *George being the Psychology Department chair and PHIL201-Section-100 being a section of PHIL201 and the topic of PHIL201 being Ethics and Ethics being a branch of Psychology and the Philosophy Department being responsible for Psychology*

can be represented as the conjunction of the situations:

> *George being the Psychology Department chair and PHIL201-section-3 being a section of PHIL201 and the topic of PHIL201 being Ethics*

and

> *Ethics being in the general area of Psychology and the Philosophy Department being responsible for Psychology.*

We can always subdivide complex situations in this way. We simply describe them and break them at the "ands." Each component situation describes some state-of-affairs which obtains if the whole situation obtains.

3.3. Subject features, object features, and subject/object relationships

It is useful to conceptually divide situations involving security subjects and protected objects into the following components.

1. *Object features*

    This includes all security relevant properties and relations of the object, the statement of which does not require reference to any security subjects. One may think of them as all features of the object which can remain the same when one subject is replaced by another. For example *that the subject matter of PHIL201-Section-100 is Ethics* is a situation which makes no reference to the subject Fred.

2. *Subject features*

    This includes all security relevant properties of security subjects, the statement of which does not require reference to a protected object. For example, *that Fred is in the school of Arts and Sciences*

3. *Relationships between subject and object*

    This includes everything else. These are connections between *this* subject and *this* object. For example, *that Fred teaches PHIL201-Section-100* is a situation which involves both the subject Fred and the object PHIL201-Section-100.

Every situation involving a subject and an object can be exhaustively broken into these three components. So we may represent the third dimension of our logical access matrix as a triplet of object features, subject features, and subject/object relationships. The problem of authorization incorporates the mechanisms for representing security relevant object features, subject features, and relationships.

4. Access control lists

A security matrix such as that shown above, let alone a three dimensional matrix, is too unwieldy for actual use.

An access matrix contains many empty cells -- many subjects can take no actions with respect to many objects. The empty cells can be eliminated by representing the matrix as a set of *access control lists (ACLs),* one for each column. An access control list represents a single column of an access matrix, with empty cells dropped. Empty cells may be dropped if the rule is adapted that whoever is not explicitly granted access is implicitly denied it. The cells of an access control list are called *access control list entries (ACL entries).*

5. Representing actions

An *action* is a logical categorization of something that a protected object can do. In our Smalltalk implementation actions are represented by Symbols. The symbols may either be method selectors, or they may be more abstract.

Many actions are equivalent for security purposes. It would be strange if access to the *firstName* and *lastName* were allowed, but not access to the *middleName*. So it would be desirable, in order to reduce the number of actions which must be listed in ACL cells, to categorize actions.

A subject can perform an action if the subject has *rights* the possession of which is sufficient to permit the subject to perform it. Consequently we can categorize actions according to the rights required by subjects in order to perform them. Actions are equivalent for security purposes if their performance requires the same rights.

5.1. Atomic Access Rights

Certain rights imply other rights. For example, the right to *read and write* implies the right to *read.* *Atomic rights* are rights which are logically independent, i.e. those which do not imply other rights. You cannot infer one atomic right from another.

An action is categorized for security purposes if the set of atomic rights its performance requires is specified. An action may require the possession of more than one right. A right may permit the execution of more than one action.

In our implementation atomic rights are represented by ASCII characters. There are 256 separate possible representations of atomic rights.

A protected object is expected to be able to answer the atomic access rights required for execution of any of the actions it can perform.

There is a standard mechanism for determining the access rights for an action. Each class of protected object holds a dictionary of associations between symbols for actions and sets of characters representing atomic access rights. If the set of required permissions is not found in the class of the object, then the dictionary of the superclass of the object is accessed.

5.2. Permissions and prohibitions

A *permission* is the granting of an atomic access right. Each access control list entry contains a set of permissions for a classification of security subjects.

A *prohibition* is the refusal of an access right, the taking away of a permission. Prohibitions serve two purposes:

- Prohibitions allow a security administrator to give blanket rights to everyone in a large group, and take away rights from a sub-group. This is mainly for convenience. It would always be possible to handle the same situation by defining three groups, one with the common permissions, and the others with the differences.

- Prohibitions allow the expression of negative rules for occupants of certain roles. For example consider the rules:

  - *The payee on an expense voucher cannot approve the voucher.*

  - *Patients cannot assign themselves the role of primary physician in their own case.*

  These rules can only be represented as a withdrawal of a permission. This not a matter of mere convenience. There is no way to express the rule except as the withdrawal of rights which the occupant of the role might otherwise have had.

Just as access control entries can grant rights by listing permissions so also they can take them away by listing prohibitions.

6. Representing features of protected objects

Creating a separate access control list for every column of an access matrix would mean a lot of access control lists. There is an additional problem that individual objects are dynamically created and destroyed. The access control lists should be comparatively stable. However, in the majority of cases, protected objects may placed into categories which are equivalent for security purposes.

- *In many cases all objects of a single class are equivalent.*

  For example, imagine a system which is determines market values of vehicles. Such a system would utilize a table of vehicle makes, entries in which are represented by instances of VehicleMake. Probably anyone who can access one vehicle make can access another.

- *In some cases objects of different classes have the same profile, whether or not they happen to be in the same class hierarchy.*

  Suppose our vehicle appraisal system includes VehicleModels and VehicleBodyTypes. It is extremely unlikely that different users would be granted the right to update models but not body types. It's imaginable, but it wouldn't happen in reality. So VehicleModels and BodyTypes would be given a common security categorization. Whether VehicleModels and VehicleBodyTypes they are in the same inheritance hierarchy is of no relevance to this categorization. Inheritance is for code reuse, not for security categorization.

- *The classification may be based upon instance characteristics which cut across class boundaries.*

  For example, suppose a real estate appraisal system in which only very experienced appraisers may appraise very complicated buildings. In such a system there might be a VictorianHouse class, a RowHouse class, a RanchStyleHouse class, but there probably there isn't a VeryComplicatedBuilding class. Very complicated buildings are probably just buildings, of whatever class, which answer the *veryComplicated* message with *true*.

What is needed is a mechanism which will categorize objects based upon common security relevant features -- a mechanism which allows an orthogonal cut across object class hierarchies, and which allows classifications based on instance characteristics.

6.1. Security categories

A *security category* is a categorization of protected objects which share common security-relevant features, the access policies to which, within a given policy-setting organization, are enforced through a single access control list. A protected object is in only *one* security category. Each protected object must be able to identify its security category.

When we define an object category we do not make reference to any subjects. So a category represents features of an object which vary independent of relations to security subjects. Changing the subject signed- on should not cause a change in the categories of the protected objects.

Each category has a name which distinguishes it from others. Examples of category names might be:

> voucher/expense/travel
> voucher/payment.

An object's security category name is determined by sending it the message *securityCategoryName*. The standard answer concatenates two major components, *securityCategoryNamePrefix* and *securityCategoryNameSuffix*.

The prefix is by default retreived from the class of the object. The suffix is typically provided at the instance level.

Either category name component can be nil. In the above example *'voucher/expense'* might be a class-contributed prefix whereas *'/travel'* might be an instance-contributed suffix. Each major component may in turn be subdivided into minor components, i.e. substrings which separately represent independently variable features of the object. For example *voucher*, */expense,* and */payment* might be minor components of the class-contributed prefixes of the above category designations.

A subject's access to an object in a category is controlled by an access control list (ACL) associated with the category and with a policy-setting organization. The identity of the ACL associated with an object category is inferred from a table cross referencing categories and organizations to access control list identifiers. The relevant policy-setting organization is determined from the representation of user created at sign-on time.

Policy Setting Organization	Category Name	ACL
Queens Campus	voucher/expense/ travel	Queens Campus Expense Voucher ACL
Queens Campus	voucher/expense	Queens Campus Expense Voucher ACL
Queens Campus	voucher/payment	Queens Campus Payment Voucher ACL
Manhattan Campus	voucher/expense/ travel	Manhattan Campus Expense Voucher ACL
Manhattan Campus	voucher/expense	Manhattan Campus Travel Voucher ACL
Manhattan Campus	voucher/payment	Manhattan Campus PaymentVoucher ACL

The routine determining the name of the category of an object is hardcoded one of the methods of the object. Distinct classes may use distinct approaches for building the name. The association between a category and an ACL is under the control of a policy setting organization. If an organization does not see a need to distinguish certain categories, it may associate them with a single ACL.

Note that an security category is a category of protected *objects*, not of database *entities*. Consequently it is possible that the same entity, as represented by different objects, might be multiply categorized. For example a person entity represented as a Student would probably be in a different security category than the same person entity represented as an Alumnus.

6.2. Limitations of security categories

It is important that there not be too many distinct object categories. There are several reasons for this:

64

- Access to all objects in a single category is handled by a single ACL. The association between an access control list and a category is under the control of a system administrator. A great multiplicity of categories will therefore place a heavy burden on administrators, both in maintaining the additional category to ACL cross references, and potentially in maintaining the additional ACLs themselves.

- The relevant information in an ACL for a particular subject is cached when the ACL is first accessed. More categories will mean typically more ACLs, which in turn will mean either more memory to support the cache, or more I/O to access the additional ACLs, or both. An unnecessarily large number of categories is likely to cause a performance degradation.

Any feature of an object could be represented with a separate category name component, and so in theory a categorization scheme could be developed to represent all of the combined features of any set of objects. The theory does not however work well in practice. Each additional feature represented with a separate category component will double the number of component combinations, and therefore double the number of categories. An object class with 10 independently varying features would require 1024 independent categories to capture all combinations for all possible instances. An equal number of access control lists would have to be defined.

6.3. Special rights for special features

As indicated above not all of the security relevant features of a protected object can be packed into its object category. There would be too many categories. So there is a need somehow to represent those changes in the accessibility of objects based upon changes in object features not captured in categories.

The solution is based upon the claim an object feature change is irrelevant to security unless it changes the atomic rights needed to perform some actions with respect to the object. Consequently, features of the object which are not captured in its category, and not captured in its relations to subjects, may be represented as alternate sets of rights returned by the method requesting the set of atomic rights required for performance of a particular action. The standard method simply looks up the symbol for the action in a dictionary, and is therefore insensitive to the state of the object. An override to the standard method however can be made sensitive to anything.

7. Representing features of security subjects

A security subject is anything or anyone in behalf of which a protected object takes actions. It is anyone who could be signed-on to the system. The rows of an access matrix are identities of subjects. Reducing an access matrix to a set of access control lists, if nothing else were done, would leave as many entriesin the access control lists are there were subjects which could do anything with respect to the categories of object for which the list specified the access rules. That would be too many entries, and would not, in any case, account for security relevant changes in subject features. So it is useful to be able to categorize subjects as well as objects.

7.1. Subject groups

A *subject group* is a named categorization of subjects with common security-relevant features. When we define subject groups we do not make reference to any objects. The non-relational features of security subjects can be represented through subject groups. For any set of such features, there a group of subjects which possess the feature. Each subject belongs to a set of such groups. The set of groups to which a particular subject belongs fully specifies its non-relational security-relevant features. The definitions of the groups do not require reference to any protected objects.

A subject can be a member of many security groups. Groups can also be members of other groups. Membership is transitive. If A is a member of B, and B is a member of C, then A is a member of C.

Groups are defined in a Security Group Table and group memberships in a Group Membership Table.

Policy Setting Organization	Group
Queens Campus	Queens Campus Philosophy Department
Queens Campus	Queens Campus Psychology Department
Queens Campus	Queens Campus Academic Departments

Group	Member
Queens Campus Academic Departments	Queens Campus Philosophy Department
Queens Campus Academic Departments	Queens Campus Psychology Department
Queens Campus Psychology Department	Mary
Queens Campus Philosophy Department	Martha

It is expected that intergroup relationships, plus the rights of groups, would be defined by central security administrators associated with policy setting organizations. The group definitions and membership relations are part of the security policy of an organization, and for this reason should probably not be frequently changeable. A subject's *memberships* in groups might however be transient and under the control of an application, rather than under the control of a central administration. There is nothing wrong with this so long as the objects used to set group memberships are themselves protected by well-defined and enforced policies.

Note that subject groups, unlike object categories, are not subject to combinatorial explosion. A subject can be in many groups. If a subject has 10 independently varying security relevant features, this can be represented by membership in 10 groups. Only 10 groups would be needed to classify all such subjects, not 1024.

Although representing subject features with groups does not cause combinatorial explosion, it does mean extra entries in access control lists, which means extra I/O, memory, and maintenance. So they should not be multiplied beyond necessity.

8. Representing relationships between subjects and objects

Subject groups and object categories do not exhaust the aspects of situations which are needed to represent a three dimensional access matrix. The situational dimension also include a component which represents the *relations* between security subjects and protected objects. This section discusses the representation of those relations.

8.1. Roles

Think of the entities in a system as playing a game. Among the game players are the users. The game has rules or policies which say how it is played. The rules reference *roles* one or more of which may be occupied by one or more game players. The roles are typically defined in terms of one another. To play a role consists in being in a certain *relationship* to the players of other roles. Associated with each role are a collection of permissions and prohibitions.Permissions state what the occupants of a role can do. Prohibitions state what they cannot do. Rules also govern how something can assume a role and how it may vacate a role. Typically something assumes a role because the occupant of another role had the permission to assign the role, and did so. Typically roles are vacated because the occupant of another role had the permission to re-assign, or de-assign, a role, and did so. The security system sets and enforces the rules governing the actions of roles played by system users.

An example will help clarify these notions.

- A faculty member, George, holds an appointment in the Philosophy Department. He received this appointment through the action of University Personnel, acting upon the recommendation of the then Philosophy Department chair, Sam, who has since retired.

- PHIL201 is a course in ethics. Ethics is a branch of philosophy. PHIL201-Section-100 is a class section of PHIL201. The Philosophy department is responsible for teaching classes of courses whose subjects are branches of philosophy. This responsibility was assigned by the Academic Dean of the college. The departmental chair of a department is responsible for distributing teaching responsibilities for the classes for which the department is responsible. The faculty chair can also re-assign teaching responsibilities. This normally happens only in the case of sickness or termination.

- PHIL201-Section-100 is taught in Cobb Hall, room 101, MWF from 2:00-3:00 PM. This room assignment was made by Sam who is the space manager responsible for Cobb Hall. Philosophy courses are taught in Cobb hall, except in very unusual circumstances.

- The current Philosophy department chair is Martha. Martha assigns teaching responsibilities for PHIL201-Section 100 to George.

- As the instructor of PHIL201-Section-100, George is responsible for grading the students who take the class i.e. the students on the PHIL201-Section-100 class roster. A student's overall grade for a class is based upon a weighted average of scores on tests, and/or written essays, and/or classroom participation. Even when grades are calculated only from test scores, the instructor must approve the overall grade. The instructor may not delegate this responsibility.

- As the class instructor George is also responsible for scoring all tests and papers. However an instructor may delegate the responsibility for grading tests to a graduate student in the same department, so long as that graduate student is not taking the class, and is qualified to do the scoring. George delegates the responsibility to grade the tests to Sally.

- Fred, a student in the Undergraduate College, is taking the class. Fred was entered on the in the class because he registered. As it happens Fred registered over the phone which he had the right to do, because he was a student in the College, the class was available to students in the college, the class section was not full, and he met the academic prerequisites.

- Fred has the right to withdraw, without record of the withdrawal appearing on his transcript, up to the end of the first week of the class. He may also withdraw up to the third week, with an incomplete appearing on the transcript. Withdrawals of either sort may be accomplished over the phone. Thereafter withdrawals are disallowed except under extenuating circumstances, and must be approved by the Academic Dean of the College.

Subject roles are classifications of subjects according to their relationships to protected objects. A subject *plays* a role with respect an object if it stands in a certain relationship to that object. Each role has a persistent identity and a name.

For any category of protected object there is a set of *relevant* subject roles. The set of relevant roles for an object category is the set of roles reference to which may be made in an ACL associated with the category. The set may be empty. The roles associated with a category define the security-relevant relationships of subjects to the objects in the category.

For each role and category combination there is a method, which must be understood and executable by any object in the category, for determining whether a given subject plays the role with reference to the object. The method

68

takes the identity of the subject as its only parameter, and returns either *true* or *false*.

There are four ways such a method could determine whether a subject plays a role with respect to an object.

- Determine that all members of an unnamed collection play the role, and that the subject is in the collection.

- Determine that only one entity plays the role, and that entity is the subject.

- Determine that the role is played by a group, and the subject is a member of the group.

- Determine that the role is played by an unnamed collection of groups, and the subject is a member of one of the groups in the collection.

Multiple subjects can play a role vis-a-vis the same protected object, and the same subject can play the same role vis-a-vis multiple objects. The same subject can also play multiple roles vis-a-vis the same object.

The relevant roles for a category are defined in a Role Table. The following might be part of the table of roles.

Object Category	Role Name	Method	Explanation
Academic Class	Potential Member	canRegister: aSubject	Played by anyone who can take the class if it is not full.
Academic Class	Class Member	isClassMember: aSubject	Played by anyone taking the class.
Academic Class	Teaching Assistant	isTeaching Assistant: aSubject	Played by graduate students who can grade papers and tests in the class.
Academic Class	Instructor	isInstructor: aSubject	Play by the instructor of the class.
Academic Class	Department Chair	isDepartmentChair : aSubject	Played by the chair of the department responsible for the class.
RoomUse	Space Manager	isSpaceManager: aSubject	Played by whoever distributes space in the area of campus in which the responsible department generally offers its classes.

8.2. Owner role

OwningSubject is a role played by the subject which "owns" an object, and *OwningGroupMember* a role played by subjects which are members of the group which "owns" an object. There can be only one owning group and only one owning subject. Within DCE, which follows POSIX, these are the only "roles" which are handled. There are special ACL entries for the owning subject and for the owning group. "Owning subject" in particular is given special treatment. Once it is determined that the subject is the owning subject, all other permissions are ignored.

It is hard to see why this one role should be given such special treatment. It is probably harmless, and it may be commonplace in ownership-based security systems. But it complicates the processing rule, and creates a documentation exception which is hard to explain or justify. Nevertheless, in order to maintain consistency with POSIX, we have kept the notion of "ownership".

Ownership is not likely to be an important relationship in the majority of business systems. Who owns a course? Who owns a transcript? Who owns a student? Who owns an expense voucher? It is unclear what is meant by the term.

8.3. Subject identities and application identities.

Role-based security assumes that at least some of the users of the system also are "entities" within the system and that the system captures their relations to other system entities. The same entity which is represented as a SecuritySubject, may also be represented as a Doctor, a Student, a FacultyMember, etc. It must be possible to determine whether the entity represented as a SecuritySubject is the same entity as an entity represented in other application specific roles.

This could happen by maintaining a cross reference between a "security identity" and other "application identities" by which the individual is known. When an object is asked whether the security subject plays a certain role, it would access the cross reference to determine the application identity and then check to see whether something with the application identity fulfills the role.

That however is pretty ugly. It would be much preferable to have a single identity which is used both within the security system and within the application.

9. Access Control List Managers, Roles, and Rights

The term "Access Control List Manager" comes from DCE. It means a routine which controls the data entry and display of ACLs. For our purposes we may think of an ACL manager as the identifier of a set of rules governing the display of rights, and governing the list of roles appropriate for a particular ACL. For each category of protected object, there are two relevant lists:

- The list of atomic access rights which "make sense" with respect to the access control list associated with a category plus for each a translation of the right into the language of the user.

- The list of roles which make sense with respect to the ACL.

Access control list manager identifiers also fulfill another purpose. An ACL manager identifier is associated both with an access control list and with an object category. The access control list associated with an object category must have a manager id identical to that of the category. Matching these identifiers allows an appropriate level of control over the editing of access control lists for categories.

10. Interpreting access control lists

An access control list is a named collection of access control list entries. An access control list is accessed in order to determine the set of atomic access rights granted to a subject vis-a-vis the categories of protected objects associated with the list. An access control list is interpreted by matching the current security subject to the various entries, to obtain a list of applicable entries. Then the permissions and prohibitions in the entries are examined to determine a resultant set of permissions. This set is compared to the set required by any action to determine whether the action is allowed. If the permissions granted include all the rights required, the action is allowed, otherwise not.

10.1. Access Control List Entries

Each entry in an access control list specifies a rule for granting or withholding permissions to certain users. Each entry consists of five variables.

- *type*

  The entry type classifies the entry. It determines how it is edited and how it is treated when interpreting the ACL. There are seven types:

  - *owningSubject, subject, owningGroup, group, role, other, mask*

The types are explained below.

- *reference*

  References are used with subject, group, and role entries. They contain a reference to a group, an individual subject, or a role.

- *permission set*

  Permissions sets are associated with all entries. They represent atomic rights granted to subjects who match the entry. Each item in the set is a single permission.

- *prohibition set*

  Prohibitions sets are associated with *owningGroup*, *group*, *role*, and *other* entries. They represent withdrawals of permissions from subjects who match the entry.

ACL entries must be matched to a currently signed on security subject to determine whether the permissions and prohibitions associated with the entry are relevant to the subject. The entry type and reference taken together are sufficient to make this determination. The entry type determines whether the reference is relevant and how it is interpreted. The reference is either the identity of an subject, or of a group of which a subject may be a member, or of a role.

10.2. OwningSubject entries

An *owningSubject* entry specifies the permissions which apply to an owningSubject of an object. The owningSubject entry overrides all other entries. If a subject is an owning subject then the permissions granted in the owningSubject entry are all the permissions granted. No other entry is examined. This being the case there is no point to specifying prohibitions for an owning subject. It is enough not to list a permission to prohibit it. There should be is no presumption that there is only one owning subject.

Whether a subject is an owning subject is determined by asking the protected object the question *owningSubject: anIdentity* with *anIdentity* set to the identity of the currently signed-on subject.

10.3. Subject entries

A *subject entry* specifies permissions for a subject principal, identified by its own unique unsharable untransferable identity. If there is no owning subject entry, or the subject is not the owning subject, and there is a subject entry for the subject, then that entry overrides all others, *except* that only permissions are granted which are also included in the mask entry if there is one. Since all other entries are ignored if there is a subject entry for the subject there is no point to entering prohibitions in a subject entry. In the case of a subject entry it is enough not to list a permission to prohibit it.

10.4. OwningGroup entries

OwningGroup entries specify permissions and prohibitions for members of the group (or groups) that own an object. There should be no presumption that there is only one owning group. Whether a subject belongs to an owningGroup is determined by asking the protected object the question *owningGroups*. The answer must return a list of identifiers of groups. Then the groups to which the subject belongs are checked against the returned list.

10.5. Group entries

Group entries apply to any subject in a specified group. The group to which a group entry applies is listed in the entry. There was some discussion in our design meetings as to how prohibitions should be treated in group entries. Two reasonable rules are:

1. A prohibition on child group overrides a permission given to a parent group.

2. A permission given to a child group overrides a prohibition on a parent group.

It was decided that (1) would be accepted but (2) would be rejected. This considerably simplifies the rules since it means that the hierarchical ordering of the groups need not be taken into account when determining what is prohibited. Any prohibition, from whatever group it is derived, applies to all members of that group, no matter what memberships they have in other groups, and no matter what permissions the other groups may have been granted.

10.6. Role entries

Role entries apply to any subject who plays a specified role vis-a-vis an object. The referent of the ACL is a role identifier, which associates the entry with a role. The combination of the ACL manager for the ACL and the role identifier enable determination of the message to be used to determine who plays the role. Note that the same role might be accessed via different messages in different ACLs. The message takes a single parameter, the identity of a subject, and answers either *true* or *false*. Role entries include both permissions and prohibitions.

10.7. "Other" entries

"Other" entries are really special group entries which apply if no other group entry applies. If the subject is not a member of any group mentioned in an ACL, and there is an *other* entry, then the subject receives the permissions and prohibitions listed in the *other* entry. These are unioned with any permissions and prohibitions listed in role entries, and they are limited in the usual way by mask entries.

10.8. Mask entries

Mask entries list the maximal set of permissions which can be granted to anyone except the principalOwner of an object. Prohibitions are not relevant for mask entries. If there is a mask entry, and a permission is not listed in it, then no one has that permission, other than the principal owner, no matter what permissions may be granted by other entries. Mask entries are designed to place an absolute limit on the permissions that are granted in an ACL. They can serve as a quick, perhaps temporary, way to block certain sorts of access, without the need to re-work the entire list.

10.9. Efficiency problems with role entries

Intuitively one would think that subject has the union of the rights of the roles it plays, unioned with the rights it has as a member of groups, minus any prohibitions due to any group memberships it has or roles it occupies. If there is a mask entry all permissions not included in the mask are removed.

There are however some questions concerning the efficiency of a role-based security system, questions which casts a shadow on this intuition. To determine whether a subject plays a role may require a number of I/O's. For example suppose that only the *responsibleDepartmentChair* can assign teaching responsibilities for a class. To determine whether someone plays the role, one asks the question *isResponsibleDepartmentChair: anIdentity* with *anIdentity* set to the identity of the current subject. Let us suppose that each class section is a class section of a course which has a particular topic area, that the topic area of a course is in a general subject area for which a certain department has teaching responsibilities, and that the responsibleDepartmentChair is the chairperson of that department, whose database identity is answered by the *identity* method. The code for *isResponsibleDepartmentChair: anIdentity* might be:

isResponsibleDepartmentChair: anIdentity

> "Answer whether the entity identified by anIdentity plays the role of responsible department chair."

> ^anIdentity = self course topic area responsibleDepartment chair identity.

It is possible, if the code is written in above manner, that least five separate I/O statements will be executed to retrieve the result.

With denormalization of the representations of persistent entities, the amount of I/O could be considerably reduced. Instead of instantiating a series of representations, each involving SQL, we might execute a single albeit complex SQL statement within one representation. But even with this denormalization, we would achieve only a reduction in the I/O needed to determine whether someone occupied only *one* role. Suppose there are 20 potential roles which could be played with respect to an object. Do we always need to determine whether a subject fills every one of them?

One solution to this problem runs as follows:

• Check to see what rights are required to perform a particular action. Then check only the roles which grant or withhold those rights, i.e. those whose permission or prohibition sets include the rights required by the action. Other roles are irrelevant and need not be checked.

This will work only if there are no rights which are granted to the occupants of all the roles, or to a large proportion of them. Unfortunately I suspect that is not the way it is. Certain rights are harmless and likely to be widely granted, whereas others are restricted privileges available only to special individuals. If this situation is common, and I suspect it is, then the above routine will not solve the problem, although it will help sometimes.

Another proviso might be added, which would make the process a little more efficient.

• When checking roles, if the rights granted or withheld are already recorded, either thorough another role check or through a group check, then do not perform the check. And perform group checks before role checks. Also before doing anything see if the rights required are included in a mask, because if they aren't nothing else is relevant.

This rule is always valid, and if combined with the first rule, might catch most of the commonly granted rights on the first few accesses.

10.10. Business functions and roles

There is a third solution which is more radical. One might suggest that a subject does not at any given moment have the access rights of all the roles the subject *could* then occupy, but only of those in which the subject is *actively playing* while performing a particular business function. For example, when performing classroom assignment one is actively playing the *SpaceManager* role. When grading papers one is actively playing *TeachingAssistant* or *Instructor*. The same person might play both SpaceManager and TeachingAssistant with respect to the same class. But *not in the context of the same business function*. While performing a business function you "assume" some of your roles; while performing another business function you "assume" another set of roles. For each business function there is a set of roles which are "assumable" within the context of that function.

On this third model something must declare, when an ACL is being interpreted, what roles are *relevant*. This can be derived from the business function with respect to which access is being requested. Only the relevant roles would be checked, and all others ignored. While engaged in classroom assignment, only roles relevant to classroom assignment would be checked. While grading, only the roles relevant to grading would be checked. If *no* business function is specified, then *all* roles are checked, following the efficiency rules specified in the previous section.

A question arises whether only *permissions* granted to roles should be ignored, or whether also *prohibitions* on irrelevant roles should be ignored. That seems dangerous. If we apply the rule only to permissions but not to prohibitions, then the total permission set granted vis-a-vis a business function will always be a subset of the permissions granted if no business function is specified. If we ignored prohibitions associated with irrelevant roles, then a subject might have more rights while assuming a role than he has overall. Since that sounds strange, the rule should be that if a role takes away a right required by an action, then the role is checked even if it was not declared relevant to the business function, unless the rights were never granted, or were prohibited already by a relevant role or group membership.

This requires some additional metadata, namely a mechanism for identifying business functions, and a cross reference of business functions to roles. It also requires a protocol for requesting access within the context of a business function.

References

1.   OSF DCE Version 1.0 DCE User's Guide and Reference, Open Software Foundation, Cambridge, MA, 1991

2.   Talvitie J. Object Model for a Security System, Proceedings of the OOPSLA 1993 Conference Workshop on Security in Object-Oriented Systems, Washington, D.C., USA, 1993

3.   Ting, TC. Application Information Security Semantics: A Case of Mental Health Delivery. In: Spooner, D. and Landwehr C. (editors) Database Security, III, Status and Prospects, North-Holland, New York, 1990.

Part II: Multilevel Secure Systems

Multilevel Security in Object-Oriented Databases

N. Boulahia-Cuppens, F. Cuppens, A. Gabillon, K. Yazdanian
ONERA / CERT
2 avenue Edouard Belin
31055 Toulouse cedex
France

Abstract

In this paper we present the preliminary work we have done to secure an object oriented database. Faced with the difficulties to implement the existing models such as the SODA model [6], we suggest two different approaches which may be complementary. The central idea of our first approach is to provide the user with a single level *virtual* database which is derived from an object oriented database which supports multilevel entities. The second is based on the decomposition of a multilevel object oriented database into a collection of single level databases. We have not yet fully analyzed difficulties to implement these models, but we feel that they would probably considerably reduce the implementation effort in comparison with the SODA model.

1 Introduction

In this paper, we investigate two new design approaches for a secure multilevel object oriented database system. These are both based on a real object oriented database which supports multilevel entities as in [6], [9]. However, we consider that supporting multilevel entities would be impratical as such and our two proposals aim to reduce the difficulties of supporting multilevel entities.

Our first proposal shows how to manage a multilevel object oriented database using the concept of virtual database. When a real user decides to perform a given work, he has first to choose a current classification level which must always be dominated by the user's clearance. Then, this user is provided with a single level *virtual* database which is derived from the multilevel real database and depends on the current classification level chosen by the user. The database operations are performed on this virtual database within a *transaction* at this current classification level. The transaction ends by a *commit* which reflects back the updates on the real multilevel database. We argue that this approach allows us to avoid many difficulties encountered in previous works undertaking the design of object oriented database supporting multilevel entities. We call this approach *VirtualView model*.

The central idea of our second proposal is to decompose a multilevel object oriented database into a collection of single level databases. The goal is to obtain a collection of single-level base relations which are then physically stored in the database. This approach takes full advantage of the object oriented model. A real multilevel database is designed to represent the actual universe, and in our case, we consider that the universe is multilevel. As was suggested in [8], one can split up this universe into worlds corresponding to each security level. These worlds are the views of the universe by users at the corresponding levels. This paper shows how to perform this partition of the universe when we deal with a multilevel object oriented database. We call this approach *MultiView model* . The MultiView model may be seen as the actual implementation of the physical database supporting multilevel entities. In this case, using a virtual database as suggested in the VirtualView model allows to implement the multilevel security on top of the physical multilevel database. Hence, the two models described in this paper are complementary.

The remainder of this paper is organized as follows. In section 2, we begin by summarizing a model called *SingleView model* which is a generalization of the SODA model proposed in [6]. We propose a discussion of this model and investigate some drawbacks which would appear if this model were directly implemented. Section 3 and section 4 present through animations, our alternative proposals namely the *VirtualView model* for the first one and the *MultiView model* for the second one. Finally section 5 concludes this paper.

2 SingleView model

The first model we describe is called SingleView because all the information related to a given real-world entity is encapsulated in a single object. This unique object represents all the different views of the real-world entity corresponding to each security level.

In the SingleView model, each object has a sensitivity associated with its identifier and another for each of its attributes. The object-identifier classification is used to hide the existence of the object to the subjects which are not sufficiently cleared. The attribute classification classifies the association of the attribute value with the object identifier. Each attribute can be labelled independently. This principle allows us to represent multilevel entities in the model.

The object-identifier must always be assigned a classification which is dominated by the greatest lower bound of the attribute classifications of the object. With this integrity constraint, a subject must first be authorized to observe the existence of the object before being authorized to access one of its attribute values.

A central idea of this model is to support cover stories in using the so-called polyinstantiation technique. Each attribute of a class, and consequently of its instances, is assigned a set of potential levels of classification, called a polyinstantiated set. This means that each attribute is assigned a collection of labelled values. It is argued in [4] that cover stories are the only good reason for the use of polyinstantiation. We agree with the point of view that representing cover stories is the appropriate motivation for introducing the polyinstantiated sets in the SingleView model. However, even though supporting cover stories is an important requirement, using polyinstantiated sets has some drawbacks. The interpretation of the data becomes more complex because simple values are replaced by a set of values. As was noticed in [6], this complicates the understanding of the data and makes applications harder to develop.

Moreover, the mandatory access controls are difficult to express in the SingleView model. Access to an object attribute would generate a first control due to the classification assigned to the object-identifier and a second control due to the classification of the attribute. It also requires research in a set of polyinstantiated values. Hence, we feel that enforcing all these security controls in a direct implementation of the SingleView model would probably lead to performance loss.

The SODA model also allows a subject to modify data at multiple levels by raising the classification level of the subject in accordance with the access class of data it is reading or the classification requirements of data it is writing. This approach, which is closely related to the High-Water Mark model [10], provides high flexibility in the method activation. However, as was noticed in [6], it is difficult to implement this type of mechanism without allowing a storage channel. Indeed, changing the security level of a method may depend on the existence of higher classified information. This can generate a covert storage channel and, to avoid this, we need trusted enforcement mechanisms in the object layer. Other trusted mechanisms required in the SODA model are described in [6].

Finally, we feel that it would be difficult to provide a complete implementation of the SingleView model without deeply modifying the mechanisms of an existing non-secure object-oriented database.

3 VirtualView model [2]

Our objective is to propose other approaches which allow us to deal with multilevel entities in an object oriented database without some inconveniencie encountered by the previous proposals, [6], [9] for instance. The VirtualView model is a first approach based on the derivation of single-level virtual databases from a physical multilevel database. All the operations are then performed on the virtual database within a transaction at a current classification level chosen by the user.

For the sake of simplicity of the exposure, we make several hypotheses. Let us first explain how the multilevel security policy is introduced within the multilevel database. In our model the assignment of security levels is only done at the object level (instances) (see Figure 1). We assume that the database schema is not protected and each user, whatever his clearance, can have access to the overall classes of the database. Notice also that a given instance has a security level associated with its identifier and another for each of its attributes.

The object-identifier classification is used to hide the existence of the object to the

82

subjects which are not sufficiently cleared. In the above example, the security level assigned to *O1* is equal to unclassified. This means that everyone is permitted to know that *O1* has been created in the database. On the other hand, the security level assigned to *O2* is confidential, hence subjects cleared to unclassified cannot know the existence of *O2*. Notice that the object-identifier classification represents the security level at which the object has been created.

The attribute classification classifies the information represented by the association of the attribute with the object identifier. For instance, the value of the attribute Age of *O1* is associated with the level unclassified. This means that the information "the age of *O1* is equal to 35" is unclassified. Each attribute can be labelled independently. This principle allows us to represent multilevel entities in the model.

Finally, notice that the object-identifier must always be assigned a classification which is dominated by the greatest lower bound of the attribute classifications of the object. With this integrity constraint, a subject must first be authorized to observe the existence of the object before being authorized to access one of its attribute values.

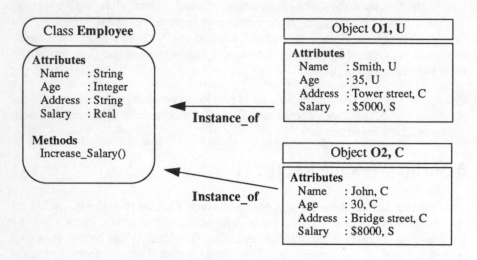

Figure 1   Multilevel Database

3.1   Virtual single level database

We create from a real multilevel database as many virtual databases as security levels. In the following we will consider three levels of classification (U(nclassified), C(onfidential), S(ecret)). Each virtual database will be classified by a unique security level. Thus, all objects inside the virtual database are implicitly classified with the same security level. A user has the possibility to choose which virtual database he wants to work on. Of course classification of the virtual database must be dominated by user's clearance.

A virtual database is derived from the multilevel database according to the level of the running transaction. Creation of a virtual database is done under the control of a classical Mandatory Security Kernel and is done as follows:

- *Rule 1.* As the schema is unclassified, it is propagated as such in any virtual database.

Once the view, i.e virtual schema, is created virtual objects are evaluated as follows:

- *Rule 2.* If an object has a security level which is not dominated by the security level of the virtual database, then this object is not propagated in the virtual database.

Notice that such a propagation would be prevented by the Mandatory Security Kernel.

- *Rule 3.* If an object has a security level dominated by the security level of the virtual database, the object may be propagated in the virtual database.

As noticed in [1], a view may be evaluated dynamically. Virtual instances are created only if a user or process wants to perform on it.

- *Rule 4.* If an attribute value of an object has a security level dominated by the security level of the virtual database, the attribute value may be propagated as such in the corresponding virtual object.

- *Rule 5.* If an attribute value of an object has a security level l_i which is not dominated by the security level of the virtual database, the attribute value is enforced to $"l_i"$ [1] in the corresponding virtual object. This is to avoid a read up.

Notice that such a read up would be prevented by the Mandatory Security Kernel.

Once a transaction has been initiated and a virtual database has been created, the user or a method can read or write attribute values in this virtual database without control or restriction. It is important to stress that as long as the user or the process does not perform a commitment, updates are not propagated in the physical database. At the end of a transaction, user or process may order a commitment. The main principle of this commitment is to propagate updates for only attribute values which are at the same level as the virtual database level. Notice that this commit does not need to be trusted since it is executed under the control of the Mandatory Security Kernel.

Figure 2 shows the confidential virtual database. Every secret attribute values in the

---

1. Each $"l_i"$ is called a *"level"* value. It is a generalization of the special symbol *restricted* used in [7] to tell users that corresponding values exist but are higher classified. Our special *"level" values* provide the user with more precise information. We assume that the attribute classification is classified at the same level of classification as the object existence classification, so the user is permitted to observe this *"level"* value.

84

multilevel database are enforced to *"secret"* in the virtual database. At the end of a transaction, commit propagates updates for Confidential attribute values only. Since it is confidential, this database is accessible by users (or process underlying a user) with clearance equal to confidential or secret.

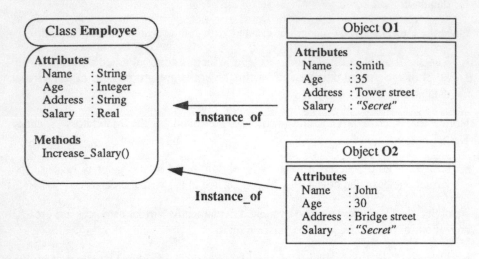

Figure 2   Virtual Confidential Database

3.2   Object creation

Object creation may be performed in any virtual database. We actually assume that the classification of the object existence is the same as the security level of the virtual database in which the object is created

The object creator is also in charge of associating the attribute values of the newly created object with sensitivities. As a user in the virtual database does not directly deal with security levels, assigning sensitivities to the attribute values is indirectly done as follows. The object creator assigned attribute values to the newly created object. Attribute values may be "level" values or "normal" values[1]. Notice that if an attribute value is associated with a level value $"l_i"$, then the corresponding security level l_i of the level value $"l_i"$ must dominate the current security level.

After commitment, the creation of the object is propagated in the physical database. The attribute values assigned to the object in the virtual database are propagated in the physical database. There are two different cases of propagation:

---

1. By "normal" value, we mean any value which is not a "level" value.

1. If, in the virtual database, the object creator has associated an attribute with a *"level"* value*"l_i"*, then, in the physical database, this attribute is associated with a *"Null"* value whose sensitivity is equal to l_i

2. If, in the virtual database, the object creator has associated an attribute with a *"normal"* value, then, in the physical database, this attribute is associated with this *"normal"* value whose sensitivity is equal to the security level of the current virtual database.

These two rules imply that the classification of the security levels assigned to the attribute values of the newly created object will be the same as the classification of the object existence (i.e. the security level of the current virtual database). This means that in knowing the object existence, a user may also observe the security levels associated with each attribute values of this object[1]. To fully instantiate the new object, the user must then successively set himself to each security level which appears in attribute values of the object. Then he may successively and normally update null values with *"normal"* values via virtual databases. The user may only update a level value *"l_i"* by a *"normal"* value if the current level of the virtual database is actually equal to l_i. Of course, to fully instantiate an object, user's clearance must dominate the least upper bound of security levels which appear in the attribute values of the object.

4 Multiview Model. [3]

This model is another approach mainly based on the decomposition of a n-level Object Oriented Database into n singlelevel databases. The MultiView model consists of a security policy and it provides a way to represent a multilevel database through a collection of singlelevel databases. Notice that this technique may be complementary with our previous VirtualView model. Each database corresponds to a given level of classification. This decomposition allows us to provide the user with a view of the database compatible with his clearance or the level of classification he chooses to perform his transaction.

In the MultiView model, the assignment of classification levels is done at the object level (instances). We assume that the database schema is not protected and each user, whatever his clearance, can have access to the overall classes of the database. He can however only have access or/and modify the values of attributes which have classification levels dominated by his clearance.

---

1. With this assumption, we do not need to use cover stories and polyinstantiation to protect the classification of an attribute. However we might introduce in the security policy of the VirtualView model the possibility to handle cover stories. Of course, in this case, multilevel objects as represented in Figure 1 would have polyinstantiated attribute values.

4.1   Object creation

Let *O1* be an object (an instance) of the class Person that *A*, a user, wants to create (see Figure 3). *A* thus assigns to each attribute stated in the class Person a value in *O1*. Of course these values belong to the corresponding types in Person. Besides this, *A* assigns a sensitivity to the object identifier and a level of classification to each attribute value. As detailed in the VirtualView model, the sensitivity assigned to the object identifier is used to hide the existence of the object to the subjects which are not sufficiently cleared, whereas the attribute classification classifies the information represented by the association of the attribute with the object identifier. Remember also that the object-identifier must always be assigned a classification which is dominated by the greatest lower bound of the attribute classifications of the object.

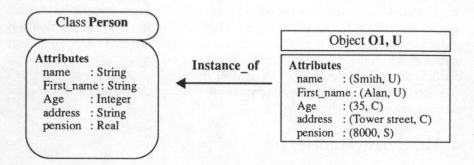

Figure 3   Multilevel Database

As the object existence is not protected and since we choose a three-level database, the creation process is done in three phases:.

Phase 1: As existence of *O1* is unclassified, *A* must downgrade his working level to unclassified if he is actually cleared at confidential or secret. Then, he creates *O1* in the unclassified database. If *A* wants to insert a cover story[1], he may assign an arbitrary value to confidential and secret attribute values, otherwise all the attribute values that possess a level of classification l_i greater than unclassified are assigned the particular *"level"* value *"l_i"*. Afterwards, in the confidential database and in the secret database, pointers to the same object_state are created. This is performed by several writes up which are allowed by the multilevel security policy. Hence, after phase 1, users cleared at secret or confidential will observe the same object_state as unclassified users

Phase 2: The confidential instance is updated in the confidential database with a minimal redundancy. Each confidential attribute which was assigned a *"Confidential"*

---

1. In the MultiView model, we introduce cover stories whereas we do not in the VirtualView model.

value in the unclassified database is now assigned the real value while each unclassified attribute points to the unclassified attribute value in the unclassified database. Notice that these updates are automatically propagated to the secret level thanks to the use of pointers.

Phase 3: Finally, the secret instance is updated in the secret database. We follow the same process as in the second phase. We then get the following Figure 4:

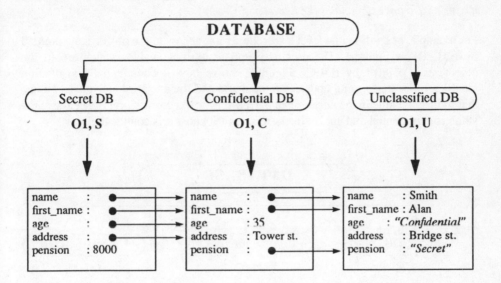

Figure 4   Three Singlelevel Databases

4.2   Consultation.

Let us consider a user who wants to consult the object *O1* belonging to the class Person in our previous database (Figure 3). Let us look at an example of a consultation process:

At unclassified level, the user acts on the unclassified database. He has access to the object_state pointed by (O1, U), so the user can learn the following:

- The name and first name of the object O1.

- He believes that the address value is unclassified and equal to 'Bridge street'. He does not know that this value is actually a cover story which hides both the real address value and its classification.

- He sees that the pension is secret and the age is confidential.

4.3   Updating

When a user updates an object, he only updates the object_state which is stored in the current classified database. As this database is single level, the user may perform updates without any restrictions. However, the following integrity constraint must be enforced:

If an attribute value is equal to "l_i", an update of this attribute value is allowed only if user's clearance dominates the l_i level.

For example, at confidential level a secret user has access to the object_state pointed by (O1, C) in Figure 4. The user may update attribute values which are in the object_state pointed by (O1,C). Figure 5 shows how a confidential consultation would be after performing updates on the name and the age attribute values. Notice that the name value in the unclassified database is now a cover story. Hence the name value is confidential and unclassified users cannot know it is confidential.

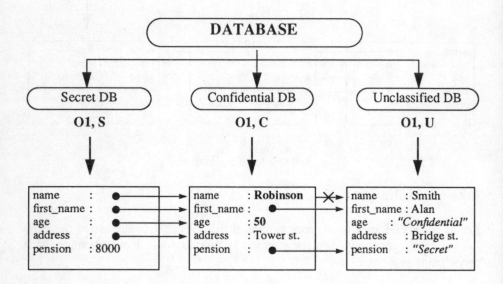

Figure 5   Updates at Confidential Level

5   Conclusion

In this paper, we have presented the preliminary work done to realize a secure object oriented database which supports multilevel entities. This preliminary work was undertaken because our first attempt to design a multilevel object oriented database using the SODA model led to the conclusion that this model introduces many difficulties and would require a complete reconception of the mechanisms used to implement a non-secure object oriented database.

Hence, we suggest two different alternatives to the SODA model: the first uses the concept of virtual database and the second is based on the decomposition of the multilevel database into single level databases. Some suggestions to implement these models were made in [2] and [3], but it is too early to draw conclusions. However, we feel that both approaches may be complementary and can be implemented with only few modifications of an existing multilevel object oriented database.

Hence, our next objective will be to analyze the difficulties to implement these two models. In particular, we need to study how to combine these two models to implement a multilevel object oriented database based on these models. The objective is at least to meet the requirements for E4 certification as outlined in the Information Technology Security Evaluation Criteria [5]. We also plan to refine these two models in several directions, in particular to include the possibility to hide some part of the database schema.

Acknowledgement

We would like to thank the STEI for its support and Jill Manning for her help.

References

1   S. Abiteboul, Cassio Souza dos Santos and C. Delobel. Virtual Schemas and Bases for dynamic Data-Intensive Systems. To be published at the next EDBT 94 conference. Cambridge. England.

2   N. Boulahia-Cuppens, F. Cuppens, A. Gabillon, K. Yazdanian. Using Virtual Databases to Design a Secure Object Oriented Databases. To be submitted.

3   N. Boulahia-Cuppens, F. Cuppens, A. Gabillon, K. Yazdanian. Multiview Model for MultiLevel Object-Oriented Database. Proc. of the Ninth Annual Computer Security Applications Conference, Orlando Florida 1993.

4   R.K. Burns. Integrity and Secrecy : Fundamental conflicts in the database environment. In proc. of the third RADC Database Security Workshop. 1990.

5   European Economic Community. Information Technology Security Evaluation Criteria (ITSEC). Technical report 1991.

6   T.F. Keefe, W.T. Tsai and M.B. Thuraisingham. SODA : A Secure Object-Oriented Database System. Computer & Security, Vol 8, N°6, 1989.

7   R. Sandhu and S. Jajodia. Polyinstantiation for cover stories. Computer security - Esorics 92, Toulouse, France. Springer Verlag.

8   B. Thuraisingham. Knowledge-Based Management Systems. In the proc. of the Computer Security Foundations Workshop IV. June 91. Franconia.

9   V. Varadharajan and S. Black. Multilevel Security in a Distributed Object-Oriented System. Computer & Security, 10 (1991).

10 C. Weissman. Security controls in the ADEPT-50 time sharing system. Proc. 1969 AFIPS Fall Jt. Computer Conf., Vol 35, AFIPS Press Arlington.

Object-Oriented Security in the Trusted Mach^{TM} Operating System

Sarbari Gupta

Trusted Information Systems, Inc.

Glenwood, MD USA

Abstract

Object-oriented (OO) design and implementation are ideally suited to the development of secure operating systems. Although an OO programming language cannot provide any subject-to-object access protection or security by its own virtue, the use of OO techniques in secure systems yields substantial benefits in meeting the assurance and security policy control objectives of the Trusted Computer System Evaluation Criteria (TCSEC.)

The Trusted Mach (TMach^{TM}) secure operating system is designed to meet the requirements of the TCSEC B3 level of trust, and the Information Technology Security Evaluation Criteria (ITSEC) E5, F-B3 rating. The fundamental features of the TMach architecture and design are its message-oriented client/server model, and heavy usage of layering, modularity, abstraction and data hiding. Thus, the choice of an object-oriented language for the implementation of the TMach system, was a natural consequence of its design requirements.

1   Overview

The Trusted Mach (TMach) secure operating system, currently under development, is intended to meet the requirements of the Trusted Computer System Evaluation Criteria (TCSEC [1]) B3 level of security, and the Information Technology Security Evaluation Criteria (ITSEC [2]) E5, F-B3 rating. The TMach system is derived from the Mach operating system and consists of a message passing kernel, and a set of trusted and untrusted servers, that provide a complete collection of abstractions and services that are typical of operating systems. The kernel and the trusted servers comprise the TMach Trusted Computing Base (TCB), which is largely personality-neutral, while the untrusted servers make use of the TCB services to provide a complete operating system personality to the user.

Kernel: The TMach kernel executes in a protected domain and provides the following set of basic abstractions: threads (active entities that execute machine instructions) and tasks (containers of threads and their working environments); messages (primary mechanism by which tasks communicate) and ports (where messages are queued); memory objects (blocks of read/write storage); and input/output devices (through which the system interacts with the external world.)

Tasks and threads are the basic units of execution. Threads within a task share the same address space and execution environment. The TMach kernel guarantees task isolation through separate address spaces. The kernel does not perform any security related access control. It does however, attach a security identity (ID) to each task, which is not interpreted by the kernel, but is a handle to the complete security characteristics of the task for use by the trusted servers. Tasks communicate through shared memory and by sending/retrieving messages to/from kernel ports; the kernel attaches the sender's security ID to every such message.

Trusted Servers: The TMach trusted servers are tasks that have special capabilities and privileges; each provides a distinct operating system service to clients inside or outside the TCB. The Root Name Server (RNS) is the focal point of all name resolutions and access mediation between *subjects* and *objects*. In the TMach system, a collection of tasks with the same security ID is called a *subject*. The *objects* are the shared named entities in the name space and are called *items*. Items may be of various types, e.g., files, devices, directories, etc.; all items of a certain type are managed by a server which is an *item manager*. When a subject resolves to the name of an object (item) in the name space, the RNS mediates the access by performing both discretionary and mandatory checks. If mediation is successful, the RNS creates a port on which the client and the item manager for that item can communicate directly for service requests.

Untrusted Servers: The set of untrusted servers and tasks provide the user-level interface to a particular operating system personality that is being emulated on top of the TMach TCB.

2   Object-Oriented Design and Security

Although the TMach kernel is encoded in the non-object-oriented C programming language, the trusted servers and shared libraries are written almost exclusively in the object-oriented C++ language. Use of an object-oriented approach has resulted in substantial benefits in meeting the security policy and assurance control objectives of the TCSEC B3 level of trust.

The C++ language and the TMach kernel together give the TMach trusted servers the foundations required to implement a multilevel secure operating system based on the client/server model. The kernel provides task identification and isolation, and allows inter-task communication through messages. The C++ language provides the constructs to allow the implementation of message-oriented objects with restricted interfaces and considerable abstraction and data hiding.

2.1   Security Policy

The TMach system implements two access control policies - a mandatory policy that is based on clearances and classifications, and a discretionary policy that is based on user/group identities and access control lists on shared objects. The security policy is implemented in two parts. In the first part, the RNS mediates all accesses of subjects to objects and returns a descriptor back to the subject. This descriptor allows the subject to send messages to the item manager for the object (item) being accessed. The RNS also informs the item manager of the identity of the client and the accesses that have been granted. The second part of access control is performed by the item manager when the client sends service requests over the mediated descriptor. The item manager enforces the RNS access control mediation decision by allowing only the specified subject to use the particular descriptor, and to invoke only those calls which are allowed by the access rights granted by the RNS.

Thus, in the TMach system, access control mediation is centralized within the RNS, whereas the enforcement of the mediation decision is done in a distributed fashion by the various trusted item managers. With the help of object-oriented design, however, the latter is also centralized to a large extent, through the use of a common set of code modules of the trusted Class Library to enforce the RNS mediation. The modules that are responsible for receiving messages from ports, checking that the sender of the message matches the identity of the intended sender, and checking whether the granted access rights are sufficient to invoke a particular service call, are all designed as C++ classes which are a part of the Class Library. The modules are designed with significant use of data hiding and abstraction and have controlled interfaces that allow the item manager to perform only those actions necessary to enforce the access control decision. Thus all of the trusted item managers enforce access control by using the same set of classes from the class library.

2.2   Assurance

The greatest benefits of using the object-oriented approach to design a highly secure operating system are in achieving the assurance control objective of the TCSEC [7]. Some of the subdivisions within the assurance control objective of the class B3 are discussed in greater detail below with reference to the object-oriented design of the TMach system.

2.2.1   System Architecture

Modularity. Use of the C++ language to implement the TMach trusted servers has resulted in a very highly modular system. C++ provides the basic language support needed for the development of distinct code modules specifying user-defined data types and their operations. Inheritance and polymorphism introduce dependencies between code modules. Inheritance causes a dependency from a derived class to a base class, whereas, polymorphism may cause a dependency from a base class to a derived class. However, inheritance and polymorphism do not cause interdependencies between active modules (trusted servers) in the system, since they execute in separate address spaces.

Layering. The TCSEC mandates that at the B3 level of trust, systems should incorporate significant use of layering among other things. In the TMach TCB, there are two independent levels of layering - layering between the active entities (trusted servers) and layering within the active entities themselves. The inter-server layering is defined by the client/server relations required within the system, and is not impacted by the object-oriented design. The servers communicate only by messages and shared memory, and they are designed so that lower layer servers are not dependent on higher layer servers in order to meet their specifications. The intra-server layering, on the other hand, is based on the OO implementation of the server. Typically, base classes constitute a lower layer than the derived classes. Polymorphism of base class operations within the derived classes could result in a dependency that negates the layering. However, even in such cases, each polymorphic function is designed to have a default implementation in the base class, so that the base class meets its specification whether or not the derived class redefines this function. In this way, layering between the code modules within a server is preserved in spite of the potential layering difficulties that may be caused by use of polymorphism.

Abstraction and Data Hiding. OO implementation is ideal for developing user-defined data types. Abstractions relevant to security, such as security labels, access control lists, mandatory and discretionary access check algorithms, sending and receiving of TMach messages, etc., are representable as new data types with well-defined sets of operations. Other modules that may need the services of these data types only need to know the public interface to the data types and do not need to be aware of the implementation details. Encapsulation of critical data within the private members of a class also helps in the robustness of the system, since clients may only access this data through the defined interface functions for the class. Additionally, as long as the interface to an user-defined data type remains the same, modules using the data type are unaffected by changes to its implementation.

TCB Minimization. OO design also proves useful to the efforts of minimizing the Trusted Computing Base as required at the B3 level of trust. Since the TCB consists mainly of well-defined modules that represent concepts, it is relatively straightforward to identify the concepts and hence modules that are not necessary for the basic operational and security aspects of the system. In the TMach system, many such modules and collections of modules have been moved outside the TCB - for example, the line printer job queuing/dequeuing mechanisms.

2.2.2 Security Testing

Security testing aims to show that the security policy of a system is implemented correctly and cannot be bypassed by untrusted clients through the TCB interface. The trusted servers implement the TMach security policy - they are implemented using C++ classes which have a very clearly defined public interface. Thus, identification of the security-relevant TCB interface calls translates to the relatively easy task of identifying the public interfaces of the C++ objects visible at the TCB boundary.

The shared variables of a procedure-oriented monolithic system are typically implemented as "global" variables. In the object-oriented TMach system, most such variables are encapsulated as private data within classes, which can only be modified or viewed through the public functions for those classes. This design approach eases the analysis and testing of covert storage channels, since the various paths to a variable (which is conceptually shared) are easier to trace if the variable is a private data member.

The hierarchical nature of the inheritance relation allows the use of incremental testing techniques to test derived classes [5]. The grey box testing approach [3] allows the efficient testing of the TCB by taking advantage of the high degree of reuse of code components. The modular design of the TMach system also makes it easier to use automated tools for security testing and execution path tracing - since each module is reasonably self-contained and there are far fewer "global" variables and functions to be kept track of. In general, dependencies between different modules of a OO program are much more explicit and tractable. However, the abundant use of polymorphism and C++ *friend* functions and classes adds to the complexity of the dependency relations, and may make greater demands on automated tools than a comparable procedure-oriented design. When flaws are discovered and corrected in an OO system, the effects to other modules and subsystems will be minimal if the correction does not change the public interface of the object involved. Thus, retesting efforts are often localized in nature.

Based on the degree of encapsulation and data hiding incorporated into the design of the system, the TCB may become more resistant to penetration [4]. This is because a large number of penetration scenarios are caused by untrusted users being able to modify critical global system data in ways that were not intended by the system designers. If most such critical data are encapsulated as private members of objects, and controlled interface functions are provided to view and modify these data variables, a lot of penetration scenarios are either nullified or easily detectable. A second major class of penetration scenarios involve those related to inadequate parameter checking for TCB calls. Since the C++ language itself eliminates a lot of parameter checking errors by static type checking and static analysis, these scenarios are less successful at system penetration.

2.2.3   Design Specification and Verification

Typically, object-oriented systems are more structured than procedure-oriented systems, and there is greater concept-to-code correspondence. In the TMach system, most of the security relevant concepts are implemented as C++ classes, so defining the formal model of the security policy and maintaining it over the life-cycle of the system is somewhat easier. Showing that the descriptive top-level specification (DTLS) is consistent with the security model is also facilitated by OO design, for the same reason. It is also easier to maintain the DTLS through the life cycle of the system, since the DTLS will comprise largely of the descriptions of the public interfaces of the C++ classes that are visible at the TCB interface.

2.2.4   Configuration Management

The configuration management of the TMach system has benefited to some extent through the use of an object-oriented design approach. The modularity, extensibility and reusability of code generated by OO techniques, results in changes being much less drastic than in procedure-oriented designs. Implementation changes in derived classes usually do not affect the base class; changes in a base class also may not affect the derived classes if the base class interface is well-designed and is stable. Thus maintaining control over code versions becomes much easier. In general, object-oriented designs are resilient to change, and are well suited for parallel development. It is also far easier to debug and maintain object-oriented code as compared to procedure-oriented code.

Typically, the implementation of a secure system is more complex than a comparable non-secure system. OO implementation helps to manage this complexity by allowing modular components that have relatively few inter-component connections.

3 Conclusions

From the TMach experience, it has been found that the use of object-oriented techniques and an object-oriented programming language has had a positive impact on the design of a multilevel secure system. It is a well-known fact that the use of an object-oriented language does not afford any protection against malicious penetrators on its own [6]. For example, recasting an object to another may allow access to the private data members of the former object. However, in the TMach system, the combination of the client/server architecture, task isolation, and use of an object-oriented programming language with strong static type checking, has yielded a design which is very effective in implementing a highly secure operating system.

References

[1] National Computer Security Center, **Department of Defense Trusted Computer System Evaluation Criteria**, DoD 5200.28-STD, December 1985.

[2] **Information Technology Evaluation Criteria, Harmonized Criteria for France - Germany - the Netherlands - the United Kingdom**, Draft June, 1991.

[3] Gligor VD, Chandersekaran CS, Jiang WD et al., A New Security Testing Method and Its Application to the Secure Xenix Kernel, **IEEE Trans. Software Engg** 1987, SE-13, No. 2, pp 169-183.

[4] Gupta S, Gligor VD, Towards a Theory of Penetration-Resistant Systems and its Applications, **Journal of Computer Security** 1992, Vol 1 No 2, pp 133-158.

[5] Harrold MJ, McGregor JD, Fitzpatrick KJ, Incremental Testing of Object-Oriented Class Structures, **Proc. of Fourteenth Intl. Conf. on Software Engg**, May 11-15, 1992 - Melbourne, Australia, pp 68-80.

[6] Stroustrup B, **The C++ Programming Language** Second Edition, Addison-wEsley Publishing Company, 1991.

[7] Tajalli H, Badger L, Graham J, The Trusted Mach Object-Oriented Operating System, **Proc. of NATO Workshop on Object Oriented Modeling of Distributed Systems** 1992 - Quebec City, Canada.

Enforcing Mandatory Access Control in Object Bases

Elisa Bertino*

Dipartimento di Scienze dell'Informazione, Università di Milano

Via Comelico, 39/41, 20135 Milano, Italy

Sushil Jajodia[†]

Center for Secure Information Systems

Department of Information and Software Systems Engineering

George Mason University, Fairfax, VA 22030-4444, U.S.A.

Pierangela Samarati*

Dipartimento di Scienze dell'Informazione, Università di Milano

Via Comelico, 39/41, 20135 Milano, Italy

Abstract

Enforcement of mandatory policies in object-oriented systems generally requires objects to be single level; i.e., all attributes of an object must have the same security level. However, entities in real world are often multilevel and, therefore, support must be provided for representing these entities. In this paper, we show how multilevel entities can be represented using single level objects. The approach, which extends an earlier proposal by Bertino and Jajodia [4], is based on the notions of composite objects and delegations. We also discuss how our approach can be implemented by extending the message filter proposed by Jajodia and Kogan in [15].

1   Introduction

Object-oriented database management systems (OODBMSs) today represent one of the most active areas in both academic and industrial worlds. OODBMSs combine object-oriented programming technology with database technology, thus combining the strengths of both. The need for those systems has been driven by several advanced applications, such as CAD/CAM, cartography,and multimedia, for which relational systems have been proven inadequate. However, at the current state of the art, those systems do not provide mandatory security. Actually, in most cases, they do not even provide adequate discretionary authorization facilities (a notable exception is presented by the ORION/ITASCA system [19]). We can expect, however, that the broadening of application scope of those systems will require them to enforce both mandatory and discretionary security requirements.

---

*The work of Elisa Bertino and Pierangela Samarati was carried out while visiting George Mason University during summer 1993.

[†]Supported in part by the National Science Foundation under grant IRI-9303416.

A basic model of security is represented by the Bell-LaPadula paradigm [1]. This paradigm is based on the notion of *subjects* and *objects*. An object is a passive entity storing information and is assigned a classification. A subject is an active entity requiring access to objects and is assigned a clearance. Classifications and clearances are collectively referred to as *security levels*. Security levels are partially ordered. A subject can read an object only if the level of the latter is lower than or equal to the level of the former ("no read up"). A subject can write an object only if the level of the latter is higher than or equal to the level of the former ("no write down").

Applying the Bell-LaPadula paradigm to object-oriented data models is not straightforward. Objects of the object-oriented data model combine the properties of passive information repositories, represented by attributes and their values, with the properties of active entities, represented by methods and their invocations. Moreover, the inclusion of notions such as complex objects and inheritance hierarchies, which must be accounted for when designing a secure object-oriented database model, makes the object-oriented data model intrinsically complex [15,18,22]. However, despite this complexity, the use of an object-oriented approach offers several advantages from the security perspective. The notion of encapsulation, which was originally introduced in object-oriented systems to facilitate modular design, can be used to express security requirements in a way that is comprehensible to the users. Moreover, the fact that messages are the only means by which objects can exchange information makes information flow in object-oriented system have a very concrete and natural embodiment in terms of messages and their replies [15]. Then, information flow in object-oriented systems can be controlled by mediating message exchanges among objects. A filtering algorithm mediating all messages exchanged among objects to ensure the satisfaction of the "no read-up" "no write-down" Bell La Padula principles, has been proposed by Jajodia and Kogan in [15]. The message filter intercepts every message exchanged among objects in the system and, based on the security level of the sender and of the receiver, as well as some auxiliary information, decides how to handle the message. Possible actions include: letting the message pass unaltered, blocking the message, let the message pass but constraint the execution of the corresponding method, or filtering the reply to be returned by the message.

Some approaches have been proposed for applying of mandatory policies to object-oriented systems [17,18,15,22]. An aspect common to all these proposals is the requirement that objects be single-level, i.e., all attributes of an object must have the same level. Indeed, supporting access to multilevel objects would significantly increase the complexity of the security monitor. By contrast, a model based on single-level objects has the important advantage of making the security monitor small enough so that it can be easily verified. However, entities in real world are often multilevel, i.e., attributes of a same entity may have different security levels. Much modeling flexibility would be lost if multilevel entities could not be represented in the database. Then, the problem arises of representing these entities with single-level objects. Some solutions have been proposed to this problem [18,15,22].

The approach proposed by Millen and Lunt [18] for handling multilevel entities is based on using references to relate objects corresponding to the same entity. However, the problems of managing objects representing a same entity are not investigated.

The approaches proposed in [22,15] for modeling multilevel entities in terms of single level objects are based on the use of the inheritance hierarchies. However, this solution has several problems. First, it leads to a replication of information. Since a multilevel entity is modeled as several single-level objects in a class inheritance hierarchy, some attributes of high level objects are replicas of attributes of low level objects (because of inheritance). Second, if not carefully monitored, updates may lead to mutual inconsistency of replicated data. In particular, changes to low level copies of the information must be propagated to the corresponding high level copies. Changes to high level copies of the data should not be allowed because they cannot be propagated to low level copies (no write-down) and would therefore introduce inconsistencies. Finally, this approach overloads the notion of inheritance hierarchy, which is used both for conceptual specialization and for supporting multilevel entities.

In this paper, we propose an approach for modeling multilevel entities in terms of single level objects based on the use of composite objects and delegation. The model extends an earlier work by Bertino and Jajodia [4]. The notion of composite object is a modeling construct that allows an object and a set of component objects to be viewed as a single object [12]. Delegation allows an object to perform some of its functions by simply delegating their executions to other objects. Moreover, we discuss how our approach can be implemented by using the message filter proposed by Jajodia and Kogan in [15].

The paper is organized as follows. Section 2 introduces the reference object-oriented data model which will be used throughout the paper. Section 3 illustrates how multilevel entities can be mapped onto single-level objects in the reference model considered. Section 4 extends the reference model to the consideration of new requirements introduced by security classifications. Section 5 discusses the execution of update and delete operations in our model. Section 6 outlines a specification language for the definition of security requirements. Section 7 concludes the paper.

2 A reference object-oriented data model

In this section we characterize the object-oriented data model referring to the model introduced in [3]. This reference model, which will be used in the remainder of the paper for the discussion, is similar to the core model described by Kim [14] and has most features commonly found in various object-oriented data models.

In object-oriented systems, each real-world entity is represented by an object. Each object is associated with a unique object identifier (oid), which is fixed for the whole life of the object, a set of instance attributes (also called instance variables), and a set of procedures, called methods. The value of an attribute can be an object or a set of objects. The values of the attributes of an object represents the object's state. The set of methods of an object represent the object's behavior. The state of an object can be accessed (and possibly modified) by invoking some method on the object. Methods are invoked by sending the object the appropriate messages.

Objects sharing the same structure and behavior are grouped into classes. A class represents a template for a set of similar objects. Each object is an instance of some class. Classes are related by a subclass-superclass relationship called *is-a*. If a class C is defined as a subclass (*is-a*) another class C', then C inherits the attributes and methods specified for C'. Every class is defined as a subclass of some classes existing in the database. We consider a class, called TOP-CLASS, which is the root of an inheritance hierarchy. TOP-CLASS is the default superclass if no superclasses are specified for a class. Multiple inheritance allows a class to have more than one direct superclass. In this case, the class inherits the attributes and methods of all its superclasses.

In the following, we distinguish between *instance* and *member* objects. An object which is an instance of class C is considered as a member of all the superclasses of C. We assume that an object can be *instance* of only one class. An object, however, can be *member* of several classes through the inheritance hierarchy [2].

Each class is defined by specifying its name, attributes, and methods, and the names of its superclass(es).

An attribute is defined by specifying its name and its domain. Attributes can be single-valued or multi-valued. In defining multi-valued attributes, the various object-oriented data models use different constructors such as set, list, tree, and array. We assume that multi-valued attributes are defined by using a constructor denoted as *set-of*. The following definitions specify the notations for the reference model.

If a_i is an attribute name and C_i is a class name then:

- $A_i = a_i : C_i$ is the definition of a single-valued attribute;

- $A_i = a_i :$ **set-of** C_i is the definition of a multi-valued attribute.

A method definition consists of a *signature* and a *body*. The signature specifies the method name and the classes of the objects that are input and output parameters for the method. The body provides the implementation of the method and consists of a sequence of statements written in some programming language. If m is a method name, In_i, $(1 \le i \le n)$, is an input parameter specification, and Out is an output parameter specification, then $m(In_1, In_2, ..., In_n) \to Out$ is a method signature definition. An input parameter specification consists of the parameter name and the parameter domain. The parameter domain is either a class name or a collection of instances of a class, in the same manner as attributes are specified. An output parameter is either a class name or a collection of instances of a class. The invocation of a method m on an object o has the form $o.m(o_1, o_2, \ldots, o_n)$ where $o_1, o_2, \ldots, o_n$ are objects that are passed as input parameters.

Classes are recursively defined as follows:

- Integers, floats, strings, text, and Boolean are classes (called *primitive* classes).

- There is a special class, called TOP-CLASS, which has no superclass; it is default for superclass if no superclasses are specified.

- If $A_1, A_2, ..., A_n$ $(n \ge 1)$ are attribute definitions, with distinct names; if $M_1, M_2, ..., M_k$ $(k \ge 0)$ are method definitions, with distinct names; and $C_1, C_2, ..., C_h$ $(h \ge 0)$ are distinct class names;

then **Class** C

      Attributes $A_1; A_2; ....; A_n;$

      Methods $M_1; M_2; .....; M_k;$

      Superclasses $C_1, C_2, ..., C_h$

End

is a class definition.

If the domain of attribute A_i of class C is a non primitive class C', in the instances of C, attribute A_i assumes, as values, *oid*s of objects of class C'. The instances of C, referencing instances of C', are said to be *composite* objects. The instances of C', which are referenced by instances of C are said *component* objects.

Several types of composite references can be supported. These can be categorized as follows [12]:

Exclusive dependent reference If an object o is component of an object o', it cannot be component of another object. If o' is removed, o is also removed.

Exclusive independent reference If an object o is component of an object o', it cannot be component of another object. The deletion of o' does not imply the deletion of o.

Shared dependent reference An object o can be component of several objects. Object o is removed when all parent objects, on which o depends for existence, are removed.

Shared independent reference An object o can be component of several objects. The deletion of the parent object does not imply the deletion of o.

In the paper we use the graphical notation for OODB schema's from [2]. For simplicity we do not indicate the methods specification in the class representation. Classes and entities are represented by a box with two regions. The first region contains the class (entity) name, the second the attribute definitions. A bold type arc from a class C to a class C' denotes that class C' is a subclass of class C'. A dotted arc from a class C to a class C' denotes that C' is the domain of a composite attribute of C.

3 Modeling multilevel entities using composite objects

In this section we review the approach proposed by Bertino and Jajodia in [4] for modeling multilevel entities with single level objects by using the composite object relationship. We then extend that approach to the case of entities organized in inheritance hierarchies and illustrate how information stored in different objects can be retrieved by defining the appropriate methods. Using the composite object approach together with the generation of the appropriate accessor methods, the resulting objects are able to provide the same interface as if multilevel objects were directly supported.

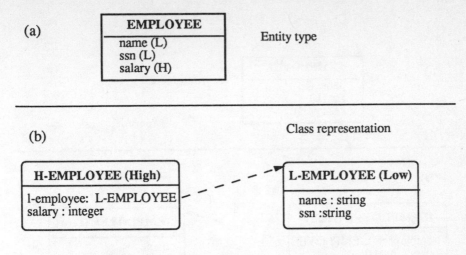

Figure 1: An example of representation of a multilevel entity type

Let E be a multilevel entity type having properties with different security levels $L_1, \ldots, L_n$. The entity is represented as follows. For each security level L_i, $(i = 1, \ldots, n)$, a class C_i with level L_i is defined. Each class C_i contains the properties with level L_i. Moreover, for each class C_j with level L_j such that $L_j < L_i$ and $\not\exists C_k$ with level $L_k, L_j < L_k < L_i$, a composite attribute a_j is defined in C_i with class C_j as domain.

As an example, consider two security levels Low (L) and High (H) such that $L < H$. Moreover, consider entity type EMPLOYEE with properties "name" and "ssn" classified Low and "salary" classified High (Figure 1(a)). This entity is represented by two classes: class L-EMPLOYEE, with security level Low, and class H-EMPLOYEE with security level High. Class L-EMPLOYEE contains attributes "name" and "ssn". Class H-EMPLOYEE contains attribute "salary" and composite attribute "l-employee" whose domain is class L-EMPLOYEE. The resulting schema is illustrated in Figure 1(b). An example of an instance of entity type EMPLOYEE, and the instance objects representing it, is illustrated in Figure 2.

Note that class H-EMPLOYEE contains attribute, "l-employee" that was not contained in the original entity. This attribute is a composite attribute used by the objects of class H-EMPLOYEE to refer to their component objects belonging to class L-EMPLOYEE.

If the entity type to be represented has multi-valued attributes, in the representation with classes, each multi-valued attribute is partitioned into several attributes, one for each possible level of classification which can be assigned to the attribute's values. Each attribute stores the values at a given level. For instance, consider entity type EMPLOYEE represented in Figure 3(a) obtained by 1(a) by adding multi-valued property "skills". This entity type is represented by class L-EMPLOYEE, classified Low, with attributes "name", "ssn", and "low-skills" and by class H-EMPLOYEE, classified High, with attributes "salary" and "high-skills", and composite attribute "l-employee". The resulting schema is illustrated in Figure 3(b).

102

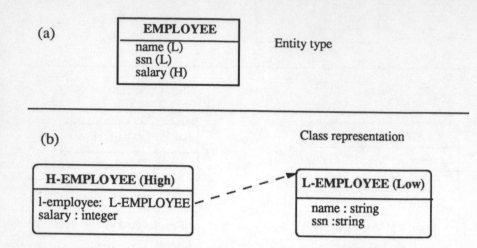

(a)

EMPLOYEE
name (L)
ssn (L)
salary (H)

Entity type

(b)   Class representation

H-EMPLOYEE (High)
l-employee: L-EMPLOYEE
salary : integer

L-EMPLOYEE (Low)
name : string
ssn :string

Figure 2: An example of representation of a multilevel entity

(a)

EMPLOYEE
name (L)
ssn (L)
salary (H)
skills {(L), (H)}

Entity type

(b)   Class representation

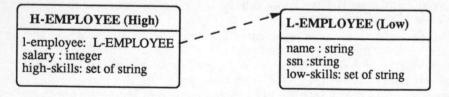

H-EMPLOYEE (High)
l-employee: L-EMPLOYEE
salary : integer
high-skills: set of string

L-EMPLOYEE (Low)
name : string
ssn :string
low-skills: set of string

Figure 3: An example of representation of a multilevel entity

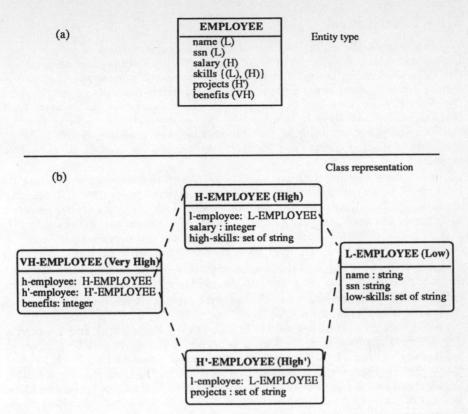

(a)

EMPLOYEE
name (L)
ssn (L)
salary (H)
skills {(L), (H)}
projects (H')
benefits (VH)

Entity type

Class representation

(b)

H-EMPLOYEE (High)
l-employee: L-EMPLOYEE
salary : integer
high-skills: set of string

VH-EMPLOYEE (Very High)
h-employee: H-EMPLOYEE
h'-employee: H'-EMPLOYEE
benefits: integer

L-EMPLOYEE (Low)
name : string
ssn :string
low-skills: set of string

H'-EMPLOYEE (High')
l-employee: L-EMPLOYEE
projects : set of string

Figure 4: An example of representation of a multilevel entity type with properties with incomparable security levels

Note that if an entity type has properties with incomparable classifications, the objects representing the entities may have multiple direct components. For instance, consider the entity type illustrated in Figure 4(a), where the relationships among the security levels are as follows: $L < H < VH$, and $L < H' < VH$, i.e., levels H and H' are incomparable. This entity type is represented as illustrated in Figure 4(b). Class VH-EMPLOYEE has two composite attributes, attribute "h-employee' whose domain is class H-EMPLOYEE and attribute "h'-employee" whose domain is class H'-EMPLOYEE.

We require the composite object hierarchy to satisfy the constraint that the security level of a composite object dominates the security level of its component objects. This is expressed as follows.

Composite Object Constraint-1

For any two objects o and o', if o' is a component of o then $L(o) \geq L(o')$.

3.1   Inheritance

We now discuss the representation of inheritance hierarchies of entity types. Inheritance hierarchies allow to specify an entity as a subtype of another entity. The first entity (called subentity) inherits the attributes specified in the second entity (called superentity). Additional attributes can be specified in the subentity. In the following, we make the hypothesis that the security level of an inherited attribute in a subentity cannot override the security level of the corresponding attribute in the superentity. For example, if the "salary" attribute is High in entity type EMPLOYEE, it cannot be Low in its subentity STUDENT.

Let E be a multilevel entity and $C_1, \ldots C_n$ be the classes representing it. Let now E' be an entity subtype of E having additional properties with security levels $L_1, \ldots L_m$. Entity E', and its relationship with entity E, are represented as follows. For each level L_i, $(i = 1, \ldots, m)$, of some properties of entity E', a class C_i' is defined. Each class C_i' contains the properties with level L_i. Moreover, for each class C_j' with level L_j such that with $L_j < L_i$ and $\nexists C_k'$ with level $L_k, L_j < L_k < L_i$, a composite attribute a_j is defined in C_i' with domain class C_j'. Then, to represent the subtype relationship with entity E, each class C_i' is defined as a subclass of each class C_j such that $L_j < L_i$ and $\nexists C_k$ with level $L_k, L_j < L_k < L_i$.

As an example, consider entity EMPLOYEE of Figure 2(a) and suppose a new entity STUDENT is defined as a subtype of EMPLOYEE with properties "university" classified as Low and "assistantship" classified as High (Figure 5(a)). Entity EMPLOYEE is represented as already illustrated in Figure 2(b). Entity STUDENT is represented by two classes: class L-STUDENT, classified Low and containing attribute "university", and class H-STUDENT, classified High, containing attribute "assistantship" and composite attribute "l-student" whose domain is class L-STUDENT. Then, class H-STUDENT is defined as a subclass of (is-a) class H-EMPLOYEE. Class L-STUDENT is similarly defined as a subclass of class L-EMPLOYEE. The resulting schema is as illustrated in Figure 5(b).

3.2   Class design

A main disadvantage of our approach is that a high user, in order to see all attributes of a multilevel entity, may need to access multiple objects, e.g., all the objects representing the entity. For instance, with reference to the example illustrated in Figure 2, a High user, in order to retrieve entity e, needs to access both object o_h and object o_l.

The need for multiple accesses by users can be avoided by providing appropriate methods which traverse the composite link to retrieve the values of nested attributes, i.e., attributes stored into lower component objects. The retrieval of information from component objects is enforced by invoking the corresponding methods on the component objects. Methods, defined in the composite objects, whose purpose is to retrieve the values of nested attributes are called *nested accessor method*. Methods whose purpose is to return the value of attributes stored in the object are called *accessor methods*. In case of multi-valued attribute, methods may need to return values stored in the object as well as nested values stored in component objects. These methods are called *combined accessor methods*.

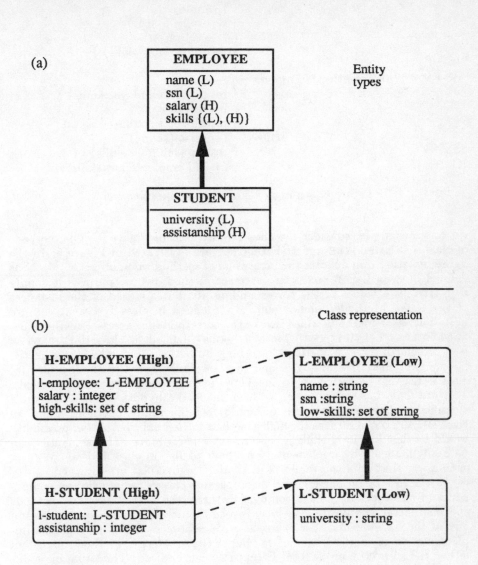

Figure 5: An example of representation of hierarchy of entity types

L-EMPLOYEE's **methods**:   *name*   ( ) $\rightarrow$ string
$\{$ return(self.name)$\}$

ssn   ( ) $\rightarrow$ integer
$\{$ return(self.ssn) $\}$

skills   ( ) $\rightarrow$ set-of(string)
$\{$ return(self.low-skills) $\}$

H-EMPLOYEE's **methods**:   *name*   ( )$\rightarrow$ string
$\{$ return(self.employee.name) $\}$

ssn   ( )$\rightarrow$ integer
$\{$ return(self.l-employee.ssn) $\}$

skills   ( )$\rightarrow$ set-of(string)
$\{$ return($\{$self.high-skills$\}$ $\bigcup$
$\{$self.l-employee.low-skills$\}$)$\}$

Figure 6: An example of method specification

As an example, consider the classes illustrated in Figure 2. The methods of classes L-EMPLOYEE and H-EMPLOYEE are illustrated in Figure 6. In the figure, notation $o.m$ denotes the invocation of method m on object o. Methods defined in class L-EMPLOYEE are accessor methods whose purpose is simply to retrieve the values of the corresponding attributes stored in the instances of the class. Methods "name" and "ssn" defined in class H-EMPLOYEE are nested accessor methods which invoke the corresponding accessor methods defined in class L-EMPLOYEE. Method "skills" defined in class H-EMPLOYEE is a combined accessor methods returning both the High skills stored in the instances of class H-EMPLOYEE and the Low skills stored in the instances of class L-EMPLOYEE (retrieved by invoking the corresponding accessor method).

Note that, in this example, we have made the hypothesis that the skills classified as Low are real skills of employees. Therefore, method "skills" of class H-EMPLOYEE returns the high as well as the low skills. Another possibility would be that low level skills just represent a *cover story*. This semantics can be easily modeled by implementing method "skills" in class H-EMPLOYEE in such a way that only the values of attribute "'high-skills" are returned.

In the case of properties with incomparable classes, where several components of an object may have common features, the nested accessor methods specified in the composite class may invoke the accessor methods specified in any of the components. For example, with reference to Figure 4, in the implementation of method "name" in class VH-EMPLOYEE, method "name" of either H-EMPLOYEE or class H'-EMPLOYEE can be used. The situation is different for method "skills". In this case, in order to retrieve all the skills, class VH-EMPLOYEE must invoke method "skills" defined in class H-EMPLOYEE and not the one defined in class H'-EMPLOYEE. Class H'-EMPLOYEE, indeed, only sees the Low skills, whereas class H-EMPLOYEE sees both High and Low skills.

4   Composite objects and semantic integrity

In Section 2, we have illustrated the types of composite references which can be defined. In this section we extend the composite reference model to the consideration of additional types of composite references. The reason for this extension is that the exclusivity constraints as originally formulated for the Orion model may bring some inference problems. For instance, consider the constraint that an instance of class L-EMPLOYEE should be referenced only by one instance of class H-EMPLOYEE. In absence of security concerns, this can be easily accomplished by using the exclusive composite references. However, exclusive composite references cannot always be used in a secure environment since they may allow low users to infer the existence of objects at higher levels. For example, suppose that an additional entity type, called DEPARTMENT, with level Low, must be stored into the database. Suppose that DEPARTMENT has an attribute whose value in a DEPARTMENT's instance is the set of employees working in the department. If composite references from class H-EMPLOYEE to class L-EMPLOYEE were exclusive, an attempt to add an employee to the list of employees working in a department would be rejected. Then, a Low user would be able to infer the existence of the High object referencing the employee.

To express the above type of constraint without introducing inference channels, we introduce a new type of composite reference which is exclusive with respect to a class, i.e., no two instances of the same class can share a component object. The above constraint can therefore be represented by declaring attribute "l-employee' of class H-EMPLOYEE exclusive with respect to class H-EMPLOYEE itself. Hence, no two instances of class H-EMPLOYEE are allowed to share a component object of type L-EMPLOYEE. However, instances of H-EMPLOYEE may share component objects with instances of other classes.

The exclusivity constraint just introduced prevents two instances of class H-EMPLOYEE from sharing a common L-EMPLOYEE component. However, in some cases this may not be sufficient. In particular, for integrity reasons, instances of class H-EMPLOYEE should not be allowed to share L-EMPLOYEE components with instances of class H-STUDENT. To enforce this type of constraint, we introduce another type of composite reference which is exclusive with respect to a class hierarchy, i.e., no two members of a same class can share a component.

The two additional types of composite references we introduce can be summarized as follows:

Exclusive independent reference with respect to a class. If an object o is component of an object o' instance of class C, it cannot be component of any other object instance of class C. That is, no two instances of the same class can share a component. However, there could be instances of other classes with references to that component.

Exclusive independent reference with respect to a hierarchy. If an object o is component of an object o' member of class C, it cannot be component of any other object member of class C. That is, no two members of the same class can share a reference to the same component.

With respect to the above example, the reference of H-EMPLOYEE to class L-EMPLOYEE, exclusive with respect to class H-EMPLOYEE, can be represented by declaring attribute "l-employee" in class H-EMPLOYEE as follows:
  "l-employee: L-EMPLOYEE **composite exclusive**(self-class)"
  where the pseudo-variable *self-class* indicates the exclusivity with respect to the class itself.

Analogously, the reference of H-EMPLOYEE to class L-EMPLOYEE exclusive with respect to the hierarchy rooted at class H-EMPLOYEE can be represented by declaring attribute "l-employee" in class H-EMPLOYEE as follows:

"l-employee: Employee composite exclusive(self-class*)".

The character "*" associated with the pseudo-variable *self-class* indicates that the reference is exclusive with respect to the hierarchy rooted at class H-EMPLOYEE.

Note that references exclusive with respect to a class are allowed only if all instances of the class have the same security level. Analogously, references exclusive with respect to a class hierarchy can be allowed only if all members of the hierarchy's root have the same security level. Let $\mathcal{H}(C)$ denote the set of classes in the class inheritance hierarchy rooted at C (including C itself). Then, the concepts above are represented by the following two constraints.

Composite Object Constraint-2

Given two classes C and C', C' can be an exclusive component of class C with respect to C if, for each instance o of C, $L(o) = L(C)$.

Composite Object Constraint-3

Given two classes C and C', C' can be an exclusive component of class C with respect to $\mathcal{H}(C)$ if, for each instance o of C'', $C'' \in \mathcal{H}(C)$, $L(o) = L(C)$.

5 Update and delete operations

In this section we describe possible approaches for dealing with update and delete operations in our model.

Since low level information is not replicated (but simply referenced) at higher levels, update operations do not introduce any problem. In particular, updates to the attributes of a low object o are directly visible (through the nested accessor methods) to all higher objects of which o is a component. As an example, suppose that attribute "low-skills" of object o_l in Figure 2 is modified by adding to it a new skill. If, after this update, method "skills" is invoked on object o_h, the new skill will be returned together with the other skills.

The delete operation is more difficult to deal with because of the different approaches the various OODBMSs use with respect to object removal. There are basically two categories of systems: systems allowing users to perform explicit delete operations (like ORION [13], and Iris [8]), and systems using a garbage collection mechanism to remove objects that are not any more reachable from other objects (like GemStone [5] and O_2 [7]). In systems belonging to the second category, no explicit delete operation is available to users. Let us now discuss the two cases in more details.

5.1 Explicit delete operation

Systems with explicit delete operation allow an object to be deleted even if
there are references to it. If a message is sent to a deleted object, the system
returns a *notification* to the invoker object. Therefore, the invoker object must
be ready to deal with the exception arising from a dangling reference. This
approach, which is used by the ORION system and it is also suggested by
Zdonik [23], works well with our composite object approach. For example,
consider objects o_h and o_l of Figure 2 and suppose object o_l is removed. Next
time a message is sent from object o_h to object o_l, object o_h will be notified
that the referenced object does not exist. It is possible to further refine this
method in two directions.

The first approach, called *upward cascading delete*, is similar to the approach
proposed by Jajodia and Sandhu [16] for dealing with delete operations in
multilevel relational databases. In that approach, each time a tuple t of a given
security level l is removed, all polyinstantiated tuples corresponding to t and
with security levels greater than l are also removed. A similar approach can
be applied in our framework by requiring the deletion of a composite object
every time any of its component is deleted. For example, with reference to the
objects illustrated in Figure 2, if object o_l is removed, object o_h will also be
removed.

The second approach, called here *conservative delete*, avoids actual deletion
of low information if there exist some references to it from objects at higher
level. Under this approach, every time a low level object is deleted, a copy
of it is created at higher levels. For example, with reference to the objects
illustrated in Figure 2, if object o_l is removed, a new object o'_h is created with
same status as o_l but with same security level as o_h.

In the following subsections, we illustrate how these two approaches can be
enforced by using the message filter proposed by Jajodia and Kogan in [15].

5.1.1 Upward cascading delete

The upward cascading delete approach can be supported as follows. A special
object, called *keeper object*, is kept at each security level, except the lowest
one. The message filter knows the *oid*s of all keeper objects at all levels. The
keeper object at level L_i maintains a list, called *correspondence list*, of pairs of
the form $\langle oid_i, oid_j \rangle$. Pair $\langle oid_i, oid_j \rangle$ in the correspondence list of keeper H_i
indicates that lower object oid_j is a component of object oid_i. For instance,
with reference to Figure 2, pair $\langle o_h, o_l \rangle$ is stored in the correspondence list of
the keeper object at level High.

Delete operations are dealt with as follows. Suppose subject s sends a
delete message to object o. This message is intercepted by the message filter.
If the subject cannot delete the object[1], the message is ignored and no action
is executed. Otherwise, if subject s can delete object o, the delete message is
forwarded the object (which will therefore be removed). Moreover, message
"deleted(o)" is sent to each keeper object whose level strictly dominates (i.e.,
is greater than) the level of o. Upon reception of message "deleted(o)" each

---

[1] The condition for the delete operation can be that the security level of the subject be
dominated the security level of the object or that the security level of the subject be the same
as the security level of the object, depending on whether writing up is allowed in the model.

110

Actions of the message filter

1. **If** s cannot delete o **then** exit

2. send message "delete(o)" to object o

3. send message "deleted(o)" to all keeper H_i such that $L(H_i) > L(o)$

Actions of keeper H_i (upon reception of message "deleted(o)" by the message filter)

1. send message "delete(o')" to all object o' such that there exists a pair $\langle o', o \rangle$ in the *correspondence list* of H_i.

Figure 7: Deletion of object o by subject s in the upward cascading delete approach

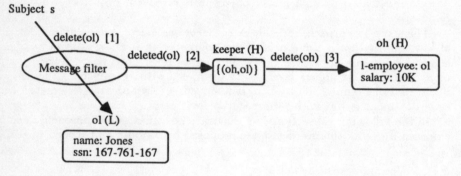

Figure 8: An example of message exchange for upward cascading delete

keeper object determines, from the correspondence list, the objects referencing o and sends them a delete message. Figure 7 illustrates the actions executed by the message filter and by the keeper objects upon the sending of a delete message from subject s to object o.

As an example, consider the objects in Figure 2 and suppose object o_l must be deleted. The messages to be exchanged are illustrated in Figure 8. In the figure, each message is denoted by a labeled arc oriented from the sender to the receiver. The label associated with the arc indicates the name of the message and the parameters (if any). The numbers between square brackets associated with the arcs indicates the relative order in which the messages are sent. Note that the keeper object before deleting object o_h should be sure that object o_l has been removed. Indeed, it may happen that the request of deleting o_l passes the filtering algorithm but some other error causes the method execution to be aborted.

5.1.2 Conservative delete

The upward cascading delete approach can be supported as follows. Like in the case of the upward cascading delete a *keeper object* is kept at each level, except the lowest one.

The keeper object at each level maintains a *correspondence list* as illustrated above. Moreover, each keeper object maintains an additional list, called *shadow list*, of pairs of the form $\langle oid_j, oid_i \rangle$. Pair $\langle oid_j, oid_i \rangle$ in the shadow list indicates that object oid_i is a copy of a lower object oid_j which has been removed.

Delete operations are dealt with as follows. Suppose subject s sends a delete message to object o. This message is intercepted by the message filter. If the subject cannot delete the object, the message is ignored and no action is executed. Otherwise, if s can delete the object, the message filter sends message "deleted(o)" to all keeper objects whose level directly dominates the security level of o. Each keeper will return reply "EX" if an object exists at its level referencing the deleted object, will return "NON-EX" otherwise. If there exist some keeper H_i which returned "NON-EX", message "deleted(o)" will be sent to all keepers H_j whose level directly dominates the level of H_i and for which all the keepers at lower levels returned "NON-EX". The process is then repeated if some keeper returns "NON-EX". Finally, message "delete(o)" is forwarded to object o. The actions executed at each keeper object H_i upon reception of message "deleted(o)" by the message filter are as follows. If, in the correspondence list of H_i, there does not exist any pair with the deleted object o as second element, then "NON-EX" is returned and no action is executed. Otherwise, if such a pair exists, a new object o' is created at the security level of the keeper, with the same status as object o. Then, pair (o, o') is added to the shadow list of keeper H_i and reply "EX" is returned to the message filter. Figure 9 illustrates the actions executed by the message filter and by the keeper objects upon the sending of a delete message from subject s to object o.

As an example, consider the objects illustrated in Figure 10(a) and suppose that object o_l is deleted. The situation resulting after the deletion of object o_l is illustrated in Figure 10(b).

A drawback of the conservative delete approach is that, in some cases, the exclusivity constraints on a composite class cannot be enforced. This happens when upon a delete operations, multiple copies of the same low object are created at higher incomparable levels.

5.2 Garbage collection

In systems based on garbage collection an object is automatically removed by the system when it is no longer referenced by any other object. This approach, if not properly enhanced, would cause some problems in a secure environment. For instance, if a low object is not removed because it is referenced by a high object, a low user may infer the existence of the high object. Therefore, a signaling channel could be established. Another serious drawback is that the garbage collector would have to access objects at various levels of security. This would require the garbage collector to be a trusted component.

To solve this problem, we propose a different approach which does not require the garbage collector to be trusted. The approach requires a garbage collector for each security level. Information needed by the garbage collectors

---

Actions of the message filter

1. **If** s cannot delete o **then** exit

2. *Keepers*:= the set of all keepers H_i such that $L(H_i)$ directly dominates $L(o)$ in the security lattice

3. send message "deleted(o)" to all keepers in set *Keepers* and wait for the replies

4. **If** all keepers returned "EX" **then** go to step 7 **else** continue

5. set *Keepers* equal to the empty set

   For each keeper H_i which returned "NON-EX" **do**

   add to set *Keepers* all keepers H_j such that $L(H_j)$ directly dominates $L(H_i)$ in the security lattice and there not exists any keeper H_l, with $L(H_l) < L(H_j)$, which returned "EX"

   endfor

6. **If** *Keepers* $\neq \emptyset$ **then** go to step 3

7. send message "delete(o)" to object o

Actions of keeper H_i (upon reception of message "deleted(o)" by the message filter)

1. **If** there exists $\langle o_i, o \rangle$ in the *correspondence list* of H_i **then** go to step 2 **else** return "NON-EX" and exit

2. create object o' as a copy of o with security level $L(H_i)$

3. add $\langle o, o' \rangle$ to the *shadow list* of H_i

4. return "EX"

Figure 9: Deletion of object o by subject s in the conservative delete approach

Initial state of objects

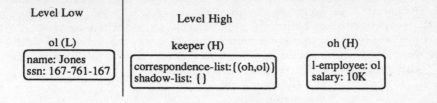

State of objects after deleting object ol

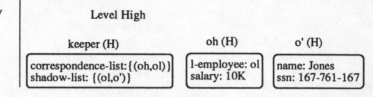

Figure 10: Object status under conservative delete

is partitioned among the different levels so that the garbage collector can access the security information only at its own level or at lower levels. Task of the garbage collector at level l is to remove objects at level l which are not referenced by any object at level l. Since the garbage collector at level l does not see references from objects at levels higher than l (because it does not see those objects at all), objects may be removed also if there exists some high level object referencing them. Therefore, this approach may cause dangling references. This problem can be solved by returning a *notification* to high objects sending messages to lower objects which have been removed. Alternatively, the *upward cascading delete* or the *conservative delete* approach could be used. However, both these approaches, would require all deletions required by the garbage collectors to pass through the message filter.

Note that the garbage collector approach is safe, i.e., does not introduce any inference problem. Indeed, delete operations at high levels do not have any effect on objects at lower levels, i.e., will not cause deletion of any object at lower levels.

6 Specification language

The approach proposed in this paper allows a large variety of application entities to be modeled. However, when dealing with real applications the number of entity types and specialization hierarchies among these can be quite large. It would therefore be desirable that the process of generating the object-oriented schema representing the real world entities be supported by some automatic tool. To support this process, a security specification language can be used to describe the entity types and the specialization hierarchies together with their security requirements. These specifications could therefore be automatically translated in terms of an object-oriented schema through a set of translation rules based on the approach we have discussed in the previous subsections.

The specification language should allow the indication of the security level of the properties of an entity. In case of multi-valued attribute it should be possible to specify whether lower values have to be considered as real values or as cover stories. As an example, entities of Figure 8 could be defined as follows.

    Entity-type EMPLOYEE
                 name: string **Low**
                 ssn: string **Low**
                 salary: integer **High**
                 skills: *set-of* string {**High, Low**}
    Entity-type STUDENT
                 assistantship: integer **High**
                 university: string **Low**
                 supertypes: EMPLOYEE

In this example, Low skills are considered as real skills and therefore are not overridden by skills at level High. The specification of the attribute skills, in case Low skills have to be considered as covert stories could instead be as follows: "*skills*: *set-of* string {**High, Low cover**}".

The specification language should also give the possibility of specifying the form of delete to be used. The possible forms of delete are: notification, upward cascading delete, conservative delete. According to the type of delete required, the translator can then generate the appropriate methods so that the keeper objects receive information concerning composite references to use in processing delete operations.

7 Conclusions and Future Work

In this paper, we have shown how composite objects can be used to model multilevel entities in terms of single level object. We have refined the composite model defined by Kim, Bertino, and Garza [12] by allowing exclusive constraints to hold with respect to a single class and to a class inheritance hierarchy. This work extends the approach proposed by Bertino and Jajodia for modeling multilevel entities in terms of single level objects by including entity types organized in inheritance hierarchies. Moreover, we have discussed possible ways of dealing with update and delete operations in such a model. Finally, we have outlined a specification language that permits incorporation of security requirements in the definition of application entities from which object-oriented database schemas can be generated.

Future work includes the implementation of the specification language and tools for the automatic derivation of the object-oriented schema representing the entities defined using the specification language. Moreover, future work will investigate the representation of entity types organized in inheritance hierarchies with multiple inheritance and attribute overriding.

References

[1] D. E. Bell and L. J. LaPadula, *Secure Computer Systems: Unified Expo-*

sition and Multics Interpretation. The Mitre Corp., March, 1976.

[2] E. Bertino and L. Martino, *Object-Oriented Database Management Systems: Concepts and Architectures*, Addison-Wesley, 1993.

[3] E. Bertino, M. Negri, G. Pelagatti, and L. Sbattella, "Object-Oriented Query Languages: the Notion and the Issues," *IEEE Trans. on Knowledge and Data Engineering*, Vol. 4, No. 3, 1992, pp. 223-237.

[4] E. Bertino and S. Jajodia, "Modeling Multilevel Entities Using Single Level Objects," in *Proc. Int. Conference on Deductive and Object Oriented Databases (DOOD'93)*, December 1993.

[5] R. Breitl, et al., "The GemStone Data Management System," in *Object-Oriented Concepts, Databases, and Applications*, W. Kim, and F. Lochovsky, eds., Addison- Wesley, 1989, pp. 283–308.

[6] V. Doshi and S. Jajodia, "Referential Integrity in Multilevel Secure Database Management System", *Proc. of the IFIP TC11 8th International Conference on Information Security*, Singapore, May 27-29, 1992.

[7] O.Deux, et Al., "The Story of O2", *IEEE Trans. on Knowledge and Data Engineering*, Vol. 2, N. 1 (1990), 91-108.

[8] D. Fishman, et Al. "Overview of the Iris DBMS", *Object-Oriented Concepts, Databases, and Applications*, W. Kim, and F. Lochovsky, eds., Addison-Wesley (1989), 219-250.

[9] T. F. Keefe, W. T. Tsai, and M. B. Thuraisingham, "A Multilevel Security Model for Object-Oriented Systems," *Proc. Eleventh National Computer Security Conference*, October 1988.

[10] T. F. Keefe and W. T. Tsai, "Prototyping the SODA Security Model" In *Database Security, III: Status and Prospects*, D.L. Spooner and C. Landwehr, eds., North-Holland, Amsterdam, 1990.

[11] W. Kim, et Al. "Composite Object Support in an Object-Oriented Database Systems", *Proc. of the Second International Conference on Object-Oriented Programming Systems, Languages, and Applications (OOPSLA)*, Orlando (Florida), October1987.

[12] W. Kim, E. Bertino, J. Garza, "Composite Objects Revisited", *Proc. of ACM-SIGMOD Conference on Management of Data*, Portland (Oregon), May 29-June 3, 1989.

[13] W. Kim, N. Ballou, H.T. Chou, J. Garza, D. Woelk, "Features of the ORION Object-Oriented Database System", *Object-Oriented Concepts, Databases, and Applications*, W. Kim, and F. Lochovsky, eds., Addison-Wesley (1989), 251-282.

[14] W.Kim, "Object-Oriented Databases: Definitions and Research Directions", *IEEE Trans. on Knowledge and Data Engineering*, Vol. 2, N.3, (1990), 327-341.

[15] S. Jajodia and B. Kogan, "Integrating an Object-Oriented Data Model with Multilevel Security", *Proc. of the 1990 IEEE Symposium on Research in Security and Privacy*, Oakland (Calif.), May 7-9, 1990.

[16] S. Jajodia and R. Sandhu, "Toward a Multilevel Secure Relational Data Model", *Proc. of ACM-SIGMOD Conference on Management of Data*, Portland (Oregon), Denver (Colorado), 1991.

[17] C. Meadows and C. Landwehr, "Designing a Trusted Application in an Object-Oriented Data Model," *Research Directions in Database Security*, T.F. Lunt, ed., Springer-Verlag, Berlin, 1992.

[18] J. Millen and T. Lunt, "Security for Object-Oriented Database Systems", *Proc. of the 1992 IEEE Symposium on Research in Security and privacy*, Oakland (Calif.), May 4-6, 1992.

[19] F. Rabitti, E. Bertino, W. Kim, and D. Woelk, "A model of Authorization for Next-Generation Database Systems", *ACM Trans. on Database Systems*, March 1991.

[20] R. Sandhu, R. Thomas, and S. Jajodia, "Supporting Timing-Channel Free Computations in Multilevel Secure Object-Oriented Databases", in *Database Security, V: Status and Prospects*, C.E. Landwehr and S. Jajodia (eds.), North-Holland, 1992.

[21] M.B. Thuraisingham, "A Multilevel Secure Object-Oriented Data Model," *Proc. Twelfth National Computer Security Conference*, October 1989.

[22] M.B. Thuraisingham, "Mandatory Security in Object-Oriented Database Systems", *Proc. of the Object-Oriented Programming Systems, Languages, and Applications*, New Orleans, Louisiana, October 1989.

[23] S. Zdonik, "Object-oriented Type Evolution", *Advances in Database Programming Languages*, F.Bancilhon, and P.Buneman, eds., Addison-Wesley, 1990, 277-288.

Information Flow Control in Object-Oriented Programs

Ciarán Bryce

IRISA-Rennes,

France

Abstract

This paper proposes an information flow control mechanism for parallel object based languages. The mechanism registers the information transmissions between program variables independently of any particular security policy. Also looked at is the range of policies that may be expressed in the security model framework, how the approach relates to traditional multi-level security and the problems related to runtime information flow control in programs.

1   Introduction

The most important aspect of computer security is the non-disclosure, or *secrecy*, of the information stored in a system. Saltzer & Schroeder [1] define a secrecy violation as occurring when

> "An unauthorized person is able to read or take advantage of information stored in the computer"

Ensuring secrecy is equivalent to saying that certain information transmissions, or *flows*, between system objects must be prohibited. There are many examples of this: a tax program must not leak (let flow) the private information it accesses to unauthorized processes in the system. A bank application has particularly strict secrecy requirements: information about a client's account may flow to the teller objects but not to other clients.

So what kind of mechanisms are needed to achieve information secrecy? Consider a mail application; each user process has a letter box object. One might consider two secrecy policies. Firstly, only the owning user is allowed to retrieve the contents of his letter box. Secondly, if a user A sends a message to user B marked FYEO (signifying For Your Eyes Only), then B must not be able to forward the contents of that message to some other user.

Access controls are universally used to control the information flows in a system [2]. To execute an operation on an object, the calling process must possess a *key* for the operation. Each process is given a set of keys, one for each of the operations on the other objects that it may legally invoke. All operating systems use this abstraction. In Unix, the key abstraction is implemented with access control lists. If a user's process has a read key for a file then the r bit for the file will be set for "world" or for that user's group. Capability based systems are a more direct implementation of the key abstraction [3].

Going back to the mail application example, access controls can be used to enforce the secrecy requirement that only the owning user can read his letter box, by only granting that user a key for the retrieve operation on the letter box. However, the problem arises with the second secrecy requirement. A user might receive a FYEO message and forward the contents in another message to some other user. Access controls do not understand how information flows in a system. The only way that access controls can stop a user A illegally forwarding a message to user B directly, or indirectly via other user objects, is to ensure that there is no sequence of user processes in the system starting with A and finishing with B such that all members of the sequence have a *send* key for the next member's letter box. Unfortunately, this solution would prohibit A from sending *anything* to B; thus, the access control solution is insufficient.

We need some other approach to preventing undesired transmission of information between program objects. An *information flow* mechanism must tag each variable with the set of variables from which it has received information flows, the effects of which have not been lost due to subsequent flows. The *flow security* of the system can then be determined from these tags. Such a mechanism requires that the behavior of each construct of the language used to program the system be precisely defined with respect to the information flows it generates. One can use the resulting semantics to statically analyze the program text for flows and reject the program if any of these flows violate the security constraints placed on the program. This analysis can be done by hand or automatically (by a compiler for example) if enough information is available about the program. Alternatively, the semantics can be used to specify a runtime mechanism. This consists of extra instructions that a compiler inserts so that the program information flows are logged at runtime. Program based information flow control supposes that an attacker has the program text; he/she thus understands the expected behavior of the program and so may be able to deduce information by examining the value of some variable.

In this paper we look at information flow control in a parallel object-oriented language. The ideas are an extension of those presented in [4] and [5]. The outline security semantics of a parallel object-oriented language are given in the next section. The third section looks at the generality of the mechanism - the issues involved in a runtime version of the mechanism, the relationship between the proposed mechanism and multi-level security and the range of information flow policies that may be expressed. The conclusions are given in section 4 along with a look at related work.

2 Object Oriented Security Semantics

2.1 Language outline

The language used to illustrate the ideas is fairly simple. To recapitulate, object-oriented programming is based on the notion of a *class* [6]. This is a specification of an abstract data type where we have data, or state, accessed only via the defined set of operations, or *methods*. Instances of classes that exist at runtime are the *objects*. An important feature of object-oriented programming is *inheritance*. This is the ability to reuse the specification and/or implementation of an existing class in the declaration of a new class. This new class, termed the sub-class, may contain new method declarations or a redefinition of methods of the defining classes.

In the language chosen, we have standard types - integers, Booleans as well as the non-standard objects (instances of classes). A class is:

$$\textbf{class } c \text{ method\_decl}^* \text{ } s \textbf{ end}$$

where c is a class name, the asterisk signifies that the class contains zero or more methods, s is the statement block executed by an object of the class when created. In the following, we do not consider that there is any special link between a class and its subclass. The relationship between inheritance and information flow needs further consideration; we want to know if there is a direct relationship between the flow specification of a class and its subclass. This is the subject of future work.

The method is:

$$\textbf{method } m \textbf{ begin } s; \textbf{ return } e^* \textbf{ end}$$

A method m executes a statement block s and returns zero or more results e^*. The remaining abstract syntax of the language is given below.

The following are the expressions:

$e ::=$	v	*variable*
$\|$	$e_1 \textbf{ op } e_2$	*arithmetic or Boolean expression*
$\|$	$e_{call}!m(e^*)$	*a method call on e_{call}, transfer parameters listed*
$\|$	$\textbf{new}(C)$	*create an object of type C*

and the commands s:

$s ::-$	$v \leftarrow e$	*assignment to variable*
$\|$	$s_1; s_2$	*sequential composition*
$\|$	$\textbf{if } e \textbf{ then } s_1 \textbf{ else } s_2 \textbf{ fi}$	*conditional*
$\|$	$\textbf{while } e \textbf{ do } s \textbf{ od}$	*repetitive statement*

On program initialization, an object of some class is automatically created and the program evolves from there. Each object has a thread of control associated.

2.2 Information flow semantics outline

There are two forms of information flows in programs [5]. There is a *direct* information flow from variables appearing on the right hand side of an assignment operator to the variable(s) on the left hand side. For example, $y := v_1 + v_2$ can lead to variety in v_1 and v_2 provoking variety in y - an information transmission [7]. An *indirect* flow captures the variety provoked by variables in the Boolean expressions of conditional commands to variables influenced by those expressions. For example, in the following alternative, where say a and b are initially 0,

$$\textbf{if } x = 0 \textbf{ then } a := 1 \textbf{ else } b := 1 \textbf{ fi}$$

there is an indirect information flow from x to **both** a and b since their subsequent values depend upon x. Note also that flows are transitive: the composition $y := x; v := y$ transfers information from x to y and from x and y to v.

120

Notation

The *flow security state* of a program is the ensemble of information flows that have occurred in the program. The flow semantics of a programming language is defined as the manner in which the constructs of the language update the flow security state. We now define the flow security state's structure.

We firstly need some way of representing the set of variables information concerning which has flown to, or influenced, a variable v. We call this set the **security variable** of v, denoted $\overline{v}$.

Indirect flows in an object are modeled by the *indirect* variable - defined as a sequence of sets of variables:

$$indirect : (\mathbf{P}variables)^+$$

(where $\mathbf{P}$ is the "set of" operator and $^+$ stands for the set of non-zero length sequences.) The empty or nil indirect is $\prec \{\} \succ$. Note that every object has its own *indirect* variable. The operators on *indirect* are now explained.

The value of the flow of *indirect*, denoted $val(indirect)$ is the set of all variables in the indirect variable. Let $indirect(i)$ denote the ith of n entries:

$$val(indirect) \triangleq \cup_{i=0}^{n-1} indirect(i)$$

where $\cup$ is the set union operator. Since *indirect* is just a sequence (of sets), we assume the $head()$, $tail()$ and concatenation ($\circ$) operators. A set of variables V may also be added to, as opposed to concatenated with, *indirect*. This is done with the $\uplus$ operator. The set V is set unioned with each entry in the *indirect* sequence.

$$V \uplus indirect \triangleq \circ_{i=0}^{n-1} (V \cup indirect(i))$$

Finally, we will need an operator for combining two *indirect* variables together. The operator is $\sqcup$. Note that it is non-commutative. Its effect is to add using the $\uplus$ operator the variables in both *indirects* to the first *indirect* argument's entries:

$$indirect_i \sqcup indirect_j \triangleq (val(indirect_i) \cup val(indirect_j)) \uplus indirect_i$$

When describing the behavior of the command types with respect to the flow security state, we will use an operational notation similar to [8]. The flow semantics are defined as a transition relation "$\rightarrow$" which maps a program segment and state pair to another. The interpretation given $(C_1, \sigma_1) \rightarrow (C_2, \sigma_2)$ is that the execution of the command block C_1 in state σ_1 can lead to a state σ_2 from which the command block C_2 executes. Composition is specified with the following rule:

$$\frac{(S_1, \sigma_1) \rightarrow (\epsilon, \sigma_2), (S_2, \sigma_2) \rightarrow (\epsilon, \sigma_3)}{(S_1; S_2, \sigma_1) \rightarrow (S_2, \sigma_2) \rightarrow (\epsilon, \sigma_3)}$$

where ϵ denotes the empty command block. We stress that all the transitions given in this paper are in terms of the flow security state, not the functional state (mapping from variables to values).

Assignment

For the assignment command, $y := e$, where e is of the form x_1 op x_2 op .. op x_n, the security semantics are:

$$(y := e, \sigma) \rightarrow (\epsilon, \sigma[(\{\, x_i \mid i = 1..n \,\} \cup \{\, \overline{x_i} \mid i = 1..n \,\} \cup val(indirect))/\overline{y}])$$

The security variable for y is updated to register the flows occurring from the x_is: $val(indirect)$ returns the set of variables in the $indirect$ of the object, the variables $\overline{x_i}$ capture the transitivity of the information flows from each x_i.

Constants are ignored in the flow calculus since they give no information concerning the values of variables. Their security variable is always the empty set $\{\}$. Thus the assignment $a:=0$ sets $\overline{a}$ to $val(indirect)$.

Sequential Alternative

Leaving aside parallelism for the present, the alternative command has the following semantics where σ is the flow security state:

$$(\text{if } e \text{ then } S_1 \text{ else } S_2 \text{ fi}, \sigma) \rightarrow (\text{update1};S_i;\text{update2},\sigma)$$

where S_i can be S_1 or S_2, depending on the functional state.

update1 $\hat{=}$
   $indirect := \{\, c \cup \overline{c} \mid c \in C_{bool} \,\} \circ indirect;$
      $\overline{l} := \overline{l} \cup \{\, c \cup \overline{c} \mid c \in C_{bool} \,\}, \forall\, l \in lhs\_vars$
update2 $\hat{=}$
   $indirect := tail(indirect)$

lhs_vars is the set of variables appearing on the left hand side of the $:=$ operator in the two branches of the command (for the example in the opening paragraph, the value of lhs_vars is the set $\{a, b\}$); C_{bool} is the set of variables appearing in the Boolean guard e. The **update1** updates the $indirect$ variable to the value of the indirect flow in the command, this change is undone in **update2** since the effect of the Boolean guard is no longer visible. Note that also in **update1**, the indirect flows to the variables in the branch not executed are registered.

Sequential Repetitive

Repetitive commands also cause indirect information flows from the variables in the guard to all variables which could possibly receive flows in the loop body since the values of the guard variables influence the values of the variables receiving assignments in the loop - even if the loop does not execute.

$$x := e;$$
$$z, y := 0, 0;$$
$$\text{while } x \neq y \text{ do } y := y + 1 \text{ od}$$
$$z := 1;$$

In this program segment, the values of y will equal x on loop termination, even if the branch does not execute.

Moreover, as Reitman [9] pointed out, since all variables receiving direct flows after the loop do so on condition that the loop terminates, the variables of the loop guards flow indirectly to these variables. This is because loop termination occurs when the guard is false - since this condition may not always be met, it signals information about the values of the guard variables. In the example above, by observing that z is 1 information concerning x and y is released: their values are equal. The following is the behavior of the repetitive command with respect to the flow security state. There are two transitions:

$$(\textbf{while } e \textbf{ do } S \textbf{ od}, \sigma) \rightarrow (\textbf{update1};S;\textbf{update2};\textbf{while } e \textbf{ do } S \textbf{ od}, \sigma)$$

$$(\textbf{while } B \textbf{ do } S \textbf{ od}, \sigma) \rightarrow (\textbf{update3}, \sigma)$$

where **update1** and **update2** are the same as in the alternative command.

update3 $\hat{=}$
$$indirect := \{ \, c \cup \bar{c} \mid c \in C_{bool} \, \} \uplus indirect;$$
$$\bar{l} := \bar{l} \cup \{ \, c \cup \bar{c} \mid c \in C_{bool} \, \} \; \forall \, l \in lhs\_vars$$

On each iteration of the loop, the flow value of the loop guard is pushed onto the *indirect* stack (**update1**) and popped at the end (**update2**). When the loop finally terminates, the indirect flow from the loop conditions to all variables that could have received a flow in the loop (*lhs_vars*) is registered to cater for the case when no iteration occurs (**update3**, ii). Also the indirect flow to all variables subsequently receiving direct flows is recorded (**update3**, i). The $\uplus$ operator is used instead of the ∘ in **update3** to capture the permanence of the change in *indirect*; in particular, the number of entries in *indirect* is the same on entry and exit since any arbitrary nesting scheme of alternative and repetitive commands must be supported.

Method Call

During a call, the caller transfers his *indirect* value to the called object, using the $\sqcup$ operator, and the reverse happens when the call returns since continuation of the execution of the two objects is dependent on Boolean expression conditions in both objects. The variables in these conditions are recorded in the two *indirects*.

On method call:
$$indirect_{callee} := indirect_{callee} \sqcup indirect_{caller}$$

On method return:
$$indirect_{caller} := indirect_{caller} \sqcup indirect_{callee}$$

A method call and return is principally an exchange of parameters by assignment. Thus the assignment semantics apply to the assignment of the actual parameter expressions to the formal input parameters with the exception that both indirects are included:

$$\overline{formal\_in} := \{actual\_in\} \cup \overline{actual\_in} \cup \mathrm{val}(indirect_{callee}) \cup \mathrm{val}(indirect_{caller})$$

Object Creation

The *indirect* of the new object is assigned that of the creator:

$$indirect_{new} := indirect_{creator}$$

because the creation comes about as a result of a set of conditions, the variables in which are recorded in $indirect_{creator}$. The objects created at initialization of the program are assigned an empty *indirect* variable. In all cases, the initial security variables of the new object are set to the empty set value.

References variables

Reference variables also need security variables. Suppose r is a variable of some class.

if b **then** $r := new$ class **else** $r := nil$ **fi**

obviously causes a transfer of information from b to r. Information is stored in r concerning the fact that an object is conditionally created. Manipulation of the security variables of references is no different to standard variables. For example, the assignment $r := ref$ in a program causes the following update of the flow security state:

$$\bar{r} := \{ref\} \cup \overline{ref} \cup val(indirect)$$

Inter-object indirect flows

It was mentioned that there is an indirect flow from conditional command guard variables to the variables which can receive flows in the body. In a similar way, when a object does a method call, there are subsequent updates and communications with other objects. The fact that one of these communications takes place, and that the updates which follow are made, gives information to each object about the condition that was met in the object that made the call. This information is contained in the object's *indirect* variable which must thus be transferred during method call. If the communication is not made, then the fact that no updates occur in a remote object can be indicative of the condition for the method call not being met in the first object. Thus, there is still an indirect flow in the absence of a method call.

As an example of how indirect flows can occur in the absence of a method call, consider the following pseudo-program extract:

object O1	object O2	object O3
$x := \exp(..);$	$m2_1(a)$ **begin**	$m3()$
if $x = 0$	$b := a$ **end**	**begin**
then $O2!m2_1(0)$ **fi**		$z := O2!m2_2();$
$y := O3!m3();$	$m2_2()$ **begin**	**return** b
	return b **end**	**end**

$b := 1$

In this example, supposing that x is 0 or 1, the variable y in object O1 will equal x after the second call even if the call to O2 is not taken. Yet unless the indirect flow to O2 is registered, x will not be added to $\bar{y}$ after the call to O3.

Mizuno & Oldehöeft recognized the problem of inter object indirect flows in an object-based system [10]. In their proposal, each time a communication with another object is skipped in a conditional command, a dummy message called a *probe* is sent to all objects which could have been transitively communicated with, had the method call been made by the object. The probe carries the information flow value (in their case the security classification - see section 3) of the variables in the condition of the command containing the communication. On arrival at the destination objects, the classification is added to the current classification of the variables which could have received a direct flow if the communication had gone ahead.

The probe message approach seems to be pessimistic for flows and to have an unacceptably high cost. For a runtime flow mechanism, sending a message each time a communication is skipped would flood the system. Another problem with it is that it is difficult to define the information flow semantics of other programming models e.g. CSP [11], for the probe message exchange. In CSP, this is due to the rendezvous communication: a receiver explicitly states when it wants a message. Thus the probe would have to be consumed at a precise point in time. Moreover, if the object receiving a flow also misses its communication, then it is not evident how and when one expresses the updating with the probe value in the receiver object.

A better solution comes from considering the causal relations that exist among objects and the way that objects view the system. An object cannot observe all the events in a system as they happen; it must be informed of these events by other objects via communication. This has important implications for the treatment of inter-object indirect flows. Consider the piece of code below. Assume that b is initially zero. If $x \neq 0$ then b is updated and the

```
        object O1                          object O2
                                           m()
        if x=0 then a:=1                    b:=1
        else O2!m()
```

indirect flow from x occurs. However, if one observes b and sees that it is zero then one cannot infer that the condition failed in the first object: the alternative command may not have executed yet in O1. The only way that the value of the condition in O1 can be inferred from any value in O2 is if a set of communications between O1 and O2 takes place, after the alternative has executed in O1. This also extends, for example, to an observer object looking at some variable in O1 and seeing that the alternative has completed and then communicating with O2 to see whether b was updated, with the intention of deducing x.

The solution proposed here is to transfer the flow value of a condition on which a communication executes, only if the communication takes place. If the communication is skipped, then the flow value of the condition is recorded in the *indirect* variable of the object and is transferred in the next method call communication. This approach works because inter-object indirect flows can only signal any useful information if an object from which the flow originates, (transitively) communicates with the object with which it should have communicated, later on. With this mechanism, we are guaranteed that the flow value of the condition in question will be transferred when this subsequent communication occurs. This approach constitutes what we call *weak information flow consistency*.

The security semantics for the alternative command when parallelism exists is the following.

$$(\text{if } e \text{ then } S_1 \text{ else } S_2 \text{ fi}, \sigma) \rightarrow (\textbf{update1};S_i;\textbf{update2'},\sigma)$$

where **update1** is the same as for the sequential case. The functionality of **update2'** is outlined below: *missed_comms* is true if the non-executed branch contains a method call. The then branch records the flow value of the condition

$$\begin{aligned} \textbf{update2'} \hat{=} \ &\textbf{if } missed\_comms \\ &\textbf{then } indirect := head(indirect) \uplus tail(indirect) \\ &\textbf{else } indirect := tail(indirect) \\ &\textbf{endif} \end{aligned}$$

for the information flow consistency.

The semantics of the repetitive command is not altered from the sequential case. For the case where zero iterations are taken the **update3** implicitly takes care of the weak consistency flow registration requirements i.e. if a method call is contained in the loop body.

$$(\textbf{while } B \textbf{ do } S \textbf{ od}, \sigma) \rightarrow (\textbf{update1};S;\textbf{update2};\textbf{while } B \textbf{ do } S \textbf{ od}, \sigma)$$

$$(\textbf{while } B \textbf{ do } S \textbf{ od}, \sigma) \rightarrow (\textbf{update3}, \sigma)$$

3 Adaptability of the Flow Control mechanism

The information flow control mechanism is based on security variables: each variable is tagged with the set of variables from which it has received a flow. This section looks at the generality of this mechanism from three points of view. We firstly explain the relationship between the security variable and traditional security level, or classification, approaches to flow control. We then look at the extra problems encountered with a runtime version of the flow mechanism. Finally, we see how the mechanism can be adapted to support coarser grained policies - flow policies where permitted flows are specified in terms of what objects or groups of objects may legally exchange data rather than what variables may do so.

3.1 Information flow control: security variables versus security levels

Information flow in programs is traditionally handled by giving each variable a security level, or classification. The set of classifications forms a lattice (see

126

below) so that the effect of the assignment $y := exp(x_1, x_2, ..., x_n)$ in the case where variables are dynamically bound to classifications, is to make the security classification of variable y, denoted $\underline{y}$, the least upper bound of the right hand side variables' classifications. In programs where security classifications are statically bound to variables, such an assignment is illegal if the resulting classification exceeds that of y.

Aside A lattice is a partially ordered set of elements S on which some relation, denoted $\leq$, is defined. The partial ordering implies *anti-symmetry* - $\forall a, b \in S, a \leq b \wedge b \leq a \Rightarrow a = b$, *reflexivity* - $\forall a \in S, a \leq a$ and *transitivity* - $a \leq b \wedge b \leq c \Rightarrow a \leq c$. In addition, for all pairs of elements a, b there is an element known as the *least upper bound* $(a \oplus b)$ and an element known as the *greatest lower bound* $(a \otimes b)$ defined as follows:
$a \oplus b = c$ if $a, b \leq c \wedge \neg \exists d$ where $a, b \leq d, d \leq c$ and $a \otimes b = c$ if $a, b \geq c \wedge \neg \exists d$ where $a, b \geq d, d \geq c$.

Theorem The relationship between the security variable approach and the classification approach is captured by the following predicate:

$$x \in \overline{y} \Rightarrow \underline{x} \leq \underline{y}$$

where $\underline{x}$ is the classification of x when the information it contained was transmitted to y. $\diamond$

The proof is given in the appendix. Note how the theorem states for $\underline{x}$ "when the information it contained was transmitted". This is because a variable named in a security variable may subsequently have its classification altered by an independent flow. For statically bound classifications, this cannot happen; the class will always be constant. Thus in this case the predicate always holds.

The reverse implication of the theorem, $\underline{x} \leq \underline{y} \Rightarrow x \in \overline{y}$, does not hold. A flow mechanism using security levels is unable to say anything about information flows between particular variables. In this sense, the traditional security level approach is poorer than the security variable approach.

3.2 Run-time detection of flow violations

For an executing program, we need some way of expressing our flow security policy since the mechanism (unlike the security classification approach) has no implicit policy. The latter means that we may also specify the points in a program where the policy is to hold.

We introduce a pragma declaration, **ENSURE**, which specifies and verifies at run-time the flow security policy. Its syntax is the following:

ENSURE Γ_v not in $\overline{v}$

where Γ_v is the set of variables forbidden to flow to v under the security policy. The axiomatic semantics of the pragma is the following:

$$\frac{P.v \cap \Gamma_v = \emptyset}{\{P\} \text{ ENSURE } \Gamma_v \text{ not in } \overline{v} \ \{P\}}$$

If the command is executed in a state satisfying P where the security variable for
v is disjoint from the set of variables forbidden to flow to it, then the command
terminates normally, still in flow security state satisfying P. The semantics are
undefined in the event of a security violation - where $P.v$ and Γ_v are not disjoint.

One of the inherent problems of a runtime mechanism is that failures can
leak information to the environment - this information being the condition that
led to the failure. Consider the following piece of code:

$$\text{if } b = 7 \text{ then } c := d \text{ fi}; \textbf{ENSURE } \{d\} \text{ not in } \overline{c}$$

The system policy forbids flows from variable d to c. During execution, should
the condition $b = 7$ be true, then the policy will be violated and the program fails. Since a failure only occurs when the value of the condition is true,
information concerning variable b is leaked to the environment.

A run-time mechanism must tackle the problem by considering the environment as part of the system. Each time an object's *indirect* is updated, an
error is signaled if information concerning the updated variables are forbidden
to flow to the environment. In the preceding example, an error is raised if the
value of b cannot be released to the environment of the object. In the case of
the alternative command, when *indirect* is updated on entry in **update1**, we
check that it contains no variables which can be leaked to the environment by
the command failing. In effect, what is happening is that we are unconditional-
izing object violations. However, there is a snag with this approach - the value
of *indirect* cannot be undone after a conditional command as is usually the
case. To see why, consider the example below. Object O2 fails if the condition

O1	O2
	$\vdots$
m(y) begin	
if $x = 0$ then $y := a$	O1 ! m(b)
else $y := 1$ fi	
end	**ENSURE** $\{a\}$ not in b

$x = 0$ is true in O1. Yet x will not be in O2's *indirect* after the call if O1's
indirect is undone after the alternative. Thus, a runtime mechanism cannot
undo the *indirect*s.

3.3 Supporting coarser grained flow policies

A feature of the security variable based mechanism is that the size of the security variables may become very large. For information flow policies expressed
in terms of the objects that may exchange information, like the Chinese Wall
model [12], rather than the variables in those objects, we have a lot of supple-
mentary information.

To verify object-based policies, we re-write the semantics. The first thing
that needs to be done is to have variables named in the security variables pre-
fixed by the name of the object in which they were declared. (This should
have been done in the first place to avoid name clashes). For example, $\overline{x} =$

{O1.s, O2.t} means that x has received a flow from variable s of object O1 and variable t of object O2. Thus, the assignment $y := e(x_i)_{i=1..N}$ would set:

$$\overline{y} = \{self.x_i \mid i = 1..N\} \cup \{self.\overline{x_i} \mid i = 1..N\} \cup \text{val}(indirect_{self})$$

where $self$ names the enclosing object. The "assignments" treating the indirect flows in the conditional commands are similarly handled. Thus, in the alternative (**update1**),

$$\overline{l} = self.\overline{l} \cup \{self.c\} \cup self.\overline{c}$$

for all variables c in the guard and all variables l in the *lhs_vars*.

For policies where only the object names are important, then one need only store the object name in the security variable. Thus, the assignment semantics above would be:

$$\overline{y} = \{self\} \cup \{self.\overline{x_i} \mid i = 1..N\} \cup \text{val}(indirect_{self})$$

One can go a step further than this. Policies on objects may be based on attributes of the objects rather than the objects themselves. In the Chinese Wall example, the attributes of interest of the object are the company name to which the object belongs. The system maintains a mapping from each object to the attributes associated with that object. One could imagine object names in the security variables being replaced by their attributes. Thus one could know the attributes of the information flow sources. The assignment semantics is the same as in the last paragraph except that $self$ and the object names now stand for the attributes that the system associates with the objects.

Examples   Consider how a multi-level secure environment might be implemented. Each object is given a classification in the set $\{c_1,....,c_N\}$ on which there is a lattice ordering $(\leq)$. We will assume here that the classification of an object is static. The security variables contain elements of the set $\{c_1,....,c_N\}$. The classification of the information that has flown to each variable is the least upper bound or maximum of the security variable entries. Therefore, to ensure multi-level secrecy in a object of classification c_i, we define Γ_{self} as follows for the variables in an object:

$$\Gamma_{self} \triangleq \{c_j \mid self < c_j \leq c_N \}$$

at the points in the program where the policy is meant to hold. In a similar way, if the set of company names in a Chinese Wall applications is denoted by the set COMPANIES, the predicate to be satisfied for variable v would be:

$$\Gamma_{self} \triangleq (\text{COMPANIES} \setminus \{self\})$$

4   Discussion

This paper has outlined the information flow semantics of a parallel object oriented language. The semantics were expressed in terms of information flows between object variables and a set of re-writing rules to support coarser grained policies was also presented. Also looked at was the relationship between security variables and security classifications in the programming language context and finally the problems related to a runtime flow control mechanism.

The ideas examined here are a continuation of a similar study made of CSP 1978 [11], see [5, 13]. In [13], a security proof system is derived from the flow semantics. More importantly, the CSP security semantics are justified in the following sense: if $x \in \overline{y}$ at some point in the program, then altering x at the start of the program can lead to variety in y, whereas $x \notin \overline{y}$ means that altering x cannot lead to variety in y. No such justification has been attempted yet for the parallel object oriented flow control version.

Denning [4] was the first to consider information flow control in programs. Using the classification approach, she describes a compile-time algorithm for ensuring that sequential programs with statically bound security classes are flow-correct - that no variable receives information whose classification is greater than that of the variable. In programs where the security classifications are dynamically bound, a runtime mechanism is introduced so that the class of y is updated with the value of the flow.

Reitman [9] describes a flow control axiomatic proof system for parallel processes communicating by shared variables as well as by message passing using the security classification approach. His assignment axiom is:

$$A_{:=}$$

$$\{ \, P[\underline{y} \leftarrow \underline{x_1} \oplus \underline{x_2} \oplus \,....\, \oplus \underline{x_n} \oplus local \oplus global] \, \}$$
$$y := exp(x_1, x_2, ..., x_n)$$
$$\{ \, P \, \}$$

where $\underline{x}$ is the security classification of x and the variables $local$ and $global$ fulfill the same role as $indirect$. Shared variable communication is treated as an extension to sequential processing. To prove a set of Pascal processes, for each process he establishes an invariant - a definition of the maximum security level of each of the variables, and then for the other processes, shows that when they communicate with the process, the invariant in the called process cannot be violated.

However, we do not believe that Reitman's flow semantics for the conditional commands are complete - he does not consider the indirect flow from the selection guard to the branch which is not executed. His selection command rule is the following,

$$\frac{\{ \, V,L',G \, \} \, S_i \, \{ \, V,L',G' \, \}, \; i=1,2}{\{ \, V,L,G \, \} \; \text{if } B \text{ then } S1 \text{ else } S2 \text{ endif } \{ \, V,L,G' \, \}}$$
$$(V,L',G) \Rightarrow L[local \leftarrow local \oplus \underline{B}]$$

$\{ \, V,L,G \, \}$ is a predicate on the security state, V a predicate on the mapping from variables to classifications, L a predicate on the value of $local$ and G a predicate on the value of $global$. In each branch, the value of $local$ which captures the indirect flow from the program guard is updated on entry: L goes to L'. Consider the following program segment where a and b are known to be 0 beforehand:

$$\{ \, \underline{a} = \underline{b} = low, \, local = low, \, global = low \, \}$$
$$\text{if } x = 0 \text{ then } a := 1 \text{ else } b := 1 \text{ endif}$$
$$\{\underline{a} \leq \underline{x}, \, \underline{b} = low, \, local = low, \, global = low\}$$

$$\bigvee$$
$$\{\underline{a} = low,\ \underline{b} \leq \underline{x},\ local = low,\ global = low\}$$

And since the post-condition allows us to conclude $\{\underline{a} \leq \underline{x},\ \underline{b} \leq \underline{x}\}$, the indirect flow in the two branches seems to be accounted for. Yet it is not. The logical or in the post-condition is in fact an exclusive-or. The predicate which holds depends on the branch which executes which is exclusive. This can be seen from an example used in [14] in which the following piece of code is given:

if b **then** $y := x$ **endif**
if $\neg b$ **then** $z := y$ **endif**

b is a Boolean expression not containing y say, both $\underline{z}$ and $\underline{y}$ are *low* beforehand. Reitman correctly points out that since only one branch can execute, there is no flow from x to z. Using his combined functional and security proofs he establishes the post-condition:

$$\{\ b \Rightarrow (\underline{y} \leq \underline{b} \oplus \underline{x},\ \underline{z} = low),\ \neg b \Rightarrow (\underline{y} = low,\ \underline{z} \leq \underline{b} \oplus \underline{x})\ \}$$

This clearly does not cater for all indirect flows since in the first case z does not have the flow from b registered, y in the second. The problem is that the logical or in the selection semantics is not logically strong enough to capture all indirect flows - as we saw it behaves as an exclusive-or. This has profounder implications for parallel programs where we must register indirect flows in other processes. Consequently, Reitman's semantics can allow an insecure program to be "proved" secure.

Mizuno & Oldehöeft [10] also use the security classification approach in the context of a distributed object oriented system. All inter-process (object) indirect flows are considered. Each time a communication is skipped in a conditional command a *probe*, or dummy message, is sent to each object which could possibly have received a flow if the method call had been made. The probe carries the security level value of the condition on which the method call was skipped which is least upper bound to the class of the variables in the objects which might have received a direct flow. However, as argued in the text, the sending of such messages is not needed.

References

[1] Saltzer J, Schroeder M. The Protection of Information in Computer Systems. IEEE Proc 1975; 63:pages 1278-1308.

[2] Lampson B. Protection. ACM OSR 1974; 8:18-24.

[3] Levy H. Capability-Based Computer Systems. Digital Press, Mass. 1984.

[4] Denning DE. Secure Information Flow in Computer Systems. Phd Thesis, Purdue University, 1975.

[5] Banâtre JP, Bryce C. Information Flow Control in a Parallel Language Framework. In: 6th IEEE Computer Security Foundations Workshop. Franconia, New Hampshire, 1993, pp 39-51.

[6] Korsen T, McGregor JD. Understanding Object-Oriented: a unifying paradigm. CACM 1990; 33:39-60.

[7] Cohen E. Information Transmission in Computational Systems. In: 6th ACM Symposium on Operating System Principles. 1977, pp 133-139.

[8] Plotkin A. An Operational Semantics of CSP. In: Björner D (ed) Formal Description of Programming Concepts - II. North Holland, 1983, pp 199-225.

[9] Reitman R. Information Flow in Parallel Programs: an Axiomatic Approach. Phd Thesis, Cornell University, 1978.

[10] Mizuno M, Oldehoeft A. Information Flow Control in a Distributed Object-Oriented System: Parts I & 2. Research Report TR-CS-88-09. Kansas State University, 1988.

[11] Hoare CAR. Communicating Sequential Processes. CACM 1978; 21:666-674.

[12] Brewer D, Nash M. The Chinese Wall Security Policy. In: IEEE Symposium on Security and Privacy. 1989, pp 206-214.

[13] Banâtre JP, Bryce C. A Security Proof System for Networks of Communicating Processes. INRIA Research Report 2042, France, 1993.

[14] Andrews GR, Reitman RP. An Axiomatic Approach to Information Flow in Programs. ACM TOPLAS 1980; 2:504-513.

A Proof of Theorem

We will prove the theorem with respect to the assignment operation:

$$y := \exp(x_1, x_2, ..., x_N)$$

The proof is by induction on the contents of the security variables. That is, we show that our property is true at step(0) - at the start of the program and that it is preserved by the initial assignment (the base step). We then show that if the property holds at step(N), then it holds at step(N+1). Step(n) denotes the flow security state after execution of the nth instruction.

After termination of the above assignment, with respect to the security classifications, where the r_is are the variables which flow indirectly in the assignment and $\oplus$ is the least upper bound operator, we have

$$\underline{y} \geq (\oplus_{i=1}^{N} x_i) \oplus (\oplus_{i=1}^{M} r_i) \qquad \text{c\_property}$$

since, for dynamic binding, the classification of y is set to the least upper bound of the right hand side variables while for static binding, the command will only terminate (without an error) if the property holds. The $\oplus$ operator allows us to re-write the c_property as $\forall i = 1..N, \underline{y} \geq \underline{x_i} \land \forall i = 1..M, \underline{y} \geq \underline{r_i}$

The security variable flow mechanism gives

$$\overline{y} = \{x_i \mid i = 1..N\} \cup \{\overline{x_i} \mid i = 1..N\} \cup \text{val}(indirect) \qquad \text{sv\_property}$$

Base Step At the start of the program, the security variables and *indirect* will be empty. Each variable will have some initial classification. The assignment $y := \exp(x_i)_{i=1..N}$ would give $\overline{y} = \{x_i\}_{i=1..N}$. Using *c_property*, the theorem is trivially satisfied for this case, that is $x \in \overline{y} \Rightarrow \underline{x} \leq \underline{y}$.

Inductive Step We assume that the property holds at the nth step.

$$\forall\, e_j \in \overline{x_i} \Rightarrow \underline{e_j} \leq \underline{x_i}$$

where e_j is the classification of the information in e_j when it was transmitted to x_i. We show that for all the entries in $\overline{y}$, the theorem holds. We take each term of *sv_property* in turn:

$\{x_i\}_{i=1..N}$

For all x_i, *c_property* tells us that $\underline{y} \geq \underline{x_i}$. Since $x_i \in \overline{y}$, the theorem holds for the x_is.

$\{\overline{x_i}\}_{i=1..N}$

The **inductive step** assumption tells us that $\underline{x_i} \geq \underline{e_j}$ for all $e_j \in \overline{x_i}$. Thus, by *c_property* and the transitivity of the $\geq$ operator,

$$\underline{y} \geq \underline{x_i} \wedge \underline{x_i} \geq \underline{e_j} \Rightarrow \underline{y} \geq \underline{e_j}$$

so the theorem also holds for the $\{\overline{x_i}\}_{i=1..N}$ terms. Note that an e_j may be the same variable as one of the x_is, this does not matter.

val(*indirect*)

This variable is of the form $\{r_i \mid i = 1..M\}$. The proof that the theorem holds for this follows directly from *c_property*.

Since the theorem holds for the inductive and the base steps, it is proven. The proof for the other program constructs easily follows. $\square$

Part III: Authorization and Access Control

A Method-Based Authorization Model for Object-Oriented Databases

Eduardo B. Fernández, María M. Larrondo-Petrie, and Ehud Gudes*

*Department of Computer Science & Engineering, Florida Atlantic University,
Boca Raton, Florida, USA*
** Department of Mathematics and Computer Science, Ben-Gurion University,
Beer-Sheva, Israel*

Abstract

We present an authorization model for object-oriented databases where access constraints are defined in terms of methods. We apply the concept of implied authorization along the data hierarchy and we develop a set of policies for the cases of generalization, aggregation, and relationship, as well as an evaluation algorithm.

1. Introduction

Object-oriented databases are a recent and important development and many studies of them have been performed. These consider aspects such as data modeling, query languages, performance, concurrency control and recovery [1, 2, 3, 4]. Relatively few studies address their security, a critical aspect in systems like these that have a complex and rich data structuring.

There are two types of security models for databases: multilevel models (also called mandatory models) and authorization models (also called discretionary models). We are concerned here with the latter type, which we call an *authorization model*.

We developed previously a model of authorization for this type of systems which includes a set of policies, a structure for authorization rules and their administration, and evaluation algorithms [5]. In that model the high-level query requests were resolved into read and writes at the data access level. Read and write primitives model adequately access to class attributes. In [6] we extended the access types to include "execute", which allows control of the execution of methods.

However, that model is based on control of low-level actions. Assuming that we use an object model such as OMT [7] as conceptual model for the database, it is clear that at the level of the object model there are no reads or writes but higher-level methods that have more meaning for applications, e.g. *add-student*, *hire-employee*, etc. We believe the security constraints must be given at the same level of the data model, e.g. a user should be authorized to add a student instead of writing directly into the relevant student attributes. This is in accordance with a basic principle for the design of secure systems: access restrictions should be defined at the highest possible level where their semantics are explicit [8]. It also follows the principle of encapsulation for objects, where access to a data structure should only be through its predefined methods [9]. Most database systems support user-oriented models on top of the conceptual model. Because the conceptual model represents the data universe of the institution and because it describes the shared data, it is clear that access restrictions should be defined at this level. If the user models differ from the conceptual model some mapping of authorization rules will be necessary.

We present here a model of authorization where access constraints are defined in terms of methods. Most of the existing object-oriented authorization models do not control access at this level [10, 11, 12, 13]. The closest model to ours is the one developed for the IRIS DBMS [14], but there accesses are controlled by the right to call a given method.

Section 2 describes the object model we use to present our authorization model, while Section 3 presents our basic policies. An evaluation algorithm is defined in Section 4. Section 5 presents some conclusions.

2. Background

As an object model we use Rumbaugh et al.'s Object Modeling Technique (OMT), a specification and design approach for object-oriented systems [7]. Figure 1 shows the definition of a class with three separate areas: the *class name*, the *class attributes*, and the *operations* or *methods* of the class. (In the following figures some of these details will be omitted if they are not of interest in their specific context.) An *object* is an instance of a class and represents a specific real-world entity. The OMT model allows three basic types of associations between classes:

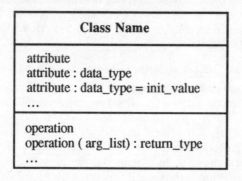

Figure 1. OMT diagram of a class.

- *Generalization* implies the definition of a superclass that collects the common characteristics of several subclasses. It describes an "is-a" association between a subclass and its superclass. For example, in Figure 2 the superclass **Person** is a generalization of the classes **Faculty**, **Student** and **Staff**; **Student**, in turn, is a generalization of **Foreign-Student**. The symbol for generalization is a triangle.

- *Aggregation (Composition)* implies the description of a class in terms of its constituent parts. The concept of aggregation defines an "is-a-part-of" relationship between a subclass and its superclass, i.e. what is known as *composite object* in some data models [1, 3]. For example, Figure 3 shows a university composed of colleges, which in turn are made up of departments.

137

Aggregation is denoted by a diamond. The black dots indicate multiplicity, e.g. a university is composed of several colleges, a college is composed of several departments.

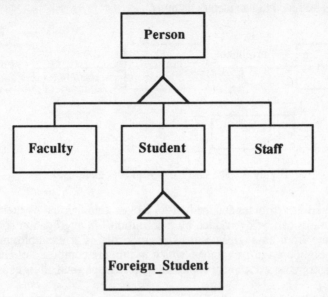

Figure 2. An OMT diagram of a generalization.

Figure 3. The OMT diagram for aggregation.

• *Relationship* describes objects belonging to different classes participating in a common semantic action. The OMT symbol for relationship is a line connecting two classes labeled with the relationship name. Relationships can be binary, ternary, or even higher order, and can have any number of attributes, e.g. **Grade** in Figure 4. For example, **Student** can enroll in courses, and **Faculty** teach courses (Figure 4). The dots at the end of relationships indicate multiplicity, e.g. students may take several courses, courses may be taken by several students, a faculty member may be assigned several courses, but each course is assigned to one faculty member.

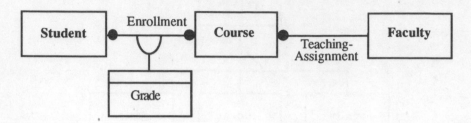

Figure 4. The OMT diagram for relationship.

In a generalization, attributes and methods of a class are inherited by their subclasses. Inherited features can be overridden by redefinition. In aggregation some methods may propagate from an aggregate to its components. For example, in Figure 5 a document is composed of paragraphs, which in turn are composed of characters. In this example, copying a document copies all its paragraphs and all its characters [7].

In addition to class modeling, the OMT model also includes dynamic modeling and functional modeling. In the *dynamic model* object behavior is addressed by representing control information, such as sequences of events and the states that can be taken by the objects. An event indicates that something has occurred and may produce a change of state. As a result of a change of state or during a state, actions may be performed. Generalization hierarchies may be used to organize states and events according to common structure and behavior. The *functional model* indicates how specific computations are performed in terms of their inputs and outputs. We utilize the functional model to express the evaluation algorithm of Section 4.

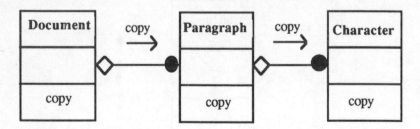

Figure 5. An example of propagation of aggregation operations.

3. Policies for Authorization

An authorization rule is a 4-tuple (s, t, o, p), where s is a subject, t an access type, o a security object (any named item in the database that can be requested by a subject), and p a predicate [8]. For object oriented databases t is a method, o is a class, and p can specify objects or instances of a class.

As shown in Figure 6, authorization rules can be represented using OMT as a relationship between **Subject** and **Data**. The "data" class shows the possible structuring of the data in an object-oriented database. The relationship attribute **Access_type** defines the operator that the user is authorized to apply to the data: The method **Check_rights** evaluates if a given request is authorized for some subject (See Section 4 for details). **Check_rights** could also be attached to **Data** if we think that its invocation is the result of accessing some specific data entity. **Get_access_type** returns the method authorized to a user for a given class. The hierarchical structure of classes and subclasses may be used to define *implied accesses* [15, 5], thus avoiding the need for a proliferation of rules. The next sections define policies for describing the access rights implied through each of the associations. From now on we will consider only rules of the form (s, t, o), leaving out the predicate (for policies with respect to combination of inherited predicates see [16]). We present these policies in an informal way; for a more precise definition see [17].

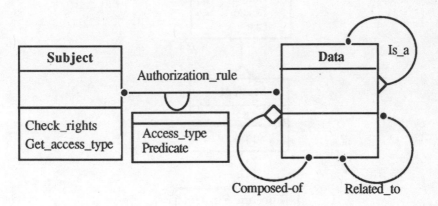

Figure 6. **Subject-Data** access authorization relationship

3.1 Policies for Generalization

We propose four basic policies which, in analogy with those in [5, 16], describe the implied access rights defined by the inheritance properties of the data model. The basic idea is that, since attributes and methods are inherited by subclasses, some access rights can be similarly inherited. We first list the policies, we then apply them in an example.

Policy P1 --*implied authorization* -- a user that is authorized to apply a given method to a class has the same right with respect to the corresponding inherited method in a subclass of that class.

Policy P2 -- *class access* -- access to a complete class implies the right to apply all the methods defined in the class as well as methods inherited from higher classes. Note that this implies a rule such that (s, All, c), where c is a class and *All* is a special method including all the applicable methods of class c.

Policy P3 -- *visibility* -- the use of methods defined in subclasses is not implied by the right to use the methods in a superclass of this class. This also applies to redefinitions of inherited methods.

Policy P4 -- *propagation control for generalization* -- the propagation of an inherited authorization for a method can be stopped by a rule specifying no access (negative authorization) to that specific method.

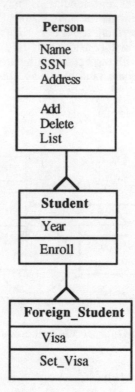

Figure 7. A part of the university database to illustrate generalization policies.

For example, given the generalization associations shown in Figure 7, a rule such as

R1: (Provost, List, Person)

would allow the provost to list foreign students (Policy P1). A rule such as

R2: (Faculty, *All*, Student)

would allow a faculty member to add, delete, and list students, as well as enroll them in courses (Policy P2). The same rule would allow **Faculty** to enroll foreign students (Policy P1), but not to set their visas (Policy P3). If we wanted to deny faculty members the right to enroll foreign students, we could do so through the rule

R3: (Faculty,¬Enroll, Foreign_Student)

which would stop the implied access from rule R2 (Policy P4). As an aditional example, consider the two rules:

R4: (Registration_Clerk, All, Student)

R5: (Foreign_Student_Advisor,{List, Set_Visa}, Foreign_Student)

The Registration_Clerk is adding students to the list of students in the university. He uses the method **Student**.Add (inherited from Person). Because the records at the level of **Student** include only 4 attributes (3 of them inherited from **Person**), his view of student records includes only these 4 fields and he fills in only those. Conceptually, the records at the **Foreign_Student** level include also a Visa attribute. The Foreign_Student_Advisor can later add values for this attribute using the method Set_Visa. If the method Add had been redefined in **Foreign_Student** it could also contain access to the extra field, Visa. In this case the semantics of the application would be different, i.e., foreign student records could only be added by the Foreign_Student_ Advisor   (this would require adding another rule: (Foreign_Student_Advisor, Add, Foreign_ Student)).

3.2 Policies for Aggregation

As indicated earlier, normally operations and attributes in aggregations do not propagate to their components, the exception being some operations that, by their effect on the whole, affect also the components. Access rights for aggregations should therefore be implied only in the latter case, as indicated by the policies below. We assume that the database keeps (as part of the schema) an explicit list of which methods propagate to the next level, e.g. in Figure 8 **Delete_College** would invoke **Delete_Dept**.

Policy P5 -- *propagation* -- Access of some type to a class only implies similar type of access for the components of the object if this type of access normally propagates to these components.

Policy P6 -- *composite objects* -- Access to all the methods of a class implies the right to apply any methods in the component classes.

Similarly to the early policies we can stop propagation of rights using negative authorization.

Policy P7 -- *propagation control for aggregation*-- A negative authorization rule can stop the propagation of implied accesses in aggregations.

The example in Figure 8 shows the use of these policies. For example, the deletion of a college implies the deletion of all its departments, and transitively the deletion of all the courses offered by the department. Listing faculty at the university level implicitly lists the faculty of the colleges and their departments. Policy P5 indicates that a rule authorizing the use of **Delete_College** in **University** implies the use of **Delete_Dept** and **Delete_Course** at the lower levels. Similarly, the right to list the faculty of the university permits listing faculties of colleges and departments. If we wanted to prevent university-wide administrators from deleting courses for example, we just need to add a negative rule at the department level, e.g.

R6:(Univ_Admin,¬Delete_Course, Department).

A rule such as: R7: (Univ_President, all, **University**) would allow the president to use any method defined in **University** and **College** and **Department**.

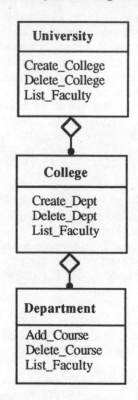

Figure 8. A part of the university database to illustrate aggregation.

3.3 Policies for Relationships

One can consider a relationship as a class and define authorization rules granting some type of access to the relationship class or to some of its attributes. Because relationships are direct associations between specific instances, an authorization given for a relationship can be inherited in the corresponding subclasses. This is summarized in the policy below

Policy P8 -- *relationship inheritance* -- Access to a relationship or to some of its attributes can be inherited with the specific restrictions (subsetting) implied by the subclasses.

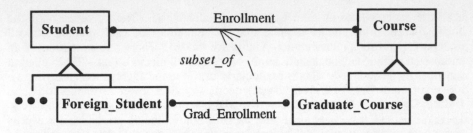

Figure 9. A part of the university database to illustrate relationships.

For example, Figure 9 shows a part of the university database showing the *Enrollment* relationship between **Student** and **Course** and the *Grad_Enrollment* relationship between **Foreign_Student** and **Graduate_Course**. Here the words "subset_of" indicate a constraint between the relationships [7]. A user authorized to List students taking courses would also be authorized to list foreign students taking graduate courses.

Similarly as for the other cases we have:

> Policy P9 --*propagation control for relationships* -- Propagation of
> inheritance in generalization relationships can be stopped by using
> negative authorization rules.

3.4 Policies for Abstract Classes.

An *abstract class* is a class without direct instances, while a *concrete class* is an instantiable class [7]. Abstract classes factor out the logical features of several classes and thus are useful for understanding a complex system. They are also convenient for reusability; for example an abstract "relation" class could collect all the logical features of the components of a relational database, such as *add-a-tuple*, *define-index* , in a generic way. Although they can occur anywhere in the class hierarchy, they usually are "roots", i.e. building blocks for more specialized classes. Many object-oriented systems provide a library of abstract classes from which users can define concrete classes tailored to their specific applications.

For example, a windowing system provides an abstract window template that any user can utilize to design their desktop configuration. All users have access to the abstract window class, however this should not imply access to read another user's window instantiation. It is then clear that implied inherited access rights should not be defined for or propagate through abstract class hierarchies. In other words,

> Policy P10 -- *instantiation*-- Authorization rules can only be defined
> for and propagated through concrete classes. Access to abstract classes
> is implicitly given by the system to all users.

3.5   Methods calling other methods

In any object-oriented model a method may call at run-time other methods. In a previous model [6] we have assumed that authorization is required for each method or

144

attribute accessed at run-time by the original method. Here , because of the encapsulation principle we assume that the semantics of each method is well understood and its implementation details are hidden. Therefore, execution of an authorized method authomatically implies access to all methods that will be called at run-time by this method. This is particularly useful in the aggregation case where a top-level method (e.g. **Delete_Dept**) needs to call a lower level method (e.g. **Delete_Course**). This policy is controversial but several authors agree with it [e.g. 18]. We believe it is consequent with the information-hiding principle, if a user is given authorization to say, add students, then he is authorized to do so, regardless of how this method accomplishes it (in fact the user should not know what other methods are called by his method invocation).

4. Evaluation Algorithm

An evaluation algorithm determines if a requested access is legal by comparing the access request from a user program or query language against the authorization rules [8]. A request can be described by the tuple (s', t', o'), where s' is the requesting subject, o' is the requested data item, and t' is the intended access type. In general, the data item is a class or an attribute of a class, although in this model it can only be a class. The access type can be a method or read/write operations on attributes but in this model we consider only method access. When considering the specific components of this model we will describe the request as (u, t, c) to indicate a user, an access type, and a class, respectively. As indicated earlier, if the user logical model is different from the conceptual model a request must first be mapped to the conceptual level. Instead of a user we can also consider a user group as the subject in the request.

Considering the policies described earlier a request may receive authorization from several possible sources:

*   There is a matching rule with $s = u, t = t, o = c$ for the requested class (Policy P2). Note that the requested class cannot be an abstract class (Policy P10).

*   Access rights are inherited from a superclass (Policy P1).

*   Access rights for a method using only a subset of the requested objects can be obtained from a rule in a subclass of the requested class (Policy P2). Note that these objects do not include new attributes defined in the subclasses (Policy P3).

*   Access rights can be inherited from a propagated aggregation right (Policies P5 and P6).

*   Access rights may exist (direct or inherited) to access a relationship involving the requested objects (Policy P8).

Similarly, considering the negative authorization policies described earlier, access to classes can be denied using the propagation control rules:

- Access rights acquired through generalization inheritance may be stopped from propagating with a negative authorization rule (Policy P4).

- Access rights acquired through aggregation may be stopped from propagating with a negative authorization rule (Policy P7).

- Access rights acquired from relationships can be similarly stopped (Policy P9)

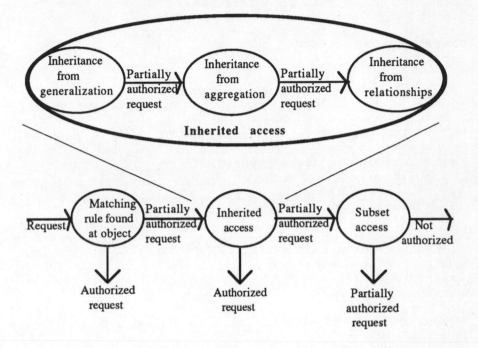

Figure 10. Functional model for evaluation of authorization

Looking at Figure 6 we can see that method **Check_rights** performs this evaluation and Figure 10 shows its functional model (data flow model). This model describes the computational structure of the algorithm. For simplicity, the effects of negative authorization and predicates are not considered in this diagram. An intermediate step in the evaluation may result in a *partial authorization*, the right to apply a method to a subset of the requested objects.

The evaluation method **Check_rights** is outlined below. The input to the algorithm is the access request $Q:(u, t, c)$ where u is the user making the request, t is the method for which authorization is requested, and c is the class of the objects on which the method is requested to be applied. The output of the algorithm is the set SO, the set of objects on which the method t is authorized. A fully authorized request has $SO = c$. This method in turn, uses the method **Subject.Get_access_type**. We assume also that the class hierarchy graph is a tree, i.e. there is no multiple inheritance. The relationship case is also not shown, it is a simple extension. An example of its use is shown below.

```
/****************** Request Evaluation **************
Does not consider multiple inheritance, predicates, and
inheritance from relationships.
  Input:      Q = (u, t, c) where
              u = user,
              t = method,
              c = class = set of objects;
  Output:    SO = set of objects on which method t
                  will be authorized.
              = [ ]  or  c  or  a subset of Q.c        */

Check_rights( Q, SO)
begin
  SO := [ ];
  PQ := Q;  /*  PQ = propagated query
                 -- query will change as it propagates  */

  /* search for a rule explicitly authorizing or denying
     access to query Q                                  */
  case Subject.Get_access_type(Q)
     positive: SO:= Q.c;
     negative: SO:= [ ];
    otherwise: search_up(PQ, Q, SO);
  endcase;

  /* search for a rule explicitly authorizing or denying
     access to a subset of Q                            */
  search_down (PQ, Q, SO);
end Check_rights;

/* Can now proceed with the call to method Q.t on data SO
   to execute query                                      */

/************* Ancestor authorization **************
  Input: SO = set of authorized objects = [ ]
         Q  = original Query = (u, t, c) where
              u = user,
              t = method,
              c = class
         PQ = propagated -- to keep track of position
              during tree traversal
              PQ.u  = Q.u
              PQ.t  = current method name
              PQ.c  = current class
  Output: SO = set of objects on which method Q.t will be
               authorized
             = [ ], if no authorization or negative
                    authorization is found.
             = Q.c, if positive authorization is found.
  Local: NPQ = next propagated query
         PC := parent class of PQ.c                     */
```

```
search_up (PQ, Q, SO)

    /* terminate recursion at root                           */
    if (PC := parent_of (PQ.c) ) is not null then

       /* adjust next propagated query for recursive call*/
       NPQ := PQ;

       case edge(PC,PQ.c)
          /* edge -- type of graph connecting 2 classes  */
          generalization: NPQ.c := PC;
             aggregation: NPQ.c := PC;
                          if PC.t implies PQ.t  then
                          /* implies -- according to
                             aggregation propagation       */
                             NPQ.t := PC.t;
                otherwise: return;
       endcase;

       /* find first rule explicitly authorizing or denying
          access to propagated query                    */
       case Subject.Get_access_type(NPQ)
          positive:  /* parent class is a superset of
                        requested objects, add only the
                        objects belonging to the original
                        requested class, and terminate
                        recursion                          */
                     SO = Q.c;
          negative:  /* stop recursion up when first
                        negative authorization found       */
                     SO = [ ];
         otherwise:  /* no rule found yet, continue
                        searching up the tree              */
                     search_up( NPQ, Q, SO);
       endcase;

    endif;
return;


/************ Descendant authorization *************
  Input:  SO = set of authorized objects
          Q  = original query =(u=user, t=method, c=class)
          PQ = propagated (current) query
                  PQ.u= Q.u
                  PQ.t= current method name
                  PQ.c= current class
  Output: SO = set of objects on which method Q.t will
                  be authorized.
  Local: NPQ = next propagated query
          CC := child class of PQ.c                    */
```

148

```
search_down ( PQ, Q,  SO)

   /* backtrack when you reach a leaf node              */
   for (CC in children_of (PQ.c) )

      /* adjust next propagated query for recursive
         call                                           */
      NPQ := PQ;
      case edge(PQ.c, CC)
         generalization: NPQ.c := CC;
            aggregation: NPQ.c := CC;
                         if PQ.t implies CC.t  then
                            NPQ.t := CC.t;
            otherwise: return;
      endcase;

   /* search for a rule explicitly authorizing or
      denying access to query NPQ                       */
   case Subject.Get_access_type(NPQ)
      positive:SO = SO + {NPQ.objects};/* + = set union*/
      negative:SO = SO - {NPQ.objects};/* - = set diff.*/
   endcase;

   /* continue searching down recursively               */
   search_down (NPQ, Q, SO);

   endfor;
return;
/****************************************************/
```

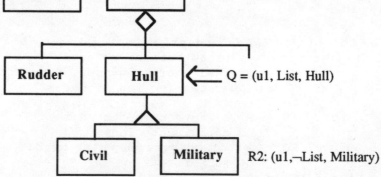

Figure 11. Example for evaluation algorithm.

Figure 11 illustrates the effect of the algorithm. The user's query is $Q:(u_1,$ **List, Hull**), i.e. user u_1 intends to list all the hulls used by this company. Rule R1 authorizes him to report **Vehicles** and it is inherited by **Boat** (Policy P1). Method **Report** from **Boat** propagates to **List** in **Hull** which would fully authorize the request. However, the negative authorization of rule R2 prevents this user from listing military type hulls.

5. Conclusions

We have presented a unified model for controlling access to object-oriented databases. In this model all security constraints are defined in terms of object methods and the authorization system itself is represented as a set of object classes. This approach provides a unified framework where the authorization system and the database are represented in similar terms. This allows the protection of the authorization information to be handled in the same way as the rest of the data.

While we have selected a coherent set of policies, these can be taken in groups and combined with other approaches. For example, policies P1, P2 and P3 could be combined with the more powerful (but also more complex) negative authorization approach of the Orion model [12].

We have left out the definition of administrative aspects, an important complement of any model; however in [5] we presented an approach that could be applied to this model. Another important aspect is the formalization of the model and we are completing it now. A further issue is user groups but it is, basically, orthogonal. We have studied that issue elsewhere [19].

References

1. E. Bertino and L. Martino, "Object-oriented database management systems: Concepts and issues," *Computer*, 24, 4 (April 1991), 33-47.

2. J. G. Hughes, *Object-oriented Databases*, Prentice Hall International (UK), 1991.

3. A. R. Hurson, and S. H. Pakzad, "Object-oriented database management systems: Evolution and performance issues," *Computer*, 26, 2 (February 1993), 48-60.

4. W. Kim, *Introduction to Object-Oriented Databases*, MIT Press, Cambridge, Massachusetts, 1990.

5. E.B. Fernandez, E. Gudes, and H. Song, "A Model for Evaluation and Administration of Security in Object-Oriented Databases", to appear in *IEEE Transactions on Knowledge and Data Engineering*, April 1994.

6. N. Gal-Oz, E. Gudes, E. B. Fernandez, "A Model of Functions Authorization in Object-Oriented Databases", in *Proc. of the 19th Int. Conf. on Very Large Data Bases*, Dublin, Ireland, 1993, 52-61.

7. J. Rumbaugh, M. Blaha, W. Premerlani, F. Eddy, W. Lorensen, *Object-Oriented Modeling and Design* , Prentice Hall, Englewood Cliffs, NJ, 1991.

8. E. B. Fernandez, R. C. Summers, and C. Wood. *Database security and integrity.* System Programming Series. Addison-Wesley, Reading, MA, 1981.

9. F. Bancilhon, C. Delobel and P. Kanellakis (eds.) *Building an object-oriented database system*, Morgan Kaufmann Pub., San Mateo, California, 1992.

10. K. R. Dittrich, M. Harting and H. Pfefferle, "Discretionary access control in structurally object-oriented databases," in *Database Security II: Status and Prospectus*, C. E. Landwehr (ed.), Elsevier Science Pub. B. V., 1989, 105-121.

11. U. Kelter, "Discretionary access controls in a high performance object management system," in *Proceedings of the IEEE Symposium on Research in Security and Privacy*, May 1991, 288-299.

12. F. Rabitti, E. Bertino, W. Kim, and D. Woelk, "A model of authorization for next-generation database systems," *ACM Transactions on Database Systems*, 16 (1) March 1991, 88-131.

13. E. Bertino and H. Weigand, "An approach to authorization modeling in object-oriented database systems," 1993, to appear.

14. R. Ahad, J. Davis, S. Gower, P. Lyngbaek, A. Marynowski, E Onuegbe, "Supporting Access Control in an Object-Oriented Database Language," in *Proceedings of the European Conference on Extending Database Technology*, Vienna, Austria, *Lecture Notes in Computer Science*, Springer-Verlag, 1992.

15. E. B. Fernandez, R. C. Summers and T. Lang, "Definition and evaluation of access rules in data management systems," in *Proceedings of the First International Conference on Very Large Databases*, Boston, Massachusetts, 1976, 268-285.

16. M. Larrondo-Petrie, E. Gudes, H. Song and E. B. Fernandez, "Security Policies in object-oriented databases," in *Database Security III: Status and Prospectus*, D. L. Spooner and C. Landwehr (eds.), Elsevier Science Pub., 1990, 257-268.

17. E. B. Fernandez and M. Larrondo-Petrie, "A method-based authorization model for object-oriented databases," Florida Atlantic University, Dept. of Computer Science and Engineering, Technical Report TR-CSE-92-31, October 1992.

18. J. Richardson, P. Schwartz, and L. F. Cabrera, "CACL: Efficient fine-grained protection for objects," in *Proceedings of the ACM OOPSLA '92*, September 1992, 263-275.

19. M. H. Fernandez, E. B. Fernandez, and J. Wu, "Subject groups for object-oriented database authorization," Florida Atlantic University, Department of Computer Science and Engineering Technical Report TR-CSE-92-40, December 1992.

The Factors that Influence Apropos Security Approaches for the Object-Oriented Paradigm

Steven A. Demurjian and T. C. Ting

Computer Science and Engineering Department

The University of Connecticut

Storrs, Connecticut, 06269-3155, USA

Abstract

Over the past several years, there has been a strong emergence of interest and increased utilization of the object-oriented paradigm in many diverse areas of computing research, design, and development. Object-oriented programming languages, database models and systems, CAD and CASE design tools, and other applications have brought the paradigm into the forefront as a valued design and development technique. A natural consequence of these efforts has been an emphases on security approaches for the object-oriented paradigm, with both traditional (mandatory access control) and newer (discretionary access control) solutions. Often many of these proposed solutions do not consider the unique and special features of the object-oriented paradigm. The premise that is promoted by this work is that the paradigm itself must be *the* guiding factor in the research, design, and development of apropos security capabilities.

1 Introduction

Historically, security in computer systems has embraced a mandatory access control (MAC) approach using the Bell and Lapadula security model [2], to protect access to information by classifying and tagging data. Multi-level secure database systems that use such an approach have been researched and developed [14, 20]. Naturally, these techniques have also spawned efforts that have investigated MAC for object-oriented systems [11, 21]. In recent years, user-role based security (URBS) has been proposed [13, 22] to focus on the rights of individuals as a guiding factor for establishing privileges. URBS is geared towards supporting discretionary access control (DAC) to offer freedom and versatility in the privilege-granting process. For object-oriented systems, some researchers have focused on DAC/URBS with an instance-based approach [3, 13, 16], while our own work has emphasized a type or design-level approach [10, 23]. In fact, these efforts are complementary, since security defined at the type level must be enforced at the instance level.

However, in extending existing approaches to security for object-oriented systems have we placed the proverbial cart before the horse? Are we mandating that security for object-oriented systems must take an existing approach, when instead we should be asking if there is a better or new choice that can be made? Moreover, are there unique characteristics and features of object-oriented systems and applications that can and should impact our approach to its security? Hence, it is appropriate to consider the not-so-rhetorical question: *Shouldn't the object-oriented paradigm influence and guide the approach for security?* The remainder of this article addresses this important question by providing a foundation for thought provoking discussion on the features of the paradigm that should impact and determine the shape and form of its security.

2 From ADTs to the Object-Oriented Paradigm

The object-oriented paradigm, while receiving recent attention, is not new. Its foundations can be traced to the emphasis in the early 1970s on modular program development via abstract data types (ADTs) [12, 17]. When using ADTs, the key is to achieve representation independence, thereby presenting a straightforward *interface* to the ADT while simultaneously hiding the *implementation*. This allows implementation changes to be made with no impact on the interface and its users. At almost the same time, similar abstraction methods were also underway in the database area, led by the classical work on aggregation and generalization by Smith and Smith [18]. The promotion of inheritance by their work and later extensions to Chen's entity-relationship model [4] were both important to transition from ADTs to the object-oriented paradigm.

Like ADTs, the object-oriented paradigm promotes the development of object types (OTs) or classes, where both the data and methods (operations) are *encapsulated*. For representation independence, the implementation is *hidden*, thereby controlling access to a type's data and methods. like ADTs, an interface provides the *visible* access capabilities. Inheritance offers a controlled sharing of data and methods between related OTs in an application. Object-oriented concepts have been covered in great detail elsewhere [24, 25]. How are these concepts related to security? Encapsulation, the binding of information (data) and behavior (methods), sets strict requirements on an OT, reducing allowable actions; a definite benefit if security is to control access to the type, with hiding playing a major role. In addition, inheritance shares information, which implicitly indicates that sharing from a security perspective is occurring. The conclusion is that any definition of security for object-oriented systems must begin with encapsulation, hiding, and inheritance, the three cornerstones of the paradigm.

3 What's in an Object-Oriented Application?

While object-oriented applications vary widely in their functionalities and capabilities, there is growing evidence that the greatest potential of its usage lies in advanced and complex systems that are large scale, heterogeneous, and distributed. Examples of such domains include health care, manufacturing, and software environments. All of these domains need to maintain high volumes of disparate data persistently, and also involve numerous individuals with varied responsibilities and needs, that must work together in a collaborative and cooperative fashion within each system. For example, in the health care domain, data varies from images (MRI, X-ray, etc.) to patient records, providers include hospitals, outpatient clinics, physician offices, etc., who all must interact with the insurance industry, and governmental and other agencies. For this domain, it has been argued [22] that URBS is the most appropriate means to support security requirements via the definition of roles and content and context based security constraints. The intent is that this domain (and others) requires a fine-grained level of control to define and maintain privileges. How can the object-oriented paradigm support such a level of control? In fact, a better question is: What feature or characteristic of the object-oriented paradigm must be explored to provide such a capability?

In the discussion of the previous section, it is apparent that the *public interface*, the set of all visible methods, their parameters, and their return types for each OT or class, may be the first place to look to answer the previous questions. The public interface, once defined, provides the access means to the OT and its instances, but is limiting from a security perspective since all users, regardless of their needs within the application, have full access to all methods in the public interface. That is, the public interface contains the union of all of the methods that need to be public for all possible users, which unfortunately, permits everyone to have access to some methods that were only intended for a select one or two users. For example, in an OT or class that maintains the medical records of patients at a hospital, physicians must be given access to methods that set the medication or treatment, requiring that these methods be part of the public interface. If that is the case, then nurses, pharmacists, technicians, and other hospital staff will also have access, since once a method is public, it is available to all. To selectively grant access to the public interface, techniques must be devised that allow different individuals to have particular access to specific subsets of the public interface at different times, based on their roles within the application. For the previous example, access by non-physicians to methods that set medication/treatment can now be prohibited, i.e., can be selectively given only to physicians. Thus, in addition to encapsulation, hiding, and inheritance, the customization of access to the public interface must also be a guiding factor in security for object-oriented systems.

In fact, there is an argument to be made that the instance characteristics of object-oriented applications also plays a significant role in guiding the appropriate security approach. Most, if not all, object-oriented applications are similar in that they depend on the development of extensive OT or class libraries. These libraries often contain multiple inheritance hierarchies for sharing code and promoting reuse. The number of OTs/classes in libraries can be quite small (in the tens), but typically contain hundreds and even thousands of different types. During runtime, the actual number of instances is also widely varying. It is not unusual to observe that the majority of classes have only a few instances (low hundreds), with a select group of classes dedicated to manage collections or sets of instances. In fact, many applications contain numerous classes with very few instances (tens or less). Therefore, in practice, there are likely a large number of types, possessing a wide range of instances (very few to thousands or more). Complicating this diverse behavior is the fact that it is not unusual for instances to change types due to inheritance, or for a type to go from having very few instances to very many instances (and back again) over time. The above discussion seems to preclude the usage of MAC for object-oriented systems, which has traditionally shown strong ties and applicability to relational and other structured data. This data has very regular characteristics; a few types (in the tens), with (tens-of-)thousands of instances per type. While the overhead to support MAC in such data is manageable, it quickly multiplies for the expansive and extensible features of object-oriented systems. Perhaps we must look for another approach to deal with these issues; one more suited to the described application needs and requirements. Clearly, the type and instance characteristics of an object-oriented application will play a pivotal role in defining and supporting security.

4 The Need to Evolve the Public Interface Concept

In the previous two sections, it has been strongly argued that the public interface can be the focal point for establishing privileges and controlling access. The public interface of an OT/class has evolved from an ADT, which in the past, has represented the unit of conceptual abstraction. That is, when ADTs were first promoted [12, 17], the unit of abstraction was a single data type. Classical examples of ADTs, Stack, Queue, etc., which are still widely utilized today, focus on a single unit of well-defined functionality. But, are these examples reflective of the current practice? Is an ADT *yesterday's* unit of conceptualization?

The overriding reality is that most, if not all, object-oriented applications, are firmly rooted in an OT/class library design and implementation, as has also been stressed in the previous two sections. These libraries are characterized by the presence of one or more inheritance hierarchies. What role does such a hierarchy play in this situation? There is strong evidence that a hierarchy is serving as a *larger* unit of conceptualization than its ADT ancestor. In the late 1970s, given the state, size, and capabilities of computing hardware and software, developing applications with multiple ADTs was both reasonable and feasible, since each ADT would represent a significant portion of the functionality at that time. However, as the mid-1990's approach, the complexity of applications and their underlying platforms has exploded! Today's class libraries capture all aspects of an application's functionality, with individual inheritance hierarchies representing substantial portions. Collectively, the hierarchies that comprise an application divide the functionality into meaningful subsets. Thus, each hierarchy represents a significant conceptual abstraction (a macroscopic view), which can be decomposed microscopically to individual OTs/classes, where each characterizes the 'older' ADT perspective.

Moreover, the individual hierarchies are used as an entire unit by different aspects of the application. That is, when a subset or tool of the application utilizes a hierarchy, it is likely to need access to most or all of its constituent OTs/classes. It would be unusual for a tool to only use one OT/class of either one or multiple hierarchies; this often indicates a poor design. An inheritance hierarchy is a conceptual unit, since it was formed on the basis of a known set of commonalities and similarities of data and/or behavior (methods) and/or usage, intended to serve specific and multiple purposes in the overall application. Therefore, it is critical that security considerations for object-oriented systems not only allow privilege definition and access on a single OT/class, but are evolved to also include an entire inheritance hierarchy. Such a larger view is crucial to simplify the privilege granting process (i.e., assign a user role or tool access to an entire hierarchy) and to coincide with the practical usage of object-oriented applications. In the process, yesterday's perspective (ADT) is retained as a part of a more appropriate view (inheritance hierarchy) of today's applications.

5 The Impact of Advanced Object-Oriented Features

Advanced object-oriented features, namely, polymorphism, dispatching, and overloading, strongly influence the design and engineering practice for object-oriented software. *Polymorphism* is important in the paradigm since it allows type-independent software to be developed. For example, instead of defining different stack classes for different data types (e.g., one stack for integer, one stack for reals, one stack for strings, etc.), a single stack can be defined that can then be utilized regardless of the data type of the stack elements. Polymorphism is supported in object-oriented languages via generics or parameterized types, and strongly promotes software reuse. *Dispatching* is the run-time or dynamic choice of the method to be called based on the type of the calling instance. For example, an inheritance hierarchy for graphical objects would contain classes for Circle, Rectangle, Triangle, etc., all children of a Shapes parent class. Each class would have its own method to graphically display the shape. For simplicity, all shapes (instances of Circle, Rectangle, Triangle, etc.) would be treated as being a collection of their common parent (Shape). Despite this commonality, when the display method is invoked on an instance, the underlying type will result in specific (and different) methods being called at runtime. Dispatching offers many different benefits to the software engineer, all related to extensibility and productivity, including: more versatility in the development of inheritance hierarchies and class libraries; the promotion of software reuse and evolution; and, the ability to more easily and effectively develop and debug generic code. Lastly, *overloading*, is the ability to define two or more methods with the same name but different signatures. In all programming languages, operations like +, −, etc., are overloaded, since they can be used for integers, reals, sets, and so on. Both object-oriented and other programming languages allow users to overload these and other operations in their user-defined data types.

How can and should these three advanced features support security? Polymorphism, through its type independence of code, might be the vehicle by which security code for object-oriented systems can be successfully implemented and reused. In a URBS solution to security, different roles must all undergo the same processes of granting privileges, authentication, and enforcement. When establishing a security policy for an application, polymorphism can be used to develop class libraries for supporting these processes, that are parameterized by type (in this case, user role!). Dispatching and overloading are strongly linked, and together allow an executing piece of object-oriented code to behave differently based on the type of the invoking instance. There is a strong parallel from a security perspective; dispatching and overloading have strong ties to promoting and supporting the execution of security code via the runtime invocation of different methods based on the involved user role. In this case, the security policy and its associated code can be extended and modified as needed when user roles (or their capabilities) change over time. The common theme of all three advanced features is geared towards class libraries that, by their nature, support software reuse, extensibility, and evolution, all of which must take a significant part in defining security for object-oriented systems.

6   Claims of the Object-Oriented Paradigm

There have been many different claims on the benefits and advantages of the object-oriented paradigm, ranging from the obvious and easily proved (stresses modularity) to the generally accepted realities (promotes software reuse and facilitates software evolution) to the difficult to verify, but hopefully true (controls data consistency and increases productivity). The claims that have the most impact on security for object-oriented systems involve software reuse and evolution, as discussed in Section 5. If these claims are true (in practice, many researchers and developers have achieved success), then these two important aspects of the paradigm must play a leading role in security design and development. These two claims are tightly linked to the definition and maintenance of OT/class libraries for object-oriented applications.

There are many possible scenarios that can form the basis of a solution. Clearly, security in object-oriented systems can be implemented through the design and development of OT or class libraries. Such an approach would be useful, whether the security is DAC, URBS, MAC, etc. Once defined, these libraries can be reused as is, extended with new capabilities, or evolved to satisfy changing needs. For a given application (like health care), as new software and tools are developed with an object-oriented approach, apropos security libraries would be included, based on the functional and security requirements for the software/tool. These libraries would provide all aspects of security, such as definition, authentication, and enforcement. For example, referring again to the health care application of Section 3, suppose that a software tool to monitor and establish treatment was to be developed for all professionals that administer care, e.g., nurses, physicians, technicians, etc. In a URBS approach, each of these professionals would have different user roles. The overall security policy for such an application would need to consider and distinguish the security requirements for each role. If such a policy for health care was implemented as a class library, then the user role for physician would be given more expansive access to the library (to allow doctors to set medication and treatment) than nurses. When such a policy is included in the software tool, the end result is that the tool behaves differently based on the user and his/her role (dispatching again).

To realize the aforementioned scenario of a class library for security, where the same tool would operate differently depending on the user role, there must be support at the implementation level in the definition of OTs/classes. One way to provide such support would be to enhance and expand the capabilities of the constructor. A constructor for an OT or class is utilized to create an instance. This could be extended to also include instances of the relevant security classes, to define the security policy for the class. In this way, we begin to bridge the gap to transition from type-level security to its instance-level realization. Another choice would be to add a *security constructor* to an OT/class, that would specifically and uniquely embody the security policy. Extensions to a class are consistent with other work that has added integrity constraints and triggers to classes [1]. Regardless of the final choice, the idea of a security class library, and its inclusion and reuse both within and across applications, can be strongly advocated as consistent and in sync with object-oriented precepts and principles.

7   One Approach to Security for Object-Oriented Models

To support DAC and URBS within the object-oriented approach, we have developed techniques that allow different individuals to have particular access to specific subsets of the public interface at different times via their roles within the application. Our approach [6, 10, 23], establishes privileges by assigning (positive) and prohibiting (negative) methods based on user roles. A role *assigned* a method can invoke the method, and by inference can also access instances on the OT on which the method is defined, and potentially read and modify private data that the method might use. A *prohibited* method restricts access in a similar fashion. The idea of defining both assigned and prohibited methods is important, since it allows the possible problem of information leakage [19] due to the inheritance between OTs to be addressed. This section reports on our prototyping efforts for the ADAM (short for Active Design and Analyses Modeling) environment that supports object-oriented design with DAC/URBS.

7.1   The ADAM Environment

ADAM was originally developed to support the automatic generation of compilable code in multiple languages from graphically/textually supplied object-oriented designs [8, 9]. ADAM currently supports code generation for two dialects of C++ (AT&T C++ and Ontos C++ – an object-oriented database system) and Ada1983 [7] (Modula-3 and Ada9X are in progress). ADAM has been extended to include the definition of security privileges for user roles [10] and for an authorization list [6]. Our approach to DAC/URBS also contains a wide range of detailed analysis techniques that operate from two perspectives to indicate: which user-roles have access to a specific aspect (OT, method, private data) of an application, and what is the access to the application by a chosen user role. These and other analyses have been detailed elsewhere [10, 23], and can be used by the designer to investigate realized privileges against the application's intended security requirements.

ADAM supports an object-oriented design model that is tightly integrated into the environment. There is no specific syntax in ADAM – choices are made via menus, browsers, etc., and text is directly entered by the designer using forms. Thus, language independence is stressed with code generation automatically providing correct syntax based on the chosen target programming language. To support incremental and iterative design, all design data can be stored persistently in the Ontos [15] database system. To track the purpose and intent of different design choices and constructs, *profiles* are utilized [9, 10]. A profile contains detailed requirements on the semantic content and context for all of the design constructs of the application. Profiles are used to force software engineers to supply detailed information as an application is designed. In addition, profiles track data that provides on-demand and automatic feedback to software engineers whenever an action in the environment results in a conflict or possible inconsistency. The current version of ADAM, supports multiple *design phases*, which are used by software engineers to define, modify, and evolve applications, and has been implemented on a Sun architecture under Unix using X windows, InterViews 3.01, AT&T C++ 2.0, and Ontos.

7.2 Object-Type Specification

In the object-type-specification phase of ADAM, the designer can define the OTs, their attributes, and methods through associated profiles [9], and establish inheritance associations among OTs. A subset of OTs for a health care application is shown in Figure 1. Visit, Prescription, and Test are subtypes of Item, and indicate procedures performed on a patient's visit to a physician. To define and track design requirements, considerations, and dependencies, profiles are utilized. *Attribute* and *method profiles* are defined for each OT by the software engineer, and from them, *OT profiles* can be automatically generated. The profiles for the OT Medical_R, the attribute Medical_History, and the method Read_Med_Rec are shown in Figure 2. Notice that in a method profile (Read_Med_Rec), its name, description, parameters, and return type are shown. In addition, the private data items that are read and/or written must be supplied, along with other public and/or private methods that will be called by its implementation. The other profiles contain analogous information that details content and context dependencies for each application feature.

7.3 URDH Specification

For DAC/URBS, the user-role definition hierarchy, URDH, characterizes the different kinds of individuals (and groups) who all require different levels of access to an application. The responsibilities of individuals are divided into three abstraction levels for the URDH: user roles, user types, and user classes. *User roles* allow the security software engineer to assign particular privileges to individual roles. To represent common responsibilities among user roles, a *user type* can be defined. Privileges that are assigned to a user type are systematically passed to all of its roles. The different user types of an application can be grouped to form one or more *user classes*. Privileges that are supplied to each class are passed on to its types and their roles.

Figure 3 shows a partial URDH created in the ADAM environment for the health care example. In the figure, the roles are defined in a two-step process of specialization (top-down definition) and generalization (bottom-up definition). From a top-down perspective in Figure 3, there are two different user types, Nurse and Physician, for defining privileges that would be common to all user roles under each type. Within each user type, one or more user roles may be defined. For example, in Figure 3, user roles for Nurse include Staff_RN, Discharge_Plng (planning), Education, and Manager. The URDH can also be examined from a bottom-up perspective to determine the common characteristics by the grouping of the user types into user classes such as Medical_Staff.

User roles are also definable from alternative perspectives. For example, user roles for care-related responsibilities (e.g., TakeVitals, CheckPatient,

159

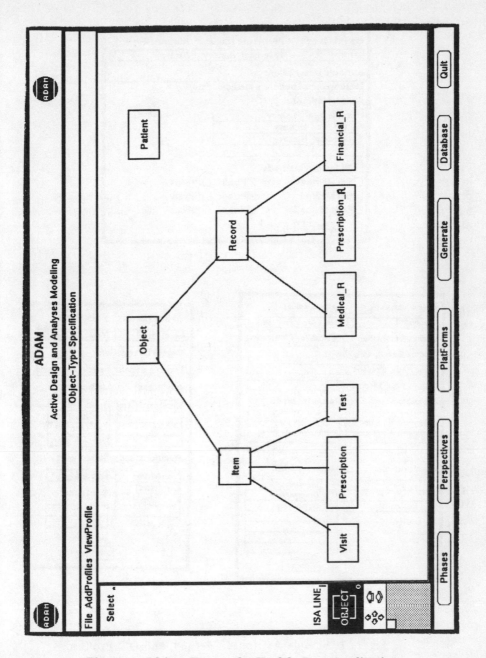

Figure 1: Object Types of a Health Care Application.

Object Name: Attribute Name: Attribute Type:
Medical_R   Medical_History   String
Attribute Description:
Description of patient's medical history
AccessMethods:
PrintMedical_History
GetMedical_History
SetMedical_History

☐ All System Methods
☐ Set Method   ☒ Public ☐ Private
☐ Get Method   ☒ Public ☐ Private
☐ Print Method   ☒ Public ☐ Private
(Done) (Cancel)

Object Name: Method Name:
Medical_R   Read_Med_Record
Access Designation :   ☒ Public ☐ Private
Method Description:
Read medical record.
Return Type: Medical_R
Parameters: Parameter Types:

Read Write Set: Methods Called:
                    Get_Treatment
                    Get_Diagnosis
                    Get_Symptoms

(Done)   (Cancel)

Object Name: Persistency:
Medical_R   Yes
Object Description:
Holds a patient's medical recor
Attributes: Methods:
Medical_Histo   Read_Med_R
                Get_Med_Hi
                Set_Med_Hi
                Get_All_Visit
Relationships: SuperType:
ContainsP   Record
ContainsT   SubTypes:
ContainsV

(Done)

Figure 2: Sample Attribute, Method, and OT Profiles.

161

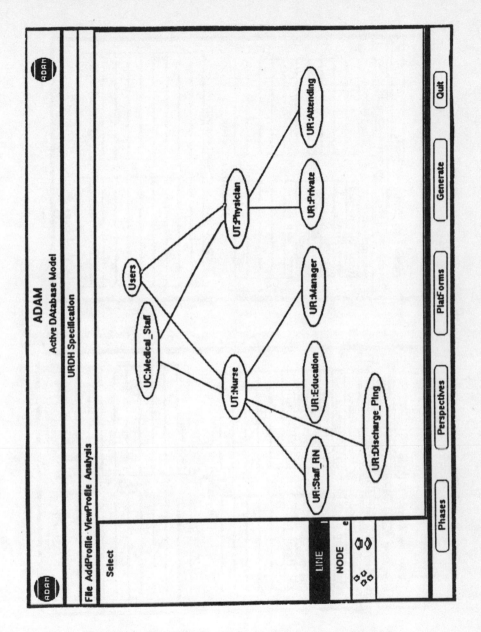

Figure 3: The URDH of the Health Care Application.

162

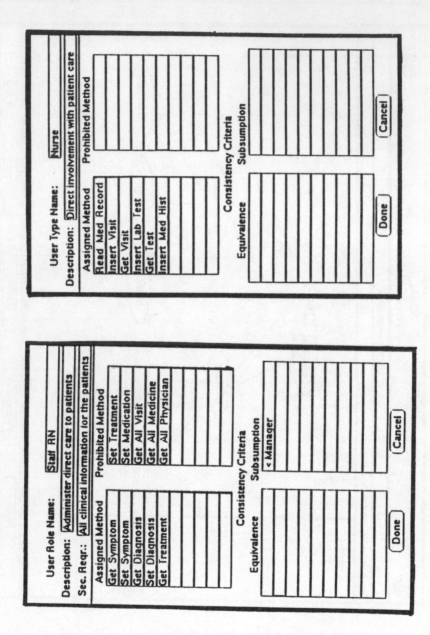

Figure 4: Node Profiles for Staff_RN and Manager.

RecordHistory, etc.) are useful since they are needed by multiple individuals (nurses, physicians, technicians, etc.). An actual nurse (say, Lois), would play multiple roles (say, Staff_RN, TakeVitals, and CheckHistory) in a hospital, and these roles would represent an authorization-list entry, as we discuss elsewhere [6].

To more accurately characterize the capabilities of user classes, user types, and user roles in the URDH, with respect to the privileges to be granted against the application, *node profiles* are defined. Sample node profiles for the user role Staff_RN and the user type Nurse are given in Figure 4. The *description* indicates the responsibilities of the role, while the security requirements detail the allowable access. Both of these displays are scrollable; the full security requirement for Staff_RN is: *All clinical information for the patients under his/her care. Can write/modify a substantial portion of clinical information to record the results/patient progress. Cannot change a Physician's orders on a patient.* The profile also contains whatever methods have been assigned (positive privileges) or prohibited (non-allowed privileges). These methods were defined as part of the definition of the OTs for the application (see Figures 1 and 2). Through assigned and prohibited methods, select access is given to OTs. In the examples of Figure 4, notice that Staff_RN has been prohibited access to methods that set the treatment or medication of a patient, which is consistent with the example from Section 3. Also notice that for the user type Nurse, all assigned methods represent shared responsibilities by all of its user roles (see Figure 3).

Lastly, consistency criteria are utilized to indicate equivalences and/or subsumptions among user classes, types, and roles, based on the assigned and prohibited methods. In ADAM, the checking on assigned/prohibited methods is performed automatically to insure that there are no conflicts, e.g., a newly assigned method cannot conflict with an earlier prohibited method. Conflicts can also occur based on subsumptions and equivalences. For example, if the roles Staff_RN and Education are equivalent, then the assignment of a method to one role must also occur to the other role, to maintain the equivalence. Conflicts and inconsistencies are automatically flagged with warning messages that require corrective actions by the designer.

8 Concluding Remarks

The intent of this article has been to open and promote discussion on the considerations and concerns that must be the guiding factors in the design and development of apropos security approaches for object-oriented systems. Our opinion is that such design and development must have strong foundations in fundamental (encapsulation, hiding, and inheritance) and advanced (polymorphism, dispatching, and overloading) object-oriented concepts, geared towards software reuse, extensibility, and evolution. There must be a concerted effort for a security approach that embodies an OT/class library solution (as argued in Section 6), providing the means to define and enforce an application's overall security policy. Moreover, the approach must be versatile enough to allow different security requirements to be realized on specific OTs/classes or on entire inheritance hierarchies (see Section 4 again), based on user roles. Such an approach will allow software and tools to be made available that appear, react, and behave in a customized fashion, based on the user role, thereby dynamically enforcing the security requirements. However, it is important to note that the thoughts in this article constitute only a starting point. There are many other important issues that must be considered, including support for concurrent engineering via cooperative and collaborative work [5]. In addition, temporal issues for object-oriented models must also be explored, to allow different user roles access to an application at different *times*. It is our intent to continue to utilize the ADAM environment (see Section 7 again) as a test-bed for examining and exploring the many issues related to security for the object-oriented paradigm as presented in this article.

References

[1] R. Agrawal and N. Gehani, "ODE (Object Database and Environment): The Language and the Data Model", *Proc. of the 1989 ACM SIGMOD Intl. Conf. on Management of Data*, June 1989.

[2] D. Bell and L. LaPadula, "Secure Computer Systems: Unified Exposition and Multics Interpretation", Technical Report MTIS AD-A023588, The MITRE Corporation, July 1975.

[3] H. H. Bruggemann, "Rights in an Object-Oriented Environment", in *Database Security, V: Status and Prospects*, C. Landwehr and S. Jajodia (eds.), North-Holland, 1992.

[4] P. Chen, "The Entity-Relationship Model - Toward a Unified View of Data", *ACM Trans. on Database Systems*, Vol. 1, No. 1, March 1976.

[5] S. Demurjian, T.C. Ting, and B. Thuraisingham, "User-Role Based Security for Collaborative Computing Environments", *Journal of Multi-Media Review*, Vol. 4, No. 2, Summer 1993.

[6] S.Demurjian and T.C. Ting, "Shouldn't the Object-Oriented Paradigm Influence and Guide the Approach for Security?", *Proc. of 1993 Workshop on Security for Object-Oriented Systems*, part of OOPSLA 1993, Sept. 1993.

[7] K. El Guemhioui, S. Demurjian, and T. Peters, "Object-Oriented Design and Automatic Ada Code Generation in the Education of Software Engineers", *Proc. of 1993 TriAda Conf.*, Seattle, WA, Sept. 1993.

[8] H. Ellis and S. Demurjian, "ADAM: A Graphical, Object-Oriented Database Design Tool and Code Generator", *Proc. of the 19th Annual ACM Computer Science Conf.*, March 1991.

[9] H. Ellis and S. Demurjian, "Object-Oriented Design and Analyses for Advanced Application Development - Progress Towards a New Frontier", *Proc. of the 21st Annual ACM Computer Science Conf.*, Feb. 1993.

[10] M.-Y. Hu, S. Demurjian, and T.C. Ting, "User-Role Based Security Profiles for an Object-Oriented Design Model", in *Database Security, VI: Status and Prospects*, C. Landwehr and B. Thuraisingham (eds.), North-Holland, 1993.

[11] T. Keefe, et al., "A Multilevel Security Model for Object-Oriented Systems", *Proc. of 11th Natl. Computer Security Conf.*, Oct. 1988.

[12] B. Liskov, et al., "Abstraction Mechanisms in CLU", *Comm. of the ACM*, Vol. 20, No. 8, Aug. 1977.

[13] F. H. Lochovsky and C. C. Woo, "Role-Based Security in Data Base Management Systems", in *Database Security: Status and Prospects*, C. Landwehr (ed.), North-Holland, 1988.

[14] T. Lunt and D. Hsieh, "The SeaView Secure Database System: A Progress Report", *Proc. of 1990 European Sym. on Research in Computer Security*, Oct. 1990.

[15] "ONTOS Object Database Documentation", Release 2.1, Ontologic, Inc., Burlington, MA, June 1991.

[16] F. Rabitti, et al., "A Model of Authorization for Next Generation Database Systems", *ACM Trans. on Database Systems*, Vol. 16, No. 1, March 1991.

[17] M. Shaw, "The Impact of Abstraction Concerns on Modern Programming Languages", *Proc. of the IEEE*, Vol. 68, No. 9, Sept. 1980.

[18] J. Smith and D. Smith, "Database Abstractions: Aggregation and Generalization", *ACM Trans. on Database Systems*, Vol. 2, No. 2, June 1977.

[19] D. Spooner, "The Impact of Inheritance on Security in Object-Oriented Database Systems", in *Database Security, II: Status and Prospects*, C. Landwehr (ed.), North-Holland, 1989.

[20] P. Stachour and B. Thuraisingham, "Design of LDV: A Multilevel Secure Relational Database Management System", *IEEE Trans. on Knowledge and Data Engineering*, Vol. 2, No. 2, June 1990.

[21] B. Thuraisingham, "Mandatory Security in Object-Oriented Database Systems", *Proc. of 1989 OOPSLA Conf.*, Oct. 1989.

[22] T.C. Ting, "A User-Role Based Data Security Approach", in *Database Security: Status and Prospects*, C. Landwehr (ed.), North-Holland, 1988.

[23] T.C. Ting, S. Demurjian, and M.-Y. Hu, "Requirements, Capabilities, and Functionalities of User-Role Based Security for an Object-Oriented Design Model", in *Database Security, V: Status and Prospects*, C. Landwehr and S. Jajodia (eds.), North-Holland, 1992.

[24] P. Wegner, "Concepts and Paradigms of Object-Oriented Programming", *OOPS Messenger*, Vol. 1, No. 1, Aug. 1990.

[25] S. Zdonik and D. Maier, "Fundamentals of Object-Oriented Databases", in *Readings in Object-Oriented Database Systems*, S. Zdonik and D. Maier (eds.), Morgan Kaufmann, 1990.

An Access Control Model for a Parallel Object-Based Programming Language

Ciarán Bryce

IRISA-Rennes,

France

Abstract

Parallel object-based languages, in general, have no way of expressing constraints on the way that objects interact at runtime. Such constraints are necessary for security, in particular. In this paper, an access control model designed for a parallel object-based language is presented and it is integrated into a small language. An example is given to show how the access control model's features are used.

1 Introduction

When designing software, some way is needed to specify and support constraints on the way that the software modules interact at run-time. Such constraints are needed for:

- *security*: program entities may contain sensitive information; access controls offer a moderate level of security though information flow controls are needed to achieve strict security.

- *reliability/integrity*: For complex entities, it may be required that access to sub-entities go through the main entity. For example, a file system directory structure has information concerning the last time a file was used. Access to the file without going through the directory violates the integrity of the directory. References to the files should be unusable outside the context of the directory.

- *Software engineering issues*: Software structured as modules aids the design and modification of applications, but as Hogg argues [1], this does not go far enough. Modules can interact in complex ways and understanding these interaction patterns can be difficult. Such an understanding is needed to engineer the application.

In this paper a parallel object-based language is presented extended with an access control model. The advantage of extending the language to incorporate access controls is that one can reason about the access control correctness of programs written in the language in the same way that one can reason about the robustness of programs written in a language furnishing an exception handling mechanism.

The object based programming model is based on the notion of a *class* [2]. This is a specification of an abstract data type where data, or state, is accessed only via a defined set of operations, or *methods*. The instances of classes that exist at runtime are the *objects*. Object oriented languages are those object based languages supporting *inheritance*. Inheritance is a mechanism for defining a new class using several pre-existing classes. The new class, the subclass of the existing classes, has a functionality which is an extension of that of the existing classes, the super-classes. Objects name other objects by *reference* values. Each reference has a class and the reference can only point to objects of that class or to objects of subclasses of the class.

One of the important features associated with object oriented programming is reuse. This has two aspects. The modular nature of the class enables one to take a class and use it in some other application. In addition, the class may be used in some new class definition using inheritance.

Regarding access control, one must be careful that the manner in which the access constraints are expressed do not hamper the individualism of objects or the reuse of classes. Access constraints to objects of the same class may differ. For example, the access constraints to a file object are set by its owner; though all files are instances of the class file, there need be no similarity between the access constraints of the different owners. Also, classes are reused on the basis of their functionality. When classes are reused they might be done so in some new application where there is a new access control policy.

The layout of this paper is as follows. A protection model for a parallel object based language is presented in the next section. In section 3, the protection model is integrated into a small parallel object based language and a programmed example is given. The conclusions are given in section 4 along with suggestions for future work.

2   The Protection Model

2.1   Model Design Considerations

An important principle that guides the model design is that programs are now "systems". This is a fundamental principle in the Hermes design [3] for example. A program thus encompasses all i/o and user interface objects. There are two important implications brought by this point of view to the access control model design.

- Systems have two classes of access constraints: *mandatory* and *discretionary*. Mandatory constraints are those put in place by the system or application administrator: in Multics [4], an object can only call another if the former's priority is greater; in a mail application, each user may only use the send command to another user's letter box, he may not read someone elses mail. Discretionary constraints are set by the participants in the system: in Unix, when a file is created, the owner decides what rights his group members have; the sender of a message in the mail example decides the list of users who may read the message. For an operation on an object to be permitted, both the discretionary and the mandatory constraints should be met.

- Applications' objects are long living. Objects created by a user during a session may outlive the session. Access constraints to long lived data may change over time. For example, a file which is top secret may over the course of time be downgraded so that more people can read it. Therefore, the access control model has to cope with access constraints changing during the lifetime of the objects, and such changes should not invalidate existing name bindings to the object.

No assumption is made about the degree of inter-object or intra-object parallelism. The access control commands operating on the access control state are atomic. The user object is part of the application; he invokes other objects using method calls, he is named via a reference and has protection attributes (see below) like any other object.

2.2   Some Language Issues

The goal of this paper is to have the protection model integrated in the language, that is, the model's operations must form part of the host language semantics. To incorporate the model in a language, two important issues must be looked at concerning the object reference - i) the information contained in the reference concerning the named object and ii) the role of the reference.

i) References should be meaningful   A reference value designates an object. Yet it gives no information concerning the named object, except its class. Imagine that a user object wishes to satisfy himself that no "suspect" object is holding a right for an owned object. He issues a review of the object's access state; the command will return the set of references for those objects with access to his object. However, the owner has no criteria upon which to discern if any suspect object has access simply by looking at the set of references he receives in the review.

To furnish more meaningful information, one could provide a directory mapping reference values to symbolic names. However, this has the problem of enforcing a symbolic naming scheme on the program which seems awkward especially if one supports dynamic object creation.

A more convenient solution is to have each application program define a set of attribute sets. One attribute set, for example, might be **secrecy level** defined as {top secret, secret, confidential, non-classified} as in military security. Every object is associated with an attribute from each attribute set. In the access control model, the *group* of an object is defined as the combination of its attributes. The class can also be a protection attribute. Thus, for an application with attribute sets security level and class, one group would be "classA;secret". An object is assigned a group at creation.

ii) The second issue related to references is the **role of a reference**. This is generally twofold in object-based languages. A reference names an object and permits the possessor to call a method on that object. To control access, some way of associating a set of method rights with an object's use of a reference is needed. There have been two approaches up to now.

The first approach is the notion of *qualified types* [5]. Each reference **variable** declared has a set of rights declared with it. These rights denote the operations which one can invoke on objects bound to that reference variable. For example, suppose the existence of a letter box type on which has send and receive operations, then

Letter_Box: my_box {*send*};

defines a variable *my_box* which references a letter box though, via the
variable *my_box*, one can only send to the letter box. By statically declaring
the access rights associated with an object's variables, access correctness can
partially be verified at compile time. However, if a dynamic mechanism is
wanted, that is, if an object does not have to have the same set of rights for
all objects named via the reference variable, then the qualified typing solution
solution is insufficient.

The second approach to fusioning references and rights is the *capability*
approach taken by McGraw and Andrews for a version of Parallel Pascal which
has access controls [6]. Here the reference **value** is a pointer to an object and
also a set of rights usable with the pointer. The approach has often been used
in operating systems [7, 8]. The capability approach, in contrast to qualified
typing, supports dynamics in the access state. The problem however is that
passing the right is linked too strongly to passing a reference. For example,
if an object temporarily stores its capability in a directory then the directory
has the object's rights while the reference is being stored. The object could
reduce the rights when passing the reference to the directory but when it gets
the reference back, it would not have the rights which it originally possessed.
In any case, the object may not receive the reference from a source where the
rights it is entitled to are available. For example, an object is created for a
certain role which may differ from its creator's; the rights needed most likely
differ according to the roles so where does the new object get the references
containing the rights that it needs?

A capability is an operating system notion; it does not work well at the
language level. The rights and reference must be handled separately. The
implication is that the access state of the program is independent of the ob-
ject/reference graph.

2.3 Existing language approaches to access control

Some definitions : The access state of a system can be represented by
an access control matrix [9]. There is a row and column for each object (by
which is meant users and entities). The matrix entry (i, j) contains the access
rights that object i holds for object j. Two generalizations of the access matrix
model exist: the *capability* model and the *access control list* (acl) model. The
capability model associates with each object the list of objects that it may
invoke and the rights which it may use on those objects. In the acl approach,
each object contains the list of objects which may call it and the rights that
those objects possess. The capability and acl approaches generalize the row
and column respectively of the access matrix. Existing language access control
models are oriented towards either capabilities or access control lists.

Language access control models

Two existing language models, qualified types [5] and the McGraw & Andrews
approach [6] were briefly looked at in the previous sub-section. Both take the
capability approach.

Mizuno & Oldhöeft [10] (acl approach) sought to incorporate access controls directly into an object based language. They extend the notion of subject S in the list entries $(S, matrix(S, O))$ to a quadruple:

$$(userID, classID, moduleID, procedureID).$$

The acl is declared in the object text. This allows a very fine degree of access - at the level of methods in the objects e.g. an object executing method m_1 might have rights set R_1 for some object O, while execution of method m_2 in the same object may give the object rights set R_2 for O. Coarser grain specifications can be got by placing "don't care" values, in the tuple entries.

Hermes [3] (capability approach) Here "a program is an entire dynamic system". Hermes is a process-oriented language. Rights are abstracted by communication ports. When a process creates another process he is responsible for passing the initial set of rights. The creator is not the owner - there is no review though there is revocation. The latter is implemented by granting the client a port to an intermediary process, instead of directly to the process of interest, which the grantor kills by requesting it to die. Rights propagation is controlled by having the passer lose the rights he transfers during the communication.

The language models presented do not fit into the object based framework outlined in the opening section. Qualified typing [5] is too static. Mizuno's approach [10] is also static, the access state dynamics is pre-determined; real dynamicism can only be got by placing "don't cares" in the extended access control list entries. McGraw & Andrews and Eden [11] are dynamic but here the reference is a capability - as was seen, this creates some problems. Hermes programming is too low level; an intermediary process has to be forked each time an owning process foresees the need for revocation and there is no review. Finally, only discretionary decisions are supported by these models; one cannot consider that constraints declared in the object's code can be classed as mandatory since this would require that the system administrator verify each class introduced.

2.4   Access control model adopted

In this section, the access control model is described at an abstract level. The **owner**ship philosophy seems sufficiently universal in existing models to adopt here. Models lacking ownership often do so for technical reasons e.g. Hydra [12] does not have ownership since ownership in the sense of the access matrix implies the ability to review the access state for an owned object. A review is costly in a capability based system since it means verifying the capability list of each object in the system. In the model here, an object's owner is discernible from its reference:

$$owner() : \text{OBJECT} \rightarrow \text{OBJECT} \cup \{system\}$$

where *system* stands for the trusted component e.g the application administrator, who creates and owns the initial objects. An object's creator becomes the owner.

An owner may **grant** and **revoke** a right for an owned object to another object. In order to be able reason about the access state, the owner's decisions should be *binding*. For example, if an object A is revoked a right and is subsequently **transfer**ed the right by a third object, then A cannot use that right. Therefore a grant of a right m gives a strong right $+m$, a transfer a normal right m and a revoke gives a strong negative right $-m$. A strong right has priority over a normal right in a decision. The discretionary access state is represented by the **Discretionary Access Control** matrix:

$$\text{DAC} : \text{OBJECT} \times \text{OBJECT}$$
$$\rightarrow$$
$$\{+m \mid m \in MName \} \cup MName \cup \{-m \mid m \in MName \}$$

where *MName* is the set of method names.

As was mentioned, each object has a **group** - the product of the object's attribute sets members. An object's inherits the attributes of his parent except for the class attribute.

$$group() : \text{OBJECT} \rightarrow \text{GROUP}$$

An owner may also grant and revoke rights on a group basis. A G_Rights table remembers what groups have been granted/revoked access so that when an object of that group is created, it will be assigned some initial rights.

$$\text{G\_Rights} : \text{OBJECT} \times \text{GROUP} \rightarrow \{+m \mid m \in MName \} \cup \{-m \mid m \in MName \}$$

A **review** typically means that the owner can read the names of all objects currently holding the right m for the owned object o. However, we have to consider the eventual implementation. Even in a centralized system such an operation would be costly (both temporally and spatially). This facility is optimized by considering two versions of review. The first, **review object**, allows the owner of an object o to ask an object a whether he has a right m for o. The second command, **review group**, enables the reviewer to see the list of groups currently holding the right m to o. The optimization seems to be sensible. Even if the owner could see the list of object names (references) holding the right, the only way that he could interpret these names is by the *group* function.

The model includes **mandatory** constraints in addition to discretionary ones. The mandatory constraints are on a group basis, are static and are set at system initialization. These constraints are represented by the **mandatory access control** matrix:

$$\text{MAC} : \text{GROUP} \times \text{GROUP} \rightarrow MName \cup \{new\}$$

The create object operator $new()$ is included in the MAC; examples suggest that one must control the classes and groups of objects that an object can create. Note that the term mandatory is not employed here in the sense of multi-level security; multi-level is just one instance of the MAC configuration.

Unlike many protection models, the *-version of the right is not employed here to control propagation e.g. access matrix [9], capability models [8]. When a reference is passed it is impossible to tell if the receiving object will need to pass the right or not to complete its task. Here, control is got by having the owner specify the groups that may be transferred the right. This information is stored in a **Rights Propagation Matrix**:

RPM : OBJECT × GROUP → BOOLEAN

The RPM is kept static for simplicity; grant and revoke decisions can override the RPM - it is only for controlling the **transfer** operation.

Note that in no model with strong binding decisions is there a need to control rights propagation. First, it should be explained why there must be a transfer operation. An object owner cannot reasonably be expected to understand how some object accomplishes some task - that is, what other objects it relies upon to complete its computation. The owner cannot just grant rights to objects which need not be refused access since one would like to keep propagation of privileges to a minimum. This is widely recognized as an important principle for access control models [13]. Thus since there is a transfer facility, it must be controlled. The RPM serves as this control.

An object o_1 may call a method m on o_2, if it possesses a discretionary right and the mandatory constraints are met.

$$\left(\left(\{m,+m\} \cap \text{DAC}(o_1, o_2) \neq \emptyset\right) \wedge \text{-}m? \notin \text{DAC}(o_1, o_2) \vee owner(o_2) = o_1 \vee o_1 = o_2 \right)$$
$$\wedge\ m \in \text{MAC}(group(o_1),\ group(o_2))$$

The discretionary clause says that o_1 must have a discretionary right or else be the owner and that recursive calls are allowed. See the appendix and [14] for a more formal description of the model and its operations.

2.5 An Editor Application Example

An editor application is considered, by nature highly interactive. *Users* use a document browser *editor* to view and update their *files*. Files have a complex structure - they contain text and *picture* objects. A user can put his file objects in a *directory* object to permit sharing between users. Each user belongs to a team - floor1, floor2 or floor3. Below are the protection requirements.

The attribute sets of the application are the <u>class</u> and <u>team</u>. As an aside, a designer might ask the question, when should some attribute of an object be declared in the object's state and when should it be made an attribute? The answer is that if the attribute in question is protection relevant, then it should be made an attribute. Of course, the program could simulate a protection attribute using the objects' state variables but in this case the access control model cannot guarantee that the constraints are met - the programmer is relying on trust.

First of all there are some integrity constraints on the application. A *picture* object only needs to be accessed by *file* objects - an editor or user accessing the picture might lead to some external integrity constraint being violated. For example, the file has a specific format for the picture objects it uses which the user or editor might not know about. The application enforces this restriction using the MAC. Thus (where * represents a don't care - i.e. any attribute)

$$\text{MAC}((*;g),\ (*;picture)) = \{\ \text{if } g = file \text{ then } all \cup \{new\} \text{ else } \{\} \text{ fi } \}$$

In a similar way a *file* object will only be accessed by the *editor* objects. Thus

$$\text{MAC}((*;g),\ (*;file)) = \{\ \text{if } g = editor \text{ then } all \text{ fi; if } g = user \text{ then } new \text{ else } \{\} \ \}$$

Note that the *new* operator on the *file* object can only be called by a user object. This is to implement the discretionary constraints. For a user to be able to control access to his files, he must be the owner, that is he must create the files and then pass them to the editor. This is one example of the access control model forcing us to think in a certain way about the application design.

The *directory* object does not have any rights (its MAC entries are set to nil), so it cannot call any object that it names. However, it may store discretionary rights for transfer to users in its DAC entry. This is how rights dispersal is achieved. When a user creates a *file* object, he passes it with full rights to the editor. He may put the reference in the directory for other users to get. He can ensure rights dispersal control by setting the RPM suitably or by putting a subset of the rights with the reference in the directory. Alternatively, he may control the access state of his files with the review, grant and revoke operations.

Finally, concerning the trustworthiness of the editors, the MAC constraints do limit the damage that a malicious editor can do. Also, the user can use his discretionary constraints if he wants to view a file but feels that the editor cannot be trusted: he simply calls the view file operation transferring only the view file right. The code of the application is looked at further on.

3   A Language with the Protection Model

3.1   Introduction

The language chosen to present the ideas is inspired by [15]. Parallelism is supported by associating a process with each object and by having an asynchronous (non-blocking) object creation command (**new**). Communication is by rendezvous. The sender names the object it is calling and the method in the object requested. The receiver names the set of methods that it is willing to service; on executing

$$\textbf{answer}(m_1, m_2)$$

the object will block until it receives calls for either method m_1 or m_2.

3.2   Language abstract syntax

Here are the principal sets of syntactic elements:

Name	Function	Elements
$IVar$	instance vars	i_1, i_2
$LVar$	local vars	l_1, l_2
$CName$	class names	c_1, c_2
$MName$	method names	m_1, m_2
$AName$	attribute names	a_1, a_2
$GName$	group names	g_1, g_2

A group name is a finite sequence of attribute names, $GName = AName^+$. Since a class can be an attribute, $CName \subseteq AName$.

Mandatory constraints must be declared in a place where they are visible to all class definitions: there is a **security definition library** for this. For example, in an application where the security attributes are the multi-level set {unclassified, confidential, secret, topsecret} and department {floor1, floor2, floor3} and where the class is an attribute, one might have:

SDL ⟨ application ⟩ =
   begin
      attribute level = { unclassified, confidential, secret, topsecret}
      attribute department = { floor1, floor2, floor3}
      class is attribute = {classA, classB, ...}

     MAC((unclassified,floor,classA), (unclassified,floor,classB)) = {new, m1 ..}
     ...etc ...
     ⋮

   end SDL.

The abstract syntax for expressions and commands are given below. The set of non-standard objects is denoted $AObj$, a typical element being α. The standard objects include only Boolean, integer and string objects and the object nil representing the value of un-initialized objects. The set of all objects is Obj:

$$Obj = AObj \cup Z \cup \{tt,\!f\!f\} \cup A^+ \cup \{nil\}$$

where A is the alphabet {a, b, c, d, ..., z, A, B, ..., Z }. In the interests of keeping the semantics simple, there are no method or group variables - though they are probably useful.

The expressions e of the language are;

$e ::=$	i	*instance variable*
|	l	*local variable*
|	$e_{call}!m(e\{m^*\}^*)$	*a method call on e_{call}, transfer parameters listed*
|	$m(e^*)$	*call the method m locally*
|	$\mathbf{new}(C, g_1, ..., g_n)$	*create an object of class C; RPM entries $g_1, ..., g_n = false$*
|	$s; e$	*execute command s, then evaluate e*
|	$\mathbf{self}$	*returns the name of the object executing the expression*
|	$\underline{\beta}$	*delivers the object β*
|	$m \textbf{ for } e_1 \textbf{ in } e_2$	*review object protection command; returns Boolean*

and the commands s:

$s ::=$	$i \leftarrow e$	*assignment to instance variable*
|	$l \leftarrow e$	*assignment to local variable*
|	$\mathbf{answer}(m_1, ..., m_n)$	*answer one of the method calls $m_1, ..., m_n$*
|	e	*evaluate the expression (for its side-effects)*
|	$s_1; s_2$	*sequential composition*
|	$\textbf{if } e \textbf{ then } s_1 \textbf{ else } s_2 \textbf{ fi}$	*conditional*
|	$\textbf{cas } e_1 : s_1 \mid .. \mid e_n : s_n \textbf{ sac}$	*case statement*
|	$\textbf{while } e \textbf{ do } s \textbf{ od}$	*repetitive statement*
|	$e\{m^*\} \Rightarrow \underline{\alpha}$	*evaluate e and send result to α; when result is nonstandard object, may pass rights also*
|	$\textbf{gt } m \textbf{ for } e_1 \textbf{ to } e_2 \textbf{ tg}$	*the grant object command*
|	$\textbf{gt } m \textbf{ for } e_1 \textbf{ to } g \textbf{ tg}$	*the grant group command*
|	$\textbf{rk } m \textbf{ for } e_1 \textbf{ from } e_2 \textbf{ kr}$	*the revoke object command*

| rk m for e_1 from g kr   *the revoke group command*
| rvw m for e
    : $(g_1, ..., g_n) \rhd (b_1, ..., b_n)$ *the review of groups command*

The review of groups command is syntactically awkward since there are no sets, sequences or arrays in the language. The idea is that there is a Boolean variable b_i for each group named in the leftmost list. On execution of the command, b_i is set to true if the group g_i has the right m for object e.

A program description is a unit U. It consists of the class definitions d_is and the security definition library sdl.

$$U \triangleq \langle\, C_1 \Leftarrow d_1, ..., C_n \Leftarrow d_n, \text{sdl} \,\rangle$$

A class definition d consists of:

$$d \triangleq \langle\, (i_1, ..., i_n), (m_1 \Leftarrow \mu_1, ..., m_k \Leftarrow \mu_k), s \,\rangle$$

where the i_is are the instance variables, m_i is a method name and μ_i is a method definition. s is the code executed by instances of the class on creation. Finally then, a method definition consists of the following:

$$\mu \triangleq \langle\, (p_1, ..., p_n), (l_1, ..., l_k), e \,\rangle$$

where the p_is are the parameters, the l_is are local variables and e is the expression evaluated by the method.

Two of the access control commands, transfer and create, are piggybacked onto existing language constructs. The following is an important abbreviation. For the method call $e_1!m(., e_2\{m_1, m_2\}, .)$ transfers rights m_1 and m_2 for object e_2 to e_1. To transfer all the discretionary rights possessed, one could write $e_1!m(., e_2\{all\}, .)$ or just $e_1!m(., e_2, .)$. To transfer no right one writes $e_1!m(., e_2\{\}, .)$. Similarly, for creation, if no groups are named in the **new** command then all the RPM entries are set to true.

The goal of this abbreviation is that objects without any explicit access control expressions can partake fully in the model. A program of the original host language [15] is thus a valid program of the extended language with a well-defined protection semantics. Moreover, there is some reusability: a program in the original language framework behaves exactly the same in the extended access control framework since all the rights are transferable and so whenever an object gets a reference, it may use it. The principle of almost "default-access" is contrary to the default refusal policy argued in the well accepted paper on protection by Saltzer and Schroeder [13]. However, it seems to be a necessary compromise in order to retain some reusability.

The operational semantics of the language are given in an extended version of this paper [14]. It is shown that the access control features do introduce extra synchronization constraints: the **new** operation which creates an object of group g is not serializable with a **grant** or **revoke** group operation on g.

3.3 The Editor Example Continued

In this section the editor application example of 2.5 is continued. An outline program is given, based on the analysis that was carried out. Firstly, here is the security definition library.

176

```
SDL EditorExample =
     begin
             attribute team = { floor1, floor2, floor3}
             class is attribute = { directory, editor, file, picture, user}

        MAC( (*, file), (*, picture) ) = {new, all}
        MAC( (*, user), (*, file) ) = { new }
        MAC( (*, user), (*, editor) ) = { new, all }
        MAC( (*, editor), (*, file) ) = { all }
        MAC( (*, *), (*, directory)) = { all}
     end SDL.
```

where entries not specified are empty by default except that a group has all rights to itself.

Class file   The state is represented simply as four paragraphs (strings) and a picture object. On creation, the object creates its picture object. The first four methods do not need any explanation. The fifth, make_copy, has the purpose of making a backup copy of the file. To save storage resources and to help achieve coherency between the backup and the original, the picture sub object is copied by reference rather than by value. To prevent unwanted changes to the picture object in the copy, only the return_image right is transferred.

```
file ⇐ ⟨ (para1, para2, para3, para4: string; figure: class picture)
        :
        /* a typical example */
        read_picture ⇐ () (buffer: string)
            (buffer ← figure ! return_image();
            buffer ← raster (buffer)) /* exp converting executable to one suiting the file */
        :
        paste_picture ⇐ ....
        :
        read_para ⇐ ....
        :
        write_para ⇐ ....
        :
        make_copy ⇐ ()(backup: class file)
            backup ← new(file);
            backup!write_para(para1);
            backup!write_para(para2);
            backup!write_para(para3);
            backup!write_para(para4);
            backup!paste_picture(figure{return_image}))
        :
        /* initialization */
figure ← new(picture);
while tt do
        answer(read_picture, paste_picture, read_para, write_para, make_copy);
od ).
```

Class picture   A very simple class. There are no discretionary access control expressions. The two methods save a text image - a string of characters - and return the text image:

picture ⇐ ⟨ (image: string)()

               save_image ⇐ (new_img: string)
                    image ← new_img)
               return_image ⇐ ()()
                    image)
               / initialization */*
image ← nil;
while *tt* do
       answer(return_image, save_image)
od).

Class Directory   The class has no explicit security expressions or commands; only an outline is given here.

directory ⇐ ⟨

        (name1,....,nameN: string; free1,...,freeN: bool; Doc1,....,DocN: **class file**;)
        ⋮
        store ⇐ ....
        ⋮
        lookup ⇐ (key:string) ()
                cas free1!and(name1!=(key)) : Doc1 |
                ⋮
                else : nil)
        ⋮
        / initialization */*
free1 ← *ff*; ...; freeN ← *ff*;
while *tt* do
       answer(lookup, store);
od).

Class Editor   It handles one file at a time which must be explicitly opened.

editor ⇐ ⟨
   (opened_file: **class file**; work_space: string;)
   ⋮
   open ⇐ (file_to_open: **class file**)()
       (opened_file ← file_to_open)
   ⋮
   close ⇐ ....
   ⋮
   view_doc ⇐ ()()
   (work_space ← (opened_file!read_picture())!concat!(opened_file!read_para($i=1..4$)))
   ⋮
   cut ⇐ ....
   ⋮
   paste ⇐ ....

178

```
        ⋮
    /* initialization */
while tt do
        answer(open, close, view_doc, cut, paste);
od ).
```

Class User   Representing the user. A user encapsulates a console - this forms part of the environmental conditions for the model. The system creates the user object with an appropriate team attribute assigned. The user waits for the initial information - an editor reference and a reference to the directory object and then receives the commands from the user himself.

```
user ⇐ ⟨ (file_to_open, command: string; file_id: class file;
                    my_ed:class editor; dir:class directory)

        ⋮
        get_info ⇐ (dir_name: class directory)()(
                my_ed ← new(editor)
                dir ← dir_name)

        ⋮
        grantfloor1 ⇐ ()()
                (gt all for file_id to (floor1;user) tg)

        ⋮
        open ⇐ ()()
                (my_ed ! open(file_id))

        ⋮
        /* initialization */
answer(get_info);
while tt do
        console!get(file_to_open);
        file_id ← dir!lookup(file_to_open);
        console!get(command);
        while (command!=("end")!not
                do cas

                ⋮
                | command!string_eq("open") : open();
                | command!string_eq("grant floor 1 team") : grantfloor1() ;

                ⋮
                console!get(command);
                sac od
od ).
```

4   Conclusions and future work

This paper has introduced an access control model for a parallel object based language. By integrating this model into the language, the goal is to be able to specify protection policies at the object level. This also gives an access control model independent of the operating system and underlying hardware.

Of course, access controls in the language does not make the language run-time secure. Issues such as encapsulation (ensuring that no object successfully generates a memory reference to the address space of another object), integrity of the operating system code and authentication must still be treated. These are perhaps orthogonal issues to the protection requirements of an abstract language machine - they should be treated at the operating system level. The philosophy adopted here is similar to that of the Opal designers [16]:

> "The kernel interface is not the programmer interface. Implement object semantics in the language and runtime system .."

To extend the model to object-oriented languages, inheritance must be treated. The first problem linked to inheritance was noted by Synder [17]. Inheritance is badly encapsulated. A change to a class can lead to adverse behavior of the subclasses' clients. The solution suggested is to treat the sub-class as a special client of the class having to access his state by a special set of methods. This should make the sub-class less susceptible to the parent class modifications.

Regarding the access control model, it was emphasised that access constraints are on an object basis and not a class basis. It is not evident that for the mandatory constraint definitions that a subclass should be treated any differently to an independent class. However, there is one aspect linked to inheritance which might be important : *dynamic binding*. This is the principle which states that a reference of a certain class may during the lifetime of the application become bound to an object of its sub-class. This seems most important for the transfer command where method rights for the referenced objects are passed as parameters during a method call. Consider the expression $e!m(e_1\{m_1\})$ where the caller transfers right m_1 for e_1 to e. If e_1 is bound to an object of a subclass of e_1, then m_1 has still meaning since methods defined in a class must also exist in the subclass by the typing rules. A priori the access control model does not interfere with inheritance. Nevertheless, a more profound investigation is needed.

In the access control model framework, two problems are caused by the introduction of new class definitions during the lifetime of the application. Firstly, classes which have been verified may be replaced by classes which are not verified. One cannot reasonably expect that classes added can be "trusted" to respect discretionary constraints. The second problem is that if the mandatory constraints are partly a function of the class (that is, if class is one of the protection attributes), then what mandatory constraints should be accorded the new classes? In the present model, "system" must intervene each time a class is introduced to update the MAC. There seems to be no nicer solution.

An area of future theoretical work might be to consider how the model answers the safety question. Basically, the safety question asks if some access state is reachable in a model, in which a certain subject possesses a right which he did not previously have. For the access matrix the safety question is undecidable [9]. However, Sandhu's results in the domain are encouraging because there seems to be some strong parallels between his SPM model [18] and this paper's: typing corresponds to groups, there is control of creation and the RPM and MAC combined closely resemble the functionality of the filter and link functions. SPM is decidable in most "practical" situations.

Another area of theoretical concern is *garbage*. Deletion of objects is implicit in object oriented systems - an object is removed from the system when it is no longer accessible by other objects (i.e. when it is garbage). One must consider if an object which is referenced but for which no object holds a right is garbage or not since no one can ever use that object. This obligation stems from the fact that the model distinguishes the naming of objects from calling the objects.

References

[1] Hogg J. Islands: Aliasing Protection in Object-Oriented Languages. In: ACM Object-Oriented Programming Systems, Languages and Applications Conference. Canada, 1991, pp 271-285.

[2] Korsen T, McGregor JD. Understanding Object-Oriented: a unifying paradigm. CACM 1990; 33: 39-60.

[3] Strom R, Bacon D, Goldberg A et al. HERMES: a Language for Distributed Computing. Prentice Hall, New Jersey, 1991.

[4] Saltzer JH. Protection and Control of Information Sharing in Multics. CACM 1974; 17:388-402.

[5] Jones AK, Liskov BH. A Language Extension for Expressing Constraints on Data Access. CACM 1978; 21:358-367.

[6] McGraw JR, Andrews GR. Access Control in Parallel Programs. IEEE TOSE 1979; 5:1-9.

[7] Dennis TD, Van Horn EC. Programming Semantics for Multiprogrammed Computations. CACM 1966; 9:337-345.

[8] Levy H. Capability-Based Computer Systems. Digital Press, Mass. 1984.

[9] Harrison MA, Ruzzo WL, Ullman JD. Protection in Operating Systems. CACM 1976; 19: 461-471.

[10] Mizuno M, Oldhöeft AE. An Access Control Language for Object-Oriented Programming Systems. Research Report. Kansas State University, 1989.

[11] Black A, Hutchinson N, Jul E et al. The Eden project: a final report. Research Report TR 86-11-01. Washington University, 1986.

[12] Cohen E, Jefferson D. Protection in the Hydra Operating System. In: 5th ACM Symposium on Operating Principles. Texas, 1975, pp 141-160.

[13] Saltzer J, Schroeder M. The Protection of Information in Computer Systems. IEEE Proc 1975; 63:1278-1308.

[14] Bryce C. An Access Control Model for an Object-Based Programming Language. IRISA Research Report, Rennes, France, 1994.

[15] America P, de Bakker J, Kok J et al. Operational Semantics of a Parallel Object-Oriented Language. In: 13th ACM Symposium on the Principles of Programming Languages. Florida, 1986, pp 194-208.

[16] Chase JS, Levy H, Lazowska ED et al. Lightweight Shared Objects in a 64-bit Operating System. In: ACM Object-Oriented Programming, Systems, Languages and Applications Conference. Canada, 1993, pp 397-413.

[17] Synder A. Encapsulation and Inheritance in Object-Oriented Programming Languages. In: ACM Object-Oriented Programming Systems, Languages and Applications Conference. 1986, pp 38-45.

[18] Sandhu RS. Expressive Power of the Schematic Protection Model. IOS Journal of Comp. Security 1992; 1:59-98.

A   Access control command semantics

The access state of the language is the following :

$\|$ MAC : (GROUP × GROUP) → $PMName \cup \{new\}$
$\|$ DAC : (OBJECT × OBJECT) → $Prights$
$\|$ RPM : (OBJECT × GROUP) → BOOLEAN
$\|$ G_Rights : (OBJECT × GROUP) → $Prights$
$\|$ $owner$: OBJECT → OBJECT $\cup \{system\}$
$\|$ $group$: OBJECT → GROUP

In the following, *self* denotes the name of the object which executes the command or expression. Non-standard objects are denoted by α-subscript.

Grant commands   The grant object command places a strong right in a DAC and removes a negative right. The operation **grant** m **for** α_1 **to** α_2 has the following effect on the access state :

$\|$ $owner(\alpha_1)$ = self /* precondition - only owner can execute */
$\|$ DAC' = DAC $\oplus$ ((α_2, α_1) $\mapsto$ ((DAC(α_2, α_1) $\cup \{+m\}$) $\setminus \{-m\}$))

The $\oplus$ is a finction override operator:

$$(\sigma_i \oplus (x \to E))(v) = \begin{cases} \sigma_i(v) & \text{si } x \neq v \\ E & \text{si } x = v \end{cases}$$

The grant group command places a strong right in a DAC for all objects of the group and also puts the right in the G_Rights table for objects of the group subsequently created. The command **grant** m **for** α_1 **to** g makes the following changes:

$\|$ self = $owner(\alpha_1)$ /* precondition - only owner can execute */
$\|$ DAC' = DAC $\oplus$ {(a : OBJECT | $group(a) = g$) •
$\qquad\qquad\qquad$ λ a, α_1. (a,α_1) $\mapsto$ (DAC(a, α_1) $\cup \{+m\}$) $\setminus \{-m\}$ }
$\|$ G_Rights' = G_Rights $\oplus$ ((α_1, g) $\mapsto$ (G_Rights(α_1, g) $\cup +m$) $\setminus -m$)

Revoke commands The two revoke commands are the reverse of the grants. For **revoke** m **for** α_1 **from** α_2:

$\|$ self $= owner(\alpha_1)$ /* *precondition - only owner can execute* */
$\|$ DAC' $=$ DAC $\oplus ((\alpha_2, \alpha_1) \mapsto ((DAC(\alpha_2, \alpha_1) \cup \{\text{-}m\}) \setminus \{m, +m\}))$

and for the revoke group command **revoke** m **for** α **from** g:

$\|$ self $= owner(\alpha_1)$ /* *precondition - only owner can execute* */
$\|$ DAC' $=$ DAC $\oplus \{(a : \text{OBJECT} \mid group(a) = g) \bullet$
$$\lambda\, a,\, \alpha_1.\ a \mapsto (DAC(a, \alpha_1) \cup \{\text{-}m\}) \setminus \{+m, m\} \}$$
$\|$ G_Rights' $=$ G_Rights $\oplus (\alpha_1, g) \mapsto (\text{G\_Rights}(\alpha_1, g) \cup \text{-}m) \setminus +m$

Review commands The review object command is an expression of the language m **for** α_1 **in** α_2:

$\|$ self $= owner(\alpha_1)$ /* *precondition - only owner can execute* */
$\|$ $\{ m, +m \} \cap DAC(a, \alpha_1) \neq \emptyset$ /* *expression evaluated* */

The review group **rvw** m **for** $\alpha : (g_1, ...,g_n) \triangleright (b_1, ...,b_n)$ is effectively a multiple assignment:

$\|$ self $= owner(\alpha)$ /* *precondition - only owner can execute* */
$\|$ b_i i=1..n $\equiv \exists\, a : \text{OBJECT},\, group(a) = g_i \mid \{ m, +m \}) \cap DAC(a, \alpha) \neq \emptyset$

Create command Let g' be the group of self, g is the group with the same attributes of g' except that if class is an attribute, then the class attribute is C in g. The effect of **new**$(C,g_1, ...,g_n)$ is

$\|$ *new* $\in$ MAC(*group*(self), g) /* *precondition - only owner can execute* */
$\|$ $n_O \notin$ dom dom DAC /* *precondition - new name must be unique* */
$\|$ DAC' $=$ DAC $\oplus \{ o \in$ dom dom DAC $\bullet$
$$\lambda\, n_O, o.\ (n_O, o) \mapsto \text{G\_Rights}(o, g) \}$$
$\|$ RPM' $=$ RPM $\oplus \{ g \in$ dom GROUP : GROUP $\bullet$
$$\lambda\, g.\ (n_O, g) \mapsto \neg(g \in \{g_i \mid i = 1..n\}) \}$$
$\|$ G_Rights' $=$ G_Rights $\cup (g \in$ dom GROUP $\bullet \lambda\, g.\ (n_O,g) \mapsto \{\} \}$
$\|$ *owner'* $=$ *owner* $\cup (n_O \mapsto$ self$)$
$\|$ *group'* $=$ *group* $\cup (n_O \mapsto g)$

Transfer command The transfer command is called each time a right is passed during a method call and return. For **transfer** m **for** α_1 **to** α_2,

$\|$ /* *passer must possess right or be the owner* */
$\|$ $\{m, +m\} \cap DAC(\text{self}, \alpha_1) \neq \emptyset \lor owner(\alpha_1) =$ self
$\|$ RPM$(\alpha_1, group(\alpha_2))$ /* *precondition - on control of transfer* */
$\|$ DAC' $=$ DAC $\oplus ((\alpha_2, \alpha_1) \mapsto DAC(\alpha_2, \alpha_1) \cup \{m\})$

Research Issues in Discretionary Authorizations for Object Bases

Elisa Bertino   Pierangela Samarati

Dipartimento di Scienze dell'Informazione, Università di Milano

Via Comelico, 39/41, 20135 Milano, Italy

Abstract

The conventional models of authorizations have been designed for database systems supporting the hierarchical, network, and relational models of data. However, these authorization models are not adequate for protection in object-oriented systems. This paper discusses the new requirements which arise in the protection of data models based on the object- oriented paradigm.

1 Introduction

The technology of object-oriented database management systems (OODBMSs) is very promising to a number of applications in business and industry. For this reason, in the last few years, object-oriented systems have been an active area of research. However, most attention has been given to the traditional database issues such as data modeling, query languages, query processing, and schema management. By contrast, less attention has been given to the problem of protection.

Many authorization models have been proposed for the protection of information in operating systems and in data base management systems. However, the application of these models in object-oriented systems is not straightforward. Indeed, the particular characteristics of object-oriented systems, such as inheritance hierarchy, versions, and composite objects, introduce new protection requirements which the traditional authorization models do not address.

Work in the area of authorization models for object-oriented databases is still in a preliminary stage. Very few OODBMSs, namely Orion [28] and Iris [2], provide authorization models comparable to the models provide by current Relational DBMSs.

In the Orion authorization model, authorizations can be specified for each group (role) of users to access objects. This authorization model takes into consideration semantic aspects of the object-oriented paradigm, such as inheritance hierarchy, versions, and composite objects. In particular, the model supports the derivation of new authorizations (called implicit) on some objects from the authorizations explicitly specified by the users on objects semantically related. Moreover, the model enforces authorization implication also on the basis of relationships among subjects and among access modes. The ORION authorization model, presented in [28], has been extended by Bertino and Weigand [7] to the consideration of content-dependent authorizations. These authorizations can include conditions which must be satisfied by the values of the attributes of the objects to be accessed. Bertino, in [5], proposes a model where authorizations specify privileges for users to execute methods on objects. The model enforces the concept of *private* methods and *protection* mode. Private methods are methods which can be invoked only by other methods. The concept of protection mode allows to grant users the privilege of executing a method m without the need of granting them the authorizations for all the methods that m may invoke during its execution. Ahad et Al., in [2], present an authorization model based on controlling function evaluation. Authorizations can be specified for users, or groups of users, to execute functions, i.e., methods over objects. *Specific functions, guard functions,* and *proxy functions* concepts are used to enforce content-dependent authorizations and to restrict the execution of given functions to some users. Another model based on authorizations to execute methods on objects is presented by Richardson et Al., in [29]. In this model, the owner of an object can control who may invoke which methods on the object. Fernandez et al., in [11,12,18,14], present an authorization model which allows the specification of positive, negative, and content-dependent authorizations. The model allows for a decentralized administration of authorizations by users.

As for object-oriented systems some work has been performed on limiting unconditional access to objects [1,16,17,15,19,26,27,31]. Most of this work is based on the approach of providing multiple interfaces to objects enforcing a sort of view mechanism. In [26,27] access constraints to objects are expressed by rules, called *laws*, each of which defines actions which the system must execute when a message is sent from an object to another object. Possible actions include: letting the message pass unaltered, sending the recipient a different message, sending the same or another message to a different object, or block the message sending. However, although all these approaches allow, in some way, to restrict or differentiate the access to objects, they do not really address the authorization problem.

All these works offer some solutions to the problem of protecting object-oriented systems. However, each of them addresses only part of the issues, therefore leaving many questions open. There is the need for a model which completely addresses the protection requirements of data models based on the object-oriented paradigm.

The goal of this paper is to discuss the issues that must be addressed in the development of an authorization model for object-oriented systems. The paper is organized as follows. In Section 2 we briefly review the main characteristics of the object-oriented data model. In Section 3 we illustrate the requirements that an authorization model for object-oriented systems must satisfy and possible approaches for it.

2 The object-oriented data model

Although every object-oriented system has its own characteristics, some basic concepts, characterizing the object-oriented paradigm, are common to all object-oriented systems. These can be summarized as follows [3]:

Object Each real-world entity is modeled by an object. Each object is associated with a unique identifier (*oid*). The object identifier is fixed for the whole life of the object.

Object's status and behavior Each object is associated a set of attributes (also called instance variables) and a set of procedures, called *methods*. The value of an attribute can be an object or a set of objects. This characteristic permits arbitrarily complex objects to be defined as aggregations of other objects. The values of the attributes of an object represents the object's *state*. The set of methods of an object represent the object's *behavior*.

Encapsulation The status of an object can be accessed, and possibly modified, by sending messages to the object. The set of messages an object can respond to is called the *interface* of the object. Upon the reception of a message by an object, the corresponding method is invoked. The execution of the method may imply the object sending messages to itself or to some other objects.

Encapsulation allows *client* objects to use the services of an object without caring how the services are implemented. Thus, changes to the implementation of an object do not affect other objects or applications using the services provided by the object.

Class Objects sharing the same structure and behavior are grouped into classes. An object belonging to a class is said to be an *instance* of the class. Each object is an instance of some class. Then, a class represents a template from which instances can be defined.

Inheritance hierarchy Classes are related by a subclass-superclass relationship called *is-a*. If class C is defined as a subclass (is-a) another class C', then C inherits the attributes and the methods specified for C'.

Composite objects The domain of the attribute of an object o can a class. In this case the attribute will assume, as value, the identifier of an instance of the class. Object o is said to be a *composite* object. The instance of the class which is reference by o is said to be a *component* object.

3 Research issues

In this section we illustrate some of the requirements to be taken into account in developing an authorization model for object-oriented systems. We start from a basic authorization model. We then discuss new requirements which must be taken into consideration and illustrate how they can be addressed by properly extending the authorization model. We also illustrate the approaches for the satisfaction of these requirements which have been proposed in recent models.

3.1 The basic authorization model

In this subsection we introduce the basic authorization model which summarizes the basic characteristics of the authorization models in the literature. In the basic authorization model, we postulate the existence of three finite sets: S, denoting the set of subjects in the system; O, denoting the set of objects in the system; and A, denoting the set of access modes in the system. The set of subjects S is composed of users and groups of users, i.e., $S = U \cup G$, where U denotes the set of users and G the set of groups in the system. The set of objects O contains the objects of the data model, i.e., instances and classes. Set A contains the following access modes: Read (R) to read an object, Write (W) to write an object, and Create (C) to create instances of an objects. The Create access modes can be referred only to classes.

An authorization is then defined as a triple $\langle s, a, o \rangle$, where $s \in S$, $a \in A$, $o \in O$. Authorization $\langle s, a, o \rangle$ states that subject s is authorized to exercise access mode a on object o.

For example, authorization $\langle \text{Jones, read, } \#o_1 \rangle$ indicates that user Jones can read object $\#o_1$. Authorization $\langle \text{Jones, create, EMPLOYEE} \rangle$ indicates that user Jones can create instances of class EMPLOYEE.

We refer to the set of authorizations holding at a given time as Authorization Base (shortly, AB). Then, $AB \subseteq S \times A \times O$.

Users are allowed to invoke any method on any object of the system. Every time an elementary operation (i.e., read, write, or execute) must be performed during the execution of a method, the authorizations of the user on behalf of whom the method is executing need to be checked. Hence, an access request is submitted to the system. An access request is characterized by a triple $\langle u, a, o \rangle$ indicating that user u requires to exercise access mode a on object o. Then, the access request is checked against the authorizations of user u. If there exists an authorization for the required access, the request is granted. Otherwise, it is denied. If the request is denied, two different approaches can be taken. Either the execution as a whole terminates, i.e., the execution of the method invoked by the user is aborted; or the execution continues with the unauthorized operation considered as ineffective, i.e., as if it has not been submitted to the system. For sake of simplicity, we consider that if any of the operations invoked during a method execution is not authorized, the execution is aborted.

In the basic authorization model, we consider administration of authorizations to be a privilege task of the administrator. We will discuss different policies which can be applied for administration of authorizations later on.

3.2   Access modes

In the basic authorization model, like in traditional access control models, we have considered authorizations to be specified for the elementary operations, i.e., read, write, and create. Users are allowed to invoke any method specified on the objects. The execution of a method invoked by a user will complete only if the user has the authorization for all the elementary operations which are required in the execution of the method. This approach has the drawback that a user can be allowed to invoke methods which will not be able to complete because the user is lacking the necessary authorizations. Morever, this approach does not take any advantage of the *encapsulation* property of object-oriented systems, meaning that objects can be accessed sending messages which invoke the appropriate methods.

To take advantage of the encapsulation property, the authorization model should support the specification of authorizations to execute methods. Indeed, specifying authorizations as privileges of executing methods would result in an extensible and more expressive authorization model. In particular, it would allow to restrict users to the execution of particular procedures on the objects.

For instance, also if a user is authorized to read and write an object, the user may not be authorized to execute some methods which access the object. For example, consider class EMPLOYEE and consider method "calculate-taxes", defined on it, which reads an employee's information (such as salary, benefits, family status) and returns the taxes the employee has to pay. A user may be authorized to read the instances of the class EMPLOYEE, and not be authorized to execute method "calculate-taxes". An advantage of considering authorizations to execute methods is that it allows to restrict the execution of method computationally very expensive only to particular users.

The consideration of authorizations to execute methods requires to extend the authorization model. In particular the access modes must be extended to the consideration of all operations (i.e., methods) which can be applied to the objects.[1] Let o be an object and let $M(o)$ be the set of methods applicable to the object. In the following we consider read, write, and create also as methods, which are applicable to any object. Let M denote the set composed of all methods $M(o)$ defined for whichever object in the system. Then, the model can be extended by considering, as access modes, all the methods executable on the objects of the system, i.e., $A = M$. For example, authorization $\langle$ Jones, calculate-taxes, $\#o_1$ $\rangle$ indicates that user "Jones" can execute method "calculate-taxes" on object $\#o_1$. Note that, for an authorization to be consistent, the authorized access must be possible, i.e., the access mode in the authorization must be applicable to the object of the authorization. For example, for the authorization just mentioned to be consistent method "calculate-taxes" must be executable on object $\#o_1$. Hence, for each authorization $\langle s, o, a \rangle$ in the Authorization Base, it must be $a \in M(o)$.

3.3   Authorizations' subject

During execution of a method invoked by a user on an object, other methods, on the same or on different objects may be invoked. The invocation of these methods is checked against the authorizations specified for the user and allowed only if the user owns the necessary authorizations. Therefore, in order for a user to successfully complete execution of a method m, the user must be authorized for all the methods which m may directly or indirectly invoke. However, giving the user the authorization for these method would give the user the possibility of invoking these methods outside the execution of m. This approach is in contrast with the least privilege principle which states that users should be given only the minimum authorizations necessary to perform their activities. For example, consider class EMPLOYEE and method "modify-salary", defined on it, which modifies the salary of employees. Moreover, consider method "review-status" which is used to update the status of employees. Suppose that, during the review of an employee's status, the need could arise of modifying the salary of the employee. Suppose then that method "review-status" automatically determines the salary change and then invokes method "modify-salary". Suppose that Jones should be authorized to execute method "review-status". Since all access requests are checked against the user on behalf of whom the method requiring the requests is executing, in order for

---

[1] Alternatively, methods can be seen as objects on which the "execute" access mode can be applied.

Jones to complete the execution of "review-status", Jones must be also given the authorization for method "modify-salary". However, doing so would allow Jones to invoke method "modify-salary" also outside the execution of method "review-status".

It would be desirable to give users authorizations to execute a method m without the need of giving them the authorization for all methods invoked during the execution of m. A solution to this problem can be the consideration of authorizations with methods as subjects. For example, an authorization can specify that a certain method m is authorized to execute another method m'. Then, if during the execution of a method m, method m' is invoked, the execution of m' will be granted also if the user on behalf of whom m is executing does not have the authorization for m'. For instance, with reference to the example just mentioned to authorization to execute method "modify-salary" can be granted to method "review-status". Then, Jones, which has the authorization for method "review-status" will be able to execute this method without need to be authorized for method "modify-salary".

Authorizations with methods as subjects have been considered by Bertino in [5]. There, the motivation for specifying authorizations for methods is that in some cases, where encapsulation is used for operation correctness, it would be desirable to avoid users to directly invoke particular methods. Therefore, the model gives the possibility of specifying that a given method cannot be invoked by clients or users, but only by other methods belonging to the same object. To allow this, the model distinguishes between *public* and *private* methods. Public methods are methods which can be explicitly invoked by end-users. Private methods can be invoked only in the executions of other methods belonging to the same objects of the private method considered. Users can be given only authorizations for public methods. Methods can be given only authorizations on private methods. Consider then that method m, executing on behalf of user u, requires the invocation of method m'. The system control if method m' is private or public. If m' is private, then the execution is allowed only if m is authorized for it. If m' is public, the authorizations of the user are checked and the execution allowed only if u has the authorization for m'.

The approach proposed by Bertino could be extended to allow to specify that a given method can be unconditionally invoked by some users and it can be invoked by some other users only inside execution of certain method. For example, with reference to the example above, user Smith can be granted an authorization for method "modify-salary". Hence, while Jones will be allowed to execute this method only inside the execution of "review-status", Smith will be also allowed to invoke it directly or inside the execution of other methods.

Considerations of authorizations to execute methods requires to extend the authorization model by including methods in the set of subjects S. Let M denote all methods defined on the objects of the system. Then, the new set of subjects is $S = U \cup G \cup M$. Since methods can be authorized to execute methods on different objects, in the specification of the authorizations the subject field must indicate also the object to which this method is referred. For example, authorization $\langle$ review-status:$\#o_1$, modify-salary, $\#o_1$ $\rangle$ states that method "review-status" executing on object $\#o_1$ is authorized to execute method "modify-salary" on object $\#o_1$.

Access requests are therefore now characterized as 4-tuple of the form $\langle u, m : o, o, a\rangle$. Tuple $\langle u, m : o, o', a\rangle$ states that method m, executing on object o on behalf of user u requires to exercise access mode a on object o'.

3.4 Authorizations' object

In the basic authorization model, the authorizations for an access mode on an object must be specified on the object itself. The authorization model should allow the specification of authorizations on objects of different granularity. In particular it should be possible to specify authorizations on single objects as well as on entire classes, or databases. Authorizations specified on an object should be considered valid on all the objects contained in it. For example, authorizations referred to a database should be considered valid on all classes contained in the database. Authorizations specified on classes should be considered valid on all the instances of the class. This would allow make easier the specification of authorizations. If a user must be authorized to execute a method on all instances of a class, just one authorization can be specified for the user for the method on the class instead that one authorization for every instance of the class. For example, authorization ⟨ Jones, read, EMPLOYEE ⟩ indicates that Jones can read all instances of class EMPLOYEE.

Authorizations referred to objects which are to be considered valid on all the objects the objects contained it have been considered by Rabitti et Al. in [28] and by Bertino and Weigand in [7]. For example, in these models, the authorizations for the read access mode on a class implies the authorizations for the read access mode on all instances of the class. These models allow also, given an authorization on an object o, to derive authorizations for the objects in which o is contained. For example, the authorization to read an instance of a class implies the authorizations to read the definition of the class.

3.5 Access control

The access control examines each access request and determines whether the request must be granted or denied on the basis of the specified authorizations. So far we have considered that every access is checked against the authorization base and granted only if the user (or the method executing on behalf of the user) has the necessary authorization. This implies that every time the execution of a method is requested, an access control must be executed. This need of multiple access control during a method execution may significantly impact on the performance of the system. It would therefore be desirable to keep the number of access controls to be executed at run time as minimum as possible.

An approach to avoid access control at run-time has been proposed by Ahad et Al. in the context of the IRIS authorization model [2]. This model distinguishes between methods with *static* authorization and methods with dynamic authorization. If a method m is defined to have static authorization, possible method invocations required during the execution of m will be allowed without need of further access controls. Then, a user authorized for method m will be able to successfully complete the execution of m also if he does not have the authorization for further methods which m may directly or indirectly invoke. By contrast, if a method m is defined to have dynamic authorization, all invocations required during execution of m will be checked and allowed only if the user has the necessary authorizations. When creating a method, a user must specify whether the authorization of the method are to be checked statically or dynamically. In either case, the method creator must have the authorization on all the methods invoked by the method being defined. If the creator of a method specifies that the method is to have static authorization, he cannot grant other users the authorization for the method unless he has the authorization to grant all methods invoked by m. Otherwise, existing security constraints could be violated.

Another approach where a user can successfully complete the execution of a method without having the authorization for all the methods which the first method may invoke has been proposed by Bertino in [5]. The approach is based on the concept of *protection mode* for method execution authorizations. When the authorization to execute a method m is granted by a user u to a user u' in protection mode, all authorization invocations made by m when executing on behalf of u' are not checked against the authorizations of u'.

The consideration of authorizations to execute method in protection model requires to extend the model by including, in the authorizations: (i) the indication of whether the authorization is granted in protection mode, and (ii) the grantor of the authorization. Then, an authorization should now be described as a 5-tuple of the form $\langle s, a, o, g, pm \rangle$. Tuple $\langle s, a, o, g, pm \rangle$ indicates that subject s can exercise access mode a on object o and that this authorization was granted by user g. Element pm indicates whether the authorization is granted in protection mode ($pm =$ "yes") or not ($pm =$ "no").

3.6   Administration of authorizations

An authorization model must include policies and mechanisms for the administration of authorizations. Administrative policies determine who is allowed to modify the Authorization Base, i.e., to grant and revoke authorizations. In the basic authorization model we have considered granting and revocation of authorizations to be privilege tasks of a special user, called *administrator*. This approach is generally called *centralized* administration. However, the centralized administration approach may be too rigid. In particular, under this approach the creator of an object is not able to autonomously managing the authorizations on his own objects. To give users the possibility of specifying authorizations, authorization models generally apply the *ownership* policy. Under this approach, the owner of an object can grant and revoke other users authorizations on his own objects.

The application of the ownership policy to object-oriented systems is not straightforward. Indeed, in object-oriented systems, classes represent just templates from which several users can derive their own instances. Then, different users can create objects belonging to the same class. As a result, instances of the same class may have different owners. The application of the ownership policy would therefore require single instances to be independently administered. Indeed, if the authorization model were not to allow single instances to be independently administered, users may have to create subclasses only for the purpose of being able to administrate their own instances. On the other hand, the decentralization at the instance level may sometimes be inconvenient for performance and also for conciseness.

Another problem concerning the application of the ownership policy in object-oriented systems is the fact that instances belonging to a class may have an owner different from the owner of the class itself. Then, the model must determine the control that the owner of a class can have on authorizations on the instances of his class which have been defined by other users.

The problem of authorization administration with particular consideration to the application of the ownership policy in object-oriented systems has been discussed by Bertino and Weigand in [7]. In the model presented in [7] it is possible to specify whether a class has to be *centrally* or *decentrally* administered. If a class is decentrally administered every user creating an instance of the class is considered the owner of the instance and can grant and revoke other users authorizations to access the instance. If a class is centrally administered, all instances of a class are considered to have the same owner, called *class administrator*. Then, instances of the class created by any user are considered to belong to the class administrator. The administration modality (decentralized vs. centralized) for a class is declared when the class is defined. It is possible, however, to change the modality later on. In particular, when the class is centrally administered, the class administrator can change the administration of the class from centralized to decentralized. Changing the class administration from decentralized to centralized requires the authority of a database administrator that can name the proper class administrator.

A similar problem concerns the control that the owner of a class should have on subclasses derived from his class by other users. In particular, a problem is whether the owner of a class should automatically receive authorizations on the subclasses and their instances. There are two approaches which can be taken with respect to this. The first approach is that the owner of a class should not automatically receive any authorization on the subclasses derived from his class by other users. The motivation behind this this approach is that object-oriented systems encourage the specialization of existing classes and thereby promote the reuse of existing specifications. This approach allows users to reuse existing classes without compromising the protection of the subclasses generated.

The second approach is that the owner of a class should automatically receive authorizations on the subclasses derived from his class by other users. This approach has the drawback that a user wishing to derive a class from another class would not have any privacy on the instances of the subclass (which are readable by the creator of the superclass). Therefore, users could be discouraged from reusing existing classes, not taking advantage of the characteristic of inheritance.

With respect to query processing, the first approach implies that an access whose scope is a class and its subclasses will be evaluated only against those classes for which the user issuing the query has the read authorization, whereas in the second approach, it would be evaluated against the class and all its subclasses.

The problem of determining the authorizations of the owner of a class on subclasses generated by other users has been discussed by Rabitti et Al. in the context of the ORION authorization model [28]. This model adopts the first of the two approaches presented above as default, and supports the second as a user option. Therefore, unless explicitly required, the owner of the class will not receive any authorization on the subclasses derived from his class by other users.

3.7 Propagation of authorizations

Object-oriented systems allow the derivation of subclasses from existing classes. Then, the problem arises of determining whether the authorizations a user owns on a class propagate along the class inheritance hierarchy; that is, whether the authorizations that a user owns on a class must be considered valid also on the subclasses of this class. For example, consider authorization ⟨ Jones, read, EMPLOYEE ⟩ stating that user Jones can read all instances of class EMPLOYEE. The problem consists in deciding whether this authorization should allow Jones to read also the instances of class MANAGER which is a subclass of class EMPLOYEE.

Propagation of authorizations along the inheritance hierarchy has some advantages and some disadvantages.

An approach in which authorizations on a class are automatically propagated to the subclasses has the advantage that in order to give a user the privilege to exercise an access mode on all classes of a hierarchy, it is sufficient to give the user the authorization for the access mode on the root of the hierarchy. Moreover, this approach is more efficient for queries applying to the members of a class and not only to its instances. This approach has been applied in the model proposed by Fernandez et Al. in [11].

However, propagation of authorizations along the inheritance hierarchy has the drawback that a user deriving a class from another class would be constrained to accept on the subclass the authorizations specified on the superclass. This may discourage re-usability of classes. In particular, a user wishing to create a class re-using another class definition would hesitate doing so, since all authorizations holding on a the superclass would automatically hold on his class. Moreover, this approach does not allow to increase the protection of subclasses with respect to superclasses. This approach has been applied in the model proposed by Rabitti et Al. in [28].

3.8 Conditional authorizations

In the basic authorization model, we have considered authorizations stating the privilege for a subject to exercise a given access mode on an object. Then, a subject is either authorized or denied (in he does not have the authorization) for a given access. In some situations it would be desirable to specify conditions which have to be satisfied for the execution of a given authorization. Then, the authorization model should also allow the specification of conditional authorizations, whose validity depend on the satisfaction of constraints on data. For example, it may be desirable to specify that a manager can update the salary only of his owns employees, that an employee can read only data regarding its own department, and so on.

The problem of conditional authorizations has been studied in the context of relational databases. There, conditional authorizations have been considered to allow specification of authorizations to hold only on a subset of the tuples in a table. Two approaches have been used to enforce conditional authorizations in relational databases. The first approach is based on the concept of *view*. If users have to be restricted to operate on the tuples of a table which satisfy some conditions, then, a view is defined with the conditions of the authorization as selection conditions for the view. Then users are given authorizations on the view instead that on the base relation. The approach based on views has some limitations. In particular, it requires the specification of a view for each possible conditional access which must be enforced. Moreover, in this approach, changes in the conditions of an access would entail changes to the view definition. The second approach is the so called *query modification mechanism*. This approach allows the specification of conditions in the authorizations. Every time a user requires to exercise an access and the authorization for the access contains some conditions, the query is modified by including such conditions. Then, enforcement of the conditions is delegated to the underlying database system. This approach has the advantage to allow an easy and flexible specification of conditions for different users.

Consideration of conditional authorizations in object-oriented systems is more problematic.

Some approaches to enforce conditional access in object-oriented systems have been proposed by Ahad et Al. in [2].

The first approach is based on the definition of derived methods.[2] This approach takes advantage of the encapsulation property of object-oriented systems by embedding the specification of conditions inside the method specification. If some conditions must be enforced for the execution of a given method m by some users, a new method m' is derived from m which checks for the satisfaction of the conditions. Then, users for which the conditions are required to hold will not be authorized to invoke method m. Instead they will be given the authorization on the derived method. For example, consider a method "salary" which returns the salary of an employee. Suppose that an employee should be authorized to see only the salary lower than \$10,000. This constraint can be enforced by deriving a new method, "restricted-salary", which invokes method salary and returns the calling user only the salary of the objects which satisfy the condition above. Then, instead of giving users the authorizations for method "salary", they are given authorization for the method "restricted-salary". However, this approach has the drawback of embedding security specification inside code specification. Therefore authorizations are no longer orthogonal to the semantics of the methods. A change in the security requirements would imply changing the method specification. Moreover, embedding security specification inside the code makes them more vulnerable from unauthorized modifications. In particular, changes to the code should be strictly controlled to avoid improper modifications of the security constraints. Furthermore, the implementation of methods becomes more complicated and unnatural because of the embedded authorization checks.

The second approach is based on the concept of *guard* methods. Guard methods are methods which can be used to restrict the execution of other methods. Each method can be associated a guard method. Suppose a guard method g is associated to another method m. Then when method m is invoked the guard method is executed first. If the guard method complete successfully method m is executed. Otherwise, method m is not executed. Then, executing method m with guard method g is equivalent to executing the expression "if g then m else return null". Conditional execution of a method can therefore be enforced by associating the method a guard method evaluating the condi-

---

[2]In [2] the term function is used instead of method. However, for consistency with the rest of the paper we prefer to use the term method.

tions. To guarantee the correctness in the application of guard methods the model requires guard methods to not be themselves guarded and to not have any side-effects on persistent data. Guard methods have the advantage that they do not modify the source code of the methods whose execution must be restricted. Hence, guard method can be installed at any time without disrupting the system. However, their application is limited. Indeed, a method can be associated only a guard method. Therefore, it is not possible, with guard methods, to enforce different conditions to be satisfied for different users or groups of users.

The third approach is based on the concept of *proxy* methods. Proxy methods provides different implementations of given methods for different users. A given method may have associated different proxy methods, each of which executable by different users (or groups of users). Proxy methods are similar to the derived methods illustrated above. The difference is that proxy methods allow also to evaluate conditions on the identity of the user invoking the method. Like derived methods, proxy methods have the drawback of adding a significant amount of overload to the implementation process.

It would be desirable to allow the specification of conditions on authorizations in the definition of the authorizations themselves. The conditions should be enforced automatically by the access control system. This would allow to keep security specification cleanly separated from the method specification. Therefore changes to authorization specifications would not imply any changes to the underlying code implementation. Then, an authorization in the authorization model would now be characterized as a 6-tuple $\langle s, a, o, u, pw, c \rangle$. Where the value of the first five elements is as illustrated in subsection 3.5 and element c indicates the conditions which have to be satisfied in order for the authorization to hold. For example suppose that class EMPLOYEE has an attribute indicating the manager of the employee. Then, the authorization for user Jones to execute method "salary" on all his employees could be expressed by the following authorization (Jones, salary, EMPLOYEE, Smith, no, Employee.manager=Jones). An approach allowing the specification of conditions inside the authorizations has been proposed by Bertino and Weigand [7].

3.9 Inter-related authorizations

Objects may be related on another. For example, instances are related to the classes to which they belong. Classes are related to the database in which they are contained, and so on. Therefore, in order to execute an operation on an object, the user may need to have some authorizations on other objects. For example, in order to execute a method on an instance a user must be able to access the class in which to which the instance belong. Analogously, in order to access a class, a user must be able to access the database in which the class is contained. Therefore, in order to exercise an access a user may need to have several authorizations. There are basically two approaches to this problem. The first approach consists in automatically giving, to the user authorized for an access, the authorizations necessary for the execution of the access. This approach has been adopted in the ORION authorization model [28]. In particular, in ORION, every time a new authorization is granted, all authorizations necessary for the execution of this new authorization are derived. For instance, according to this approach, if a user is authorized for the read access mode on an object, the user is implicitly given the authorization for the read definition access mode on the class containing the object. The other approach consists in requiring that, in order to exercise an access, a user must be esplicitly authorized for all the necessary related accesses. For instance, according to this approach, in order to read an object the user must be explicitly given, besides the authorization to read an object, the authorization to read the definition of the class containing the object. An example of this approach, in the context of operating systems, is the Unix operating system, where, for example, to exercise any privilege on a file a user needs to have the execute privilege on the directory in which the file is contained. This latter approach has the drawback that it may require the specification of many authorizations. However, it has the advantage that it allows to enforce a more strict control on the authorizations given to users.

3.10   Negative and positive authorizations

In the basic authorization model, as in most of the models existing in the literature, we have considered only positive authorizations, i.e., authorizations giving users the privilege to exercise accesses. Under this approach the lack of an authorization is interpreted as negative authorization. Therefore, whenever a user is trying to access an object, if the user does not own any authorization for the access, the access is denied. This approach has a major problem in that the lack of a given authorization for a given user does not prevent this user from receiving this authorization later on. For example, suppose that user u is not meant to access a given object. In situations where the administration of authorization is decentralized it might happen that a user possessing the right to administrate an object, by mistake grants u the authorization to that object. Therefore, it is not possible to enforce the constraint that a user is not supposed to access an object. This would be possible if negative authorizations could be specified in the authorization model. An explicit negative authorization expresses a denial for a user to exercise a given method on a given object. Beside allowing the specification of this type of constraint, negative authorizations allow the specification of exceptions to authorizations. For example, suppose that all users of a group but one must be authorized to execute a method on a given object. If only positive authorizations are considered in order to express this, all single users of the group, but u, must be given the authorization for the access. By contrast, the consideration of negative authorizations allow to specify the above constraint by giving the group the positive authorization for the access and user u the negation for it. As another example, suppose that user u must be authorized to access all instances of a class but instance $\#o_1$. This constraint can be expressed by giving the user a positive authorizations for the access on the class and a negative authorization for the access on instance $\#o_1$.

However, while negative authorizations give the authorization model more expressive power, they also introduce the possibility of conflicts among negative and positive authorizations. It is possible to have at a same time two authorizations, one stating that a given user must be authorized the execution of a given access mode on an object, and the other one stating that the user must be denied the same access mode. Therefore a policy for resolving possible conflicts must be provided. The usual approach for solving conflicts between authorizations is to adopt the *denials-take-precedence* policy. According to this policy if a user is both denied and authorized for a given access, the user will not be able to exercise the access. The advantage of this policy is that when conflicting authorizations are granted, the safest solution is taken by not allowing the user to exercise the access. However, this policy has the drawback that it does not permit exceptions to negative authorizations. For example, suppose that all members of a group must be denied for an access, except for user u, who must be authorized. If a negative authorization is specified for the group as a whole and a positive authorization is specified for u, the negative authorization specified for the group would prevent u from using the positive authorization granted him. Thus, to express the above requirement under the denials-take-precedence policy, every single member of the group, except u, must be given a negative authorization for the access; whereas a positive authorization must be granted to u. This example illustrates the rigidity of the denials-take-precedence policy.

More flexible policies for resolving possible conflicts between negative and positive authorizations have been proposed [28,11,9]. These approaches are based on the concept of more specific authorizations. Intuitively more specific authorizations are authorizations which are referred to more specific subjects (for example a user is more specific than a group to which the user belongs) and more specific object (for example an instance is more specific than a subclass).

An authorization model for the protection of information in object-oriented systems which considers positive as well as negative authorizations is the ORION authorization model. This model allows authorizations (either positive or negative) to be overridden by more specific authorizations (either negative or positive). To give users the possibility of specifying authorizations which will be certainly obeyed, the method distinguishes between *weak* and *strong* authorizations. Weak authorizations can be overridden whereas strong authorizations cannot.

Another model considering both positive and negative authorizations has been proposed by Fernandez et Al. in [11]. In this model, negative authorizations are used to stop the propagation of authorizations along the inheritance hierarchy. In particular, in the model a user authorized for an access on a class is considered authorized for that access on the subclasses of the class unless he is given an explicit negative authorization on them. For example, consider authorization ⟨ Jones, read, EMPLOYEE ⟩ . Suppose that class EMPLOYEE has subclasses MANAGER and SECRETARY. The above authorization allows Jones to read the instances of class EMPLOYEE as well as the instances of classes MANAGER and SECRETARY. Suppose now that the following authorization is specified ⟨ Jones, ¬read, MANAGER ⟩. Now user Jones will be allowed to read all instances of classes EMPLOYEE and SECRETARY. However, he will not be allowed to read the instances of class MANAGER.

The consideration of negative authorizations requires to extend the authorization model. In particular, authorizations must be extended to indicate whether an authorization is positive or negative. This can be done by extending the access modes to the consideration of negative access modes (e.g., ¬ read, ¬write) or by adding a new element to the authorization tuple stating the sign of the authorization.

4 Conclusions

Object-oriented systems, semantically richer than traditional data management systems, arise new protection requirements that conventional authorization models do not satisfy. This paper has illustrated the issues which must be considered in the development of an authorization model for the protection of object-oriented systems. In the paper, we have also discussed possible solutions for the satisfaction of the new protection requirements and illustrated how they can be expressed in the authorization model.

References

[1] S.K. Abdali, G.W. Cherry, and N. Soiffer "A Smalltalk System for Algebraic Manipulation," *Proc. of the ACM Conf. on Object-Oriented Programming Systems, Languages, and Applications (OOPSLA)*, Portland, Oregon, September 1986.

[2] R. Ahad, et al., "Supporting Access Control in an Object- Oriented Database Language," *Proc. Third International Conference on Extending Database Technology (EDBT)*, Vienna, Austria, Springer-Verlag Lecture Notes in Computer Science, Vol. 580, 1992.

[3] E. Bertino, and L. Martino, "Object-Oriented Database Management Systems: Concepts and Issues" *Computer* (IEEE), April 1991.

[4] E. Bertino, M. Negri, G. Pelagatti, L. Sbattella, "Object-Oriented Query Languages: the Notion and the Issues" *IEEE Trans. on Knowledge and Data Engineering*, Vol. 4, No. 3, 1992.

[5] E. Bertino, "Data Hiding and Security in an Object-Oriented Database System," *Proc. Eighth IEEE International Conference on Data Engineering*, Phoenix, Arizona, February 1992.

[6] E. Bertino, "A View Mechanism for Object-Oriented Databases" *Proc. of the International Conference on Extending Database Technology (EDBT)*, 1992.

[7] E.Bertino, H.Weigand, "An Approach to Authorization Modeling in Object-Oriented Database Systems" to appear in *Data and Knowledge Engineering*, (North-Holland), 1993.

[8] E. Bertino, S. Jajodia, P. Samarati, "Access Controls in Object-Oriented Database Systems - Some Approaches and Issues" in *Advanced Database Systems*, N.R. Adam and B.K. Bhargava, eds., Springer-Verlag, 1993.

[9] E. Bertino, S. Jajodia, P. Samarati, "A Flexible Authorization Mechanism for Relational Databases" submitted for publication.

[10] O.Deux, et Al., "The Story of O2" *IEEE Trans. on Knowledge and Data Engineering*, Vol. 2, N. 1, 1990.

[11] E. B. Fernandez, E. Gudes, and H. Song, "A security model for object-oriented databases," *Proc. IEEE Symposium on Security and Privacy*, May 1989, pp. 110–115.

[12] E. B. Fernandez, E. Gudes, and H. Song, "A model of evaluation and administration of security in object-oriented databases," *to appear in IEEE-TKDE*.

[13] D. Fishman, et Al. "Overview of the Iris DBMS" *Object-Oriented Concepts, Databases, and Applications*, W. Kim, and F. Lochovsky, eds., Addison-Wesley, 1989.

[14] N. Gal-Oz, E. Gudes, E. B. Fernandez, "A model of methods authorization in object-oriented databases," *Proc. Very Large Data Bases (VLDB) Conference*, Dublin, Ireland, August 1993.

[15] D. Garlan, "Views for Tools in Integrated Environments," Ph.D. dissertation, Carnegie-Mellon, University, Pittsburgh, PA, 1987.

[16] I.P. Goldstein, and D.G. Bobrow, "A Layered Approach to Software Design," Xerox Palo Alto Research Center, Tech. Rep. CSL-80-5, December 1980.

[17] I.P. Goldstein, and D.G. Bobrow, "An Experimental Description-Based Programming Environment: Four Reports," Xerox Palo Alto Research Center, Tech. Rep. CSL-81-3, December 1981.

[18] E. Gudes, H. Song, and E. B. Fernandez, "Evaluation of negative and predicate -based authorization in object-oriented databases," *Database Security Iv: Status and Prospects*, s. Jajodia and C. Landwehr (eds.), North-Holland, 1991.

[19] A.N. Habermann, C. Krueger, B. Pierce, B. Staudt, and J. Wenn "Programming with Views," Tech. Report, Dept. of Computer Science, Carnegie Mellon Uni., Pittsburgh, PA, January 1988.

[20] B. Hailpern, and H. Ossher, "Extending Objects to Support Multiple Interfaces and Access Control", *IEEE Trans. on Software Engineering*, vol. 16, no. 11, November 1990.

[21] W. Kim, et Al. "Composite Object Support in an Object-Oriented Database Systems" *Proc. of the Second International Conference on Object-Oriented Programming Systems, Languages, and Applications (OOPSLA)*, Orlando (Florida), October 1987.

[22] W. Kim, E. Bertino, J. Garza, "Composite Objects Revisited" *Proc. of ACM-SIGMOD Conference on Management of Data*, Portland, Oregon, May 29-June 3, 1989.

[23] W. Kim, N. Ballou, H.T. Chou, J. Garza, D. Woelk, "Features of the ORION Object-Oriented Database System" *Object-Oriented Concepts, Databases, and Applications*, W. Kim, and F. Lochovsky, eds., Addison-Wesley (1989).

[24] W. Kim, "Object-Oriented Databases: Definitions and Research Directions" *IEEE Trans. on Knowledge and Data Engineering*, Vol. 2, N.3, 1990.

[25] J. Millen, and T. Lunt, "Security for Object-Oriented Database Systems" *Proc. of the IEEE Symposium on Research in Security and Privacy*, Oakland, California, May 1992.

[26] N.H. Minsky, "A Law-Based Approach to Object-Oriented Programming," *Proc. of the Second International Conference on Object-Oriented Programming Systems, Languages, and Applications (OOPSLA)*, Orlando (Florida), October 1987.

[27] N.H. Minsky, "Law-Governed Systems," *Software Engineering Journal*, September 1991.

[28] F. Rabitti, E. Bertino, W. Kim, and D. Woelk, "A Model of Authorization for Next-Generation Database Systems" *ACM Trans. on Database Systems*, March 1991.

[29] J. Richardson, P. Schwarz, and L.F. Cabrera, "CACL: Efficient Fine-Grained Protection for Objects", *Proc. of the Seventh International Conference on Object-Oriented Programming Systems, Languages, and Applications (OOPSLA)*, Vancouver, British Columbia, Canada, 1992.

[30] S. Zdonik, "Object-oriented Type Evolution" *Advances in Database Programming Languages*, F.Bancilhon, and P.Buneman, eds., Addison-Wesley, 1990.

[31] S.M. Watt, R.D. Jens, R.S. Sutor, and B.M. Trager, "The Scratchpad II Type System: Domains and Subdomains," in *Computing Tools for Scientific Problem Solving*, A.M. Miola, ed., New York Academy, 1990.

Part IV: Multilevel Applications, Systems, and Issues

Using Object Modeling Techniques To Design MLS Data Models

Myong H. Kang
Judith N. Froscher
Naval Research Laboratory,
Washington, D.C. 20375

Oliver Costich
George Mason University,
Fairfax, Virginia 22030

Abstract

The expressiveness of the data model has a significant impact on the functionality of the resulting database system. The more general the data model, the less need be lost when the conceptual model is mapped onto a particular data model.

In this paper, we explain how MLS data models can lead to a loss of database functionality or the inability to model some real world phenomena if data models are not kept general and independent of other considerations. We also present our positions with respect to developing MLS data models for MLS database systems using the object modeling technique (OMT).

1 Introduction

Figure 1 shows a typical idealized approach to database development. Requirements are analyzed and represented in a conceptual model of the problem domain which is independent of any anticipated architectural or implementation features. A logical structural model, based on a particular data model, (e.g., relational, object-oriented), is then produced by the development of particular data structures, algorithms, constraints, etc. which are appropriate to a specific data model. Mapping this logical model to a particular architecture results in the system design, which is used to implement the database on a DBMS.

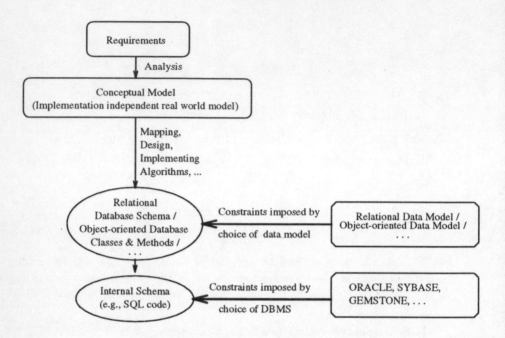

Figure 1: A Database Design Approach.

This approach relies critically on the data model to produce a database system which satisfies the requirements and can be implemented on a given architecture and platform. Thus the expressiveness of the data model has a significant impact on the functionality of the resulting database system. The more general the data model, the less need be lost when the conceptual model is mapped onto a particular data model. The data model should represent the data structures, relationships, and operations defined by a data management paradigm without imposing constraints needed for the physical representation of the system on a particular architecture.

For MLS database systems, the semantics of the security labels are a part of the system's requirements and must be carried through all stages of the development process. In particular, an MLS data model (e.g., relational, object-oriented) is now required. It is our position that this data model should be abstract and independent of other system considerations and should correctly represent security label semantics. The conventional relational data model, with its schema and relational algebra, is a good example of this level of abstraction and independence.

Below we give examples of how MLS data models can lead to a loss of database functionality or the inability to model some real world phenomena if data models are not kept general and independent of other considerations. In other words, failure to separate concerns when developing a data model can lead to loss of functionality in the expressiveness of the resulting data model. We then proceed to our second position that some object-oriented conceptual design tools (e.g., OMT) are useful for developing MLS data models.

2   Consequences of Commingling Concerns

Figure 2 shows a process for MLS data model development which appears to have been used for a relational MLS system. The conventional relational data model is augmented to incorporate the semantics of the labeling policy. This in itself does not necessarily lead to problems, but when considered simultaneously with the architectural constraints which are imposed by the MLS solution, it can lead to loss of some database functionality. Such losses may be inevitable with some architectures, but failure to separate data model issues from architectural constraints prevents detecting the cause of the losses.

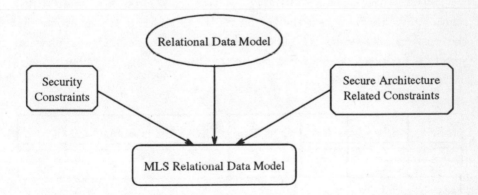

Figure 2: Architecture specific approach to define MLS Data Model.

2.1 Uniform Classification of Keys

Consider the following *many-to-many* association (figure 3) in object modeling notation [1]:

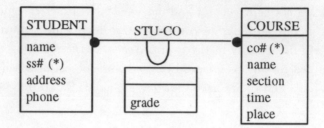

Figure 3: Many-to-many association.

If these objects and their association are mapped to the conventional relational database model, there will be three tables:

STUDENT(ss#, name, address, phone)
COURSE(co#, name, section, time, place)
STU-CO(ss#, co#, grade)

where ss# is the key for STUDENT relation, co# is the key for COURSE relation, and {ss#, co#} is the key for STU-CO relation. It is plausible that the existence of a student is confidential but the existence of some courses are secret. If a student takes a secret course then we may have the following entry in the STU-CO relation:

SS#	SS#_C	CO#	CO#_C	GRADE	GRADE_C	TL
1234	C	55	S	A	S	S

This entry shows that the student, whose SS# is 1234 and whose existence is confidential, took a secret course 55 and received a grade of A. A person whose clearance dominates secret can generate or view such a tuple without violating the security policy.

Some MLS relational data models have this restriction (i.e., that the key should be uniformly classified). We believe that this restriction stems from the decomposition and reconstruction techniques of kernelized architectures [2] rather than from any general security-imposed necessity. Other architectures[1] can support the representation and manipulation of such tuples securely.

If a MLS DBMS system enforces this restriction (i.e., uniform classification of the key), then instead of the above tuple, the following tuple will be generated:

SS#	SS#_C	CO#	CO#_C	GRADE	GRADE_C	TL
1234	S	55	S	A	S	S

First, this restriction obscures which tuple in the STUDENT relation is being referenced. Second, if the system allows polyinstantiation, and enforces referential integrity [3], then problems arise. For example, consider what happens when the STUDENT relation includes an unclassified tuple where ss# = 1234. If an unclassified user deletes a tuple whose ss# is 1234, then the system should enforce referential integrity. However, due to this confusion of labels for the same key element, the system cannot decide whether the tuple above should be deleted from STU-CO relation.

2.2 Expressive Power of Tuple-level and Element-level Classification

One of the strengths of the relational model is that new views of data can be created by combining relations through key references. It has been suggested that, for base relations, tuple-level labeling is no less (and no more) expressive than element(attribute value)-level labeling [4].

Considering again the example of the previous section, we notice that the information in STU-CO cannot be obtained from STUDENT and COURSE alone, and therefore must be a base relation. The labels of the elements of STU-CO may all be different, so that resorting to a single tuple-level label must lead to a loss of information (figure 4).

---

[1] This tuple can be produced in the replicated architecture by the following SQL statement insert into STU-CO select . . . from STUDENT, COURSE where . . .

This confusion arises, we believe, because [4] uses a concept of *well-formed referential dependency* which requires that a foreign key either be the primary key or lie in the complement of the primary key. This definition appears to be motivated by the kernelized architecture, which has difficulty in dealing with more general referential dependencies. We note that our example does not satisfy the definition of well-formed referential dependency but that ss# and co# are foreign keys in the more general use of the term [3].

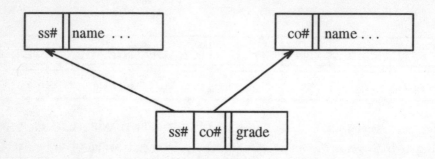

Figure 4: Referential dependencies among three tables.

2.3 Difficulty of Enforcing Referential Integrity

Briefly, the referential integrity property states that if base relation R2 includes a foreign key, FK, matching the primary key, PK, of relation R1, then every value of FK in R2 must either be equal to a value of PK in R1 or be null.

In a MLS relational database, if the deletion of one tuple can cause the deletion of another tuple with a lower security classification, a covert channel could be established. Therefore, if a tuple contains a foreign key (FKT), the security level of that tuple must dominate that of the corresponding primary key tuple (PKT).

Even though referential integrity is considered important in conventional relational databases, proposed MLS relational data models either exclude this integrity [2, 5] or consider it too difficult to enforce. For example, if a lower level operation deletes a lower level PKT, then either higher level FKTs have to be deleted or the value of FK should be set to null. Since the lower level operation has to trigger some mechanism to either delete or update higher level tuples and no other operation should be executed between these two lower-

and higher-level operations, it is considered too difficult to implement in the kernelized architecture [6]. Enforcing MLS referential integrity can be readily supported in the replicated architecture and should be investigated for the trusted subject architecture. Thus the difficulty of enforcing referential integrity is a consequence of the architecture and not inherent in data models of MLS database systems.

3 An Approach To Developing MLS Data Models

We take the following positions with respect to developing MLS data models for MLS database systems:

1. The methodology should embody separation of concerns: making decisions which constrains the development process as late as possible.

2. The semantics of security labeling is a constraint on the conceptual model and must be addressed at that stage of model development.

3. Constraints imposed by the choice of architecture should be dealt with when an architecture is chosen.

4. Object modeling techniques (e.g., OMT [1]) are very powerful in terms of expressive power at the conceptual level and are promising tools in MLS data model development.

Figure 5 represents these positions with respect to development of MLS relational or object-oriented data models. As development of the data model progresses, each imposition of further constraints reduces the expressive power of the model at the previous stage.

Separation of concerns permits one to recognize what the next set of constraints imposes on the features of the previous stage. This leads to a better understanding of the roles of constraints imposed by the security policy, data model type, or choice of architecture. In the MLS relational case, for example, the goal is to define a data model which is independent of the choice of architecture, and depends only on the relational concept. By comparing this standard MLS data model to an architecture specific data model,

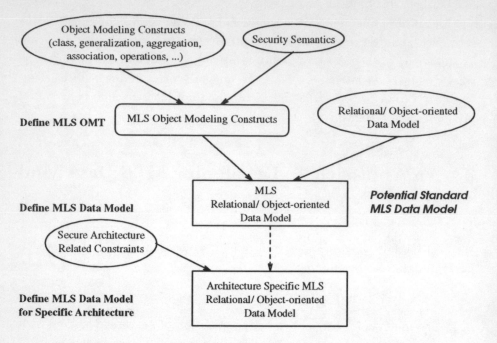

Figure 5: A MLS Data Model Development Approach.

- The restrictions due to using a particular security architecture can be easily understood.

- Interoperability among architecture specific data models is promoted.

Position 2 reflects our belief that security features should be modeled in the relationships at the conceptual level and not forced into the conventional data model for a particular type of model.

Our last position is that available object-oriented analytical tools can go a long way toward expressing the abstract concepts of data modeling; and that with little modification, most security labeling relationships can be easily expressed. In particular, the OMT of [1] seems readily adaptable: Keep in mind that the OMT, like the E-R model and its generalizations, was created to be used in system development, not data model development. However, our initial experience shows that the concepts, language, and notation of OMT can be abstracted and applied to data model development.

References

1. Rumbaugh, J., et el. Object-oriented modeling and design, Prentice Hall, 1991

2. Denning, D. E., et el. A multilevel relational data model. IEEE Symposium on Research in Security and Privacy, 1987

3. Date, C. J. An introduction to database systems, Volume I, Addison-Wesley, 1986

4. Qian, X. and Lunt, T. Tuple-level vs. element-level classification. Database Security VI: Status and Prospects, North-Holland, 1993

5. Jajodia, S. and Sandhu, R. Toward a multilevel secure relational data model. Proceedings of ACM SIGMOD International Conference on Management of Data, 1991

6. Maimone, B. and Allen R. Methods for resolving the security vs. integrity conflict. Proceedings of the Fourth RADC Database Security Workshop, 1991

Can We Do Without Monotonically Non-decreasing Levels in Class Hierarchies?

William R. Herndon
The MITRE Corporation
7525 Colshire Drive, McLean, VA 22102, USA

Abstract

Most object-oriented security models require that the security classifications applied to classes be monotonically non-decreasing as one proceeds from class to subclass in a hierarchy. However, this restriction has a number of detrimental consequences for object-oriented software developers and object-database designers. In this position paper, I attempt to demonstrate why monotonically non-decreasing class hierarchies should be avoided in object-oriented security models and then briefly discuss a number of approaches to OODBMS design that make monotonicity restrictions unnecessary.

1 Introduction

In the last 6 years a number of security models incorporating mandatory access control (MAC) for object-oriented (OO) systems and DBMSs have been proposed. Most of these models, such as [JaKo90], [MiLu92], and [Morg90] are designed to control illegal information flows through a combination of message filtering and localizing of state changes to objects. Another model, SODA [KeTs89], prevents illegal information flows through dynamic upgrading of a method's security classification based on the classifications of information read. But all of these models, in some cases implicitly and in some explicitly, have monotonicity restrictions on metadata classifications within the class hierarchy. Specifically, the models require that the classification relationship between class and subclass be monotonically non-decreasing.

Monotonically non-decreasing class hierarchies (hereafter referred to as *restricted hierarchies*) are introduced to solve problems having to do with information flows that arise from inheritance. Operations involving the run-time resolution and activation of methods, in addition to object instantiation operations, may require access to metadata. Because of inheritance, the metadata of any given object instance may exist in the object's class, or in any of its superclasses. To ensure that the metadata is always available, a restricted hierarchy is introduced so that a subject operating at level L is guaranteed to be able to read superclass metadata, all of which is classified at levels dominated by L. The restricted hierarchy also prevents models from breaking down in the presence of potentially illegal inheritance information flows. For instance, [JaKo90] treats inheritance as a series of retrieval messages sent to superclass objects, but without a restricted hierarchy, messages sent from a low subject to a high superclass object would be blocked due to the potential downward flow of information, resulting in unacceptable runtime behavior.

Even though the introduction of restricted hierarchies seems a reasonable solution to inheritance flows, it actually introduces a number of other problems that can hamper the ability of object-database designers to build class hierarchies that accurately represent real-world entities. Therefore, I devote the remainder of this paper to two topics: First, I discuss the problems for data representation that are inherent in a model that uses restricted hierarchies. Second, I discuss a number approaches to OODBMS design that might produce more functional systems than could be built using the existing secure object-oriented models. As with most attempts to increase the utility of secure data models, this one turns out to be a tradeoff between functionality and the amount of trusted code in the system. In this case, however, I believe that the tradeoff is justified.

2 Problems With Restricted Hierarchies

Most of the problems that arise because of the use of restricted hierarchies stem from the observation that specialization in a subclass does not always imply the need for greater, or even equal, sensitivity. Consider the simple class hierarchy depicted in Figure 1.

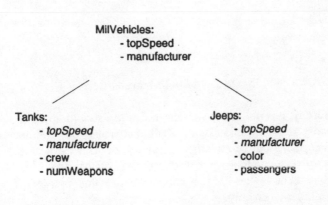

Figure 1. Example Class Hierarchy

214

In this hierarchy a class *MilVehicles* is defined that has a number of attributes with very sensitive definitions. Also depicted are classes *Jeeps* and *Tanks* which inherit the sensitive attributes of class *MilVehicles* and define attributes of their own. Although the additional attributes of class *Tanks* might also be highly sensitive, it is unlikely that the *Jeeps* attributes *color* and *passengers* will require the same high classification.

Models that support only single-level objects, such as [JaKo90] and [LuMi92], tend to force the overclassification of metadata because of the restricted hierarchy. Even if attribute definitions are encapsulated in their own objects in order to provide more realistic classification, they are still referred to by class objects at a higher level, and derived subclasses must still satisfy the monotonicity restriction. Thus overclassification is not circumvented simply by imposing a finer granularity object breakdown on the metadata.

In support of restricted hierarchies, an argument can be made that states that the *IS-A* relationship that applies between class and superclass should also be applied to classification. In other words, (using the classes defined in Figure 1) it is appropriate to classify all metadata of class *Jeeps* at least as high as class *MilVehicles* because a *Jeep* IS-A *MilVehicle*. However, this argument is not valid for all hierarchies because many contemporary OODBMS support multiple-inheritance, where a class inherits attributes and methods of two or more superclasses. Figure 2. depicts such a hierarchy.

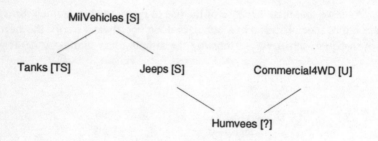

Figure 2. Multiple-Inheritance

In this hierarchy, it is not clear what classification should apply to the *Humvee* class. Presumably many of this classes attributes would be inherited from class *Commercial4WD* and could be classified similarly, perhaps even at U. However, this would not satisfy monotonicity restrictions that require that class *Humvee* be classified at level S or higher. Most models avoid this problem by explicitly assuming single-inheritance only.

Overclassification of metadata (and consequently overclassification of data) and an inability to support multiple-inheritance would reduce the utility of OODBMSs built upon models that use restricted hierarchies. In addition, the class hierarchies of legacy object-databases, designed with accurate representation in mind rather than security, are likely to be subjected to extreme over-classification or underclassification of data when imported into an MLS OODBMS that uses a restricted hierarchy. Therefore, alternatives should be explored that allow restriction free models to be built. A number of alternatives, and their consequences, are briefly covered in the next section.

3 Alternatives to Restricted Hierarchies

Approaches to eliminating monotonicity restrictions differ depending upon what type of OODBMS is to be built; will the system rely primarily on static, compile-time binding or on dynamic, run-time binding? Sections 3.1 and 3.2 discuss each of these alternatives in turn.

3.1 Static Systems

The C++ language does not support run-time polymorphism and only deals with class definitions at compile-time. Many OODBMSs such as ObjectStore and Objectivity are designed to be compatible with C++. Lack of run-time binding eliminates the need for dynamic lookup of metadata and hence the need for a restricted hierarchy. Instead, class metadata can be handled by a trusted subcomponent of the compiler. Metadata necessary for method activation or that defines object structure, but that is classified above the level of the compilation, would not be supplied by the trusted component, and the view of the class available to the application would be level dependant.

Such an approach does have some consequences though. In order to protect against frequent, unexplainable, run-time crashes, the OODBMS should operate with some tranquility restrictions on the class hierarchy. These restrictions might involve preventing updates to the existing class hierarchy by unauthorized individuals, and in order to prevent inadvertent downgrades of metadata information, authorized individuals might have to perform modifications while operating under a special role. Fortunately, such restrictions are analogous to restrictions that already exist in commercial OODBMSs that prevent unexpected changes to object structure. A number of acceptable strategies should become apparent with further study of this approach.

3.2 Dynamic Systems

Potential solutions to the restricted hierarchy problem for OODBMSs that support dynamic binding can be further divided depending on whether the OODBMS keeps tight or loose control over the data that it protects.

OODBMSs that maintain tight control over data are similar to relational DBMSs (RDBMSs) in that the internal state of objects is not available to user programs except through the execution of well defined operations. Even though such operations may be implemented through methods, return results do not take the form of whole objects that are then placed under the control of a user program. Rather, only partial object copies and attribute values are returned. But since such an OODBMS must still perform dynamic resolution in order to execute methods, trusted code must exist in the DBMS in order to overcome the necessity of having a restricted hierarchy. The trusted code must perform two functions. First, the code must filter return results in much the same way that a secure RDBMS filters the tuples returned to an untrusted application. Second, the trusted code must intervene to block the execution of, or must block return values from, method executions that would cause inferences of the existence of higher level metadata.

On the other hand, OODBMSs that maintain loose control over data are intended to allow user programs to operate on database objects directly. In order to maintain security without imposing a restricted hierarchy, the trusted code introduced into the DBMS TCB must filter objects before releasing them into the user program space, as before. But in addition, because user programs operate on the data directly, the DBMS TCB must also provide appropriately filtered metadata on demand so that user programs can perform dynamic resolution and lookup. Because filtered metadata is being supplied, user programs in this scenario might be very similar to those developed to operate against OODBMSs that require static binding, as described in the previous section. However, because the metadata is used dynamically, the user program would appear to be defining classes "on the fly", and this is interesting because the use of so called *virtual* or *lightweight* classes is an ongoing topic of discussion in the OODBMS research community. Techniques may be forthcoming or already available that can be adapted to suit the needs of this approach.

4 Conclusion

The intent of this position paper has been to stimulate thought and discussion on whether monotonicity restrictions in current secure OODBMS models are in fact necessary, and if they are not, how OODBMSs could be constructed that would be free of such restrictions. I feel that if models free of restricted hierarchies can be constructed, using the approaches that I covered in the previous section, or others not yet identified, then the resulting secure OODBMS would exhibit both the utility and security necessary to make them acceptable to a wide spectrum of users.

References

[KeTs89] Keefe, T., W. Tsai, and B. Thuraisingham, "SODA - A Secure Object-oriented Database System," *Computers and Security*, Vol. 8, No. 6, 1989.

[JaKo90] Jajodia, S. and B. Kogan, "Integrating An Object-Oriented Data Model With Multilevel Security," *Proceedings of the 1990 IEEE Symposium on Research in Security and Privacy*, IEEE Computer Society, Oakland, CA, May 1990.

[MiLu92] Millen, J. K. and T. F. Lunt, "Security for Object-Oriented Database Systems," *Proceedings of the 1992 IEEE Computer Society Symposium on Research in Security and Privacy*, IEEE Computer Society, Oakland, CA, May 1992.

[Morg90] Morgenstern, M., "A Security Model for Multilevel Objects With Bidirectional Relationships," *Proceedings of the 4th IFIP Conference on Database Security*, Elsevier/North-Holland, September 1990.

Concurrency, Synchronization, and Scheduling to Support High-assurance Write-up in Multilevel Object-based Computing

Roshan K. Thomas and Ravi S. Sandhu[1]

Center for Secure Information Systems

&

Department of Information and Software Systems Engineering
George Mason University, Fairfax, VA 22030-4444

Abstract

We discuss concurrency, synchronization, and scheduling issues that arise with the support of high-assurance RPC-based (synchronous) write-up actions in multilevel object-based environments. Such environments are characterized by objects classified at varying security levels (called classifications) and accessed by subjects with varying security clearances. A write-up action occurs when a low level object sends a message to a higher one, triggering an update in the latter. While such actions do not directly violate the security policy, their abstract nature in object-based systems poses confidentiality leaks by opening up signaling channels. We present an approach to closing such channels by executing the methods in the sender and receiver objects concurrently, whenever a write-up action is issued. However, these concurrent computations have to be synchronized and scheduled so that they preserve the semantics of the original and synchronous (sequential) execution. We utilize a multi-version synchronization scheme and various scheduling strategies to achieve this.

1 Introduction

We are currently investigating support for secure and efficient RPC-based write-up actions in multilevel object-based computing environments. Such environments are characterized by objects classified at varying security levels (also called classifications or access classes) and accessed by subjects with varying security clearances. These security levels form a lattice structure and mandatory access control is governed by a security policy. The notion of multilevel security originated in the 1960's when the U.S. Department of Defense wanted to protect classified information processed by computers. The Bell-LaPadula (BLP) [1] security model was the first one formally used to implement the military security policy, and even today remains the de facto standard. BLP characterizes (and governs) access control and information flow with the following two rules (l denotes the label of the corresponding subject (s) or object (o)).

---

[1] The work of both authors is partially supported by a grant from the National Security Agency, contract No: MDA904-92-C-5140. We are grateful to Pete Sell, Howard Stainer, and Mike Ware for their support and encouragement.

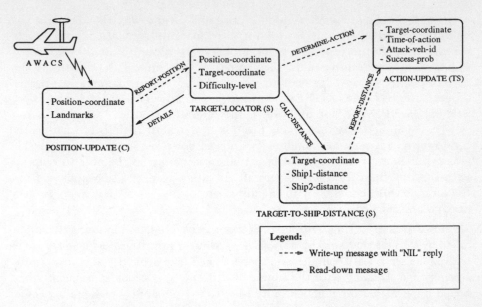

Figure 1: Write-up in situation assesement

- **Simple Security Property.** Subject s can read object o only if $l(s) \geq l(o)$.

- **⋆-Property.** Subject s can write object o only if $l(s) \leq l(o)$.

In a nutshell, the BLP rules boil down to the fact that a low subject cannot read a high object (called a read-up) and a high subject cannot write a low object (called a write-down). But the BLP mandatory rules do allow write-up actions whereby a low level subject can initiate an update in a high object. However, it is interesting to note that most multilevel (ml) systems such as relational ml DBMS's typically do not allow write-up, due to integrity problems arising from the blind nature of write-up operations in these systems.[2] In object-based computing environments, on the other hand, sending messages upwards in the security lattice does not present an integrity problem because such messages will be processed by appropriate methods in the destination object. Further, write-up operations are very useful in many applications.

Figure 1 illustrates a simple situation assessement application in the military setting. The messages REPORT-POSITION, REPORT-DISTANCE, and DETERMINE-ACTION initiate write-up actions. For example, the sending of the REPORT-POSITION message from the lower object POSITION-UPDATE (confidential) to the higher object TARGET-LOCATOR (Secret) results in the invocation of a method that locates a target and updates the attribute 'Target-

---

[2] A good discussion of the conflict between integrity and confidentiality can be found in [4].

coordinate' in the latter. It is important to understand why the above cannot be implemented neatly with read-down operations. In applications such as battle management and process control, processing is often initiated by triggered events in the environment. In such scenarios it is difficult to determine the correct polling window for read-down operations. In our example, the higher object TARGET-LOCATOR would have to periodically poll the lower object POSITION-UPDATE for updates in the aircraft's position. If it polls too slowly, the object may miss many position updates. If it polls too frequently the lower object may be inundated with read-down requests, causing considerable processing overhead, and in extreme cases may not be able to keep up with the vital updates from the aircraft. In either case, position updates from the aircraft will be missed with the disastrous consequence that many targets may go unidentified.

However, supporting write-up operations in object-based systems is complicated by the fact that such operations are no longer primitive read's and write's; but can be arbitrarily complex and therefore can take arbitrary amounts of processing time. Dealing with the timing of write-up operations consequently has broad implications on confidentiality (due to the possibility of signaling channels), integrity, and performance. Consider what happens when a write-up is initiated and methods (computations) are executed serially. Thus the method in the sender object is suspended until the method in the receiver object has finished executing and returns a reply. Now in the security context, the actual contents of the actual reply from the receiver object cannot be to the lower object (this will be prevented by trusted computing base/security kernel). However we may return an innocuous 'nil' reply. But the very timing of the reply can be observed by the low level suspended method when it is resumed, and this information can be exploited for signaling channels [5]. These channels form means through which high-level subjects can leak information to cooperating lower level subjects. It is important to address these channels since it is well known that mandatory access controls do not provide any protection against them.

We are currently investigating an asynchronous computation model to handle write-up actions. This requires concurrent computations (methods) to be generated whenever write-up actions are issued, and for them to be scheduled and synchronized so that the net effect is logically that of a sequential computation (mimicing RPC semantics). In other words, after sending a message to a higher object, the method in the lower sender object continues executing. The method in the receiver object is executed by a newly created *message manager* process. In this way, the signaling channel is closed as a lower level object never has to wait for a higher one. Our work utilizes an underlying message filter security model to enforce basic mandatory confidentiality [3, 6].

While concurrent computations can close signaling channels, we now have to pay the price of providing synchronization. Synchronization is required to ensure that the concurrent computations have the same effect as the intended serial execution. When this is guaranteed we say that the concurrent computa-

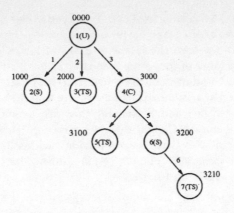

Figure 2: A tree of concurrent computations

tions preserve *serial correctness*. Further, we must ensure that synchronization itself does not cause confidentiality leaks (for otherwise we would be chasing our own tail). To see how serial correctness could be violated, consider again the REPORT-POSITION message in figure 1. Now suppose on receiving the message, the receiver object TARGET-LOCATOR requests additional information about the position identified (such as 'Landmarks') in a read-down message DE-TAILS. In a serial execution, the DETAILS message would correctly retrieve the required information from the lower object POSITION-UPDATE. This is because processing in this object is temporarily suspended and thus its state would not have been updated after the sending of the REPORT-POSITION message. Contrast this with a concurrent execution, where before the arrival of the DETAILS message, the object POSITION-UPDATE may have updated its state (as it is no longer suspended). Hence DETAILS if allowed to retrieve the 'Landmarks' attribute, would erroneously obtain the values for some later target. Our solution to this synchronization problem calls for lower level objects to save their states before sending write-up messages. The DETAILS message would now retrieve the version of POSITION-UPDATE object whose state existed before the write-up message REPORT-POSITION was issued.

2 Concurrency, Synchronization, and Serial Correctness

We now elaborate on concurrency and serial correctness in more general terms. We can visualize a set of concurrent computations as forming a tree such as the one shown in figure 2. The label on the arrows indicate the order in which the messages and the associated computations (methods) would be processed in a serial execution. Note that this order can be derived by a depth-first traversal of the tree. Serial correctness requires that a computation such as 3(TS) in the tree, see all the latest updates of lower level computations to its left, and no updates of lower level computations to its right. Thus 3(TS) should see the latest updates of 2(S) but not of 4(C) and 6(S). This is achieved in our multi-version synchronization scheme by making sure that the versions at levels C (confidential) and S (secret) that are available to 3(TS) are the ones that existed before 4(C) and 6(S) were created (forked). Further, serial correctness also mandates that a computation such as 3(TS) not get ahead of earlier forked ones to its left. Thus 3(TS) should not be started until 2(S) and its children (if any) have terminated.

If no system component has a global snapshot (such as that embedded in a tree) of the entire set of computations, then we need to explicitly capture the global serial order of messages and computations. This can be done by a scheme that assigns a unique forkstamp to each computation, as shown in figure 2. Starting with an initial forkstamp of 0000 for the root, every subsequent child of the root is given a forkstamp by progressively incrementing the most significant digit of this initial stamp by one. To generalize this for the entire tree, we require that with increasing levels, a less significant digit be incremented.

We can now succinctly state the requirements for serial correctness in terms of the following constraints that need to hold whenever a computation c is started at a level l:

- **Correctness-constraint 1:** There cannot exist any earlier forked computation (i.e. with a smaller forkstamp) at level l, that is pending execution;

- **Correctness-constraint 2:** All current non-ancestral as well as future executions of computations that have forkstamps smaller than that of c, would have to be at levels l or higher;

- **Correctness-constraint 3:** At each level below l, the object versions read by c would have to be the latest ones created by computations such as k, that have the largest forkstamp that is still less than the forkstamp of c. If k is an ancestor of c, then the latest version given to c is the one that was created by k just before c was forked.

In summary, the maintenance of serial correctness requires careful consideration on how computations are scheduled as well as on how versions are assigned to process read down requests.

Discussion

In concluding this section on concurrency and synchronization, it is important to note that approaches to synchronization across multiple security levels are heavily influenced by mandatory security rules. These approaches thus

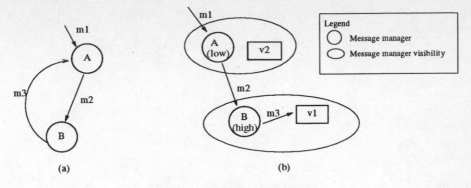

Figure 3: Handling recursion

differ (as they pose a different set of problems) from existing synchronization mechanisms proposed in the literature for general (non multilevel) object-based computing. For example, in asynchronous message passing, the sender and receiver execute concurrently and when the sender needs to access the reply to the message, synchronization is achieved through the notion of futures. When the sender wants the reply from the receiver, it pauses and accesses a *future* data structure to which the receiver would have returned a reply. In the multilevel context, there is no need for futures as a low level sender can never actually access the reply from the higher receiver since this violates mandatory security.

In [2], the authors describe an execution model for distributed object-oriented computation, where methods execute concurrently. To provide synchronization, an approach based on discrete-event simulation is pursued. They describe an interesting scenario with recursion where it may not be possible to finish processing one message before beginning another. As shown in figure 3(a), a message $m1$ is sent to object A, which in turn sends a message $m2$ to object B. A cyclical wait occurs, when B in processing the $m2$ message, sends another message $m3$ back to object A. More precisely, A cannot complete the processing of $m1$ until B completes its own processing of $m2$, and B cannot do this until A completes the processing of message $m3$. Further, if these messages are processed sequentially, serial correctness requires the following: (1) object A should process the $m3$ message with its state not reflecting any of the updates after the message $m2$ was sent; (2) when object A continues processing $m1$ after sending $m2$, its state should reflect all updates intitiated by message $m3$.

How is the above scenario handled in our model when methods execute at different security levels? To start with, we note that a low level object such as A will never have to wait for the processing of message $m2$ sent to the higher level object B. As soon as $m2$ is sent, an immediate reply is returned and A continues processing. The second requirement (listed above) for serial

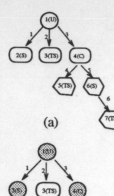
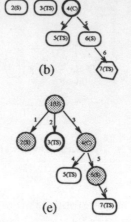
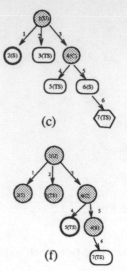

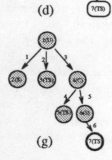

Figure 4: Conservative Scheduling

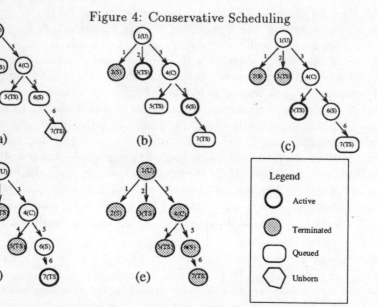

Figure 5: Aggressive Scheduling

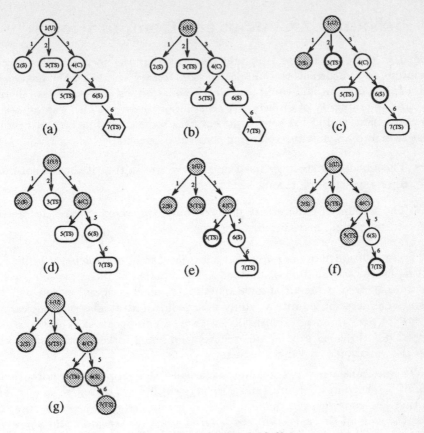

(a)   (b)   (c)

(d)   (e)   (f)

(g)

Figure 6: Hybrid Scheduling

correctness, is trivially satisfied since the message $m3$ can only be a read-down message and can never update the state of object A. The first requirement is satisfied by requiring this read-down message $m3$ to retrieve an older version of object A that existed before $m2$ was sent. This is illustrated in figure 3(b) where object A is required to archive its state as a version $(v1)$ just before the write-up message $m2$ is issued. The message manager for the method in object A resumes execution but now accesses and updates a new version $(v2)$ of object A. Meanwhile, on receiving the message $m2$, the message manager created to process this message suspends execution of the method in object B, and executes the method in object A to process message $m3$. However it now accesses (reads) the older version of $(v1)$ of object A.[3]

---

[3] Whenever this message manager accesses an object classified lower than the level of object B, it will be prevented from writing to such objects. Otherwise, a write-down violation will occur.

3 Scheduling Concurrent Computations

From the above discussion it should be clear that we need to enforce some discipline on concurrent computations as arbitrary concurrency makes synchronization difficult and could lead to the violation serial correctness (thereby affecting the integrity of objects). A scheduling strategy which guarantees serial correctness and at the same time enforces some discipline on concurrency, must take into account the following considerations.

- The scheduling strategy itself must be secure in that it should not introduce any signaling channels.

- The amount of unnecessary delay a computation experiences before it is started should be reduced.

The first condition above requires that a low-level computation never be delayed waiting for the termination of another one at a higher or incomparable level. If this were allowed, a potential for a signaling channel is again opened up. The second consideration admits a family of scheduling strategies offering varying degrees of performance. Informally, we say a computation is unnecessarily delayed if it is denied immediate execution on being forked, for reasons other than the violation of serial correctness.

We now consider two scheduling strategies that appear to approach the ends of a spectrum of secure (and correct) scheduling strategies, and a third one that lies somewhere in the middle of such a spectrum. These schemes that lie at the ends of this spectrum are referred to as *conservative* and *aggressive* schemes, and they are governed by the following invariants, respectively.

Inv-conservative: *A computation is executing at a level l only if all computations at lower levels, and all computations with smaller fork stamps at level l, have terminated.*

Inv-aggressive: *A computation is executing at a level l only if all non-ancestor computations (in the corresponding computation tree) with smaller fork stamps at levels l or lower, have terminated.*

Given a lattice of security levels, the conservative scheme essentially boils down to executing computations on a level-by-level basis in forkstamp order, starting at the lowest level in the lattice. At any point, only computations at incomparable levels can be concurrently executing. However, with the aggressive scheme, we are not following a level-by-level approach. Rather, a forked computation is denied immediate execution only if (at the time of fork) there exists at least one non-ancestral lower level computation with an earlier (smaller) forkstamp, that has not terminated. If denied execution, such a computation is queued and later released for execution when this condition is no longer true (as a result of one or more terminations). A third hybrid strategy can

be formulated by executing computations again on a level-by-level basis, but
allowing the immediate children of any executing computation to proceed as
well. Figures 4, 5, and 6 illustrate the progressive execution of the tree of concurrent computations in figure 2 under the conservative, aggressive, and hybrid
strategies, respectively. In each of these figures, the termination of one or more
computations (indicated by shaded circles) advances the tree to the next stage.
As can be seen in these figures, the tree progresses to termination fastest under
the aggressive scheme, since it induces no unnecessary delays. We conjecture
that there exists several other variations of the above three scheduling schemes.
Finally, it is important to note that the security of these schemes stem from the
fact a low level computation is never suspended (delayed) because of a higher
one.

4   Summary and Conclusions

In this paper, we have briefly discussed the problem of signaling channels in
multilevel object-based computing. The impasse formed by these channels,
appears to be fundamental due to the intrinsic abstract nature of operations in
object-based computing. We have discussed a solution to close these channels
that is based on an asynchronous model of computing and at the price of
providing synchronization. Our approach provides a solution that meets the
conflicting goals of confidentiality, integrity, and performance. We are currently
looking into the scheduling schemes to exploit more intra-level concurrency.
In particular, we are investigating how existing general mechanisms can be
harmoniously incorporated with the mechanisms to provide synchronization
across security levels.

References

[1] D.E. Bell and L.J. LaPadula. Secure computer systems: Unified Expo-
    sition and Multics Interpretation. EDS-TR-75-306, The MITRE Corp.,
    Bedford, MA., March 1976.

[2] E.H. Bensley and T.J. Brando and M.J. Prelle. An execution model for
    distributed object-oriented computation. *Proc. of the ACM OOPSLA con-
    ference*, pp. 316–322, September, 1988.

[3] S. Jajodia and B. Kogan. Integrating an object-oriented data model with
    multi-level security. *Proc. of the 1990 IEEE Symposium on Security and
    Privacy*, pp. 76–85, May 1990.

[4] B. Maimone and R. Allen. Methods for resolving the security vs. integrity
    conflict. In *Proc. of the fourth RADC Database Security Workshop*, Little
    Compton, Rhode Island, April 1991.

[5] R.S. Sandhu, R. Thomas, and S. Jajodia. Supporting timing-channel free computations in multilevel secure object-oriented databases. *Proc. of the IFIP 11.3 Workshop on Database Security,* Sheperdstown, West Virginia, November 1991.

[6] R.K. Thomas and R.S. Sandhu. Implementing the message filter object-oriented security model without trusted subjects. *Proc. of the IFIP 11.3 Workshop on Database Security*, Vancouver, Canada, August 1992.

Secure Database Interoperation via Dynamic Addition of Roles

Vicki E. Jones   Marianne Winslett

Department of Computer Science

University of Illinois at Urbana-Champaign

Urbana, Illinois USA

Abstract

Secure object-oriented database models discuss features necessary to ensure access control to object-oriented data. Discretionary and mandatory access control models have recently been proposed for object-oriented systems. One of the primary discretionary methods proposed is based on the role of a user within the system and is called user role based security. In this paper we discuss the addition of new roles at run time to facilitate interoperation between secure databases which use user role based security. We discuss a promising approach to dynamic addition of roles, and propose future research to develop a role calculus for describing and merging role lattices.

1 Introduction

In recent years many database applications have turned to object-oriented technology to seek solutions for their database needs. Object bases provide a richer set of data types and tighter coupling of the application with the data. However, these object bases do not provide security. Confidentiality is important for many object base applications including those in the health care and credit reporting domains. Databases need to prevent malicious corruption of data and unauthorized access to and use of private information.

Research into database security has been divided into two categories—discretionary access controls (DAC) and mandatory access controls (MAC). DAC systems assign privileges to users based on their particular needs within the application. MAC systems control the reading and writing of data by individuals based on their authorized security clearance level. Recently, commercial application requirements have driven a change in the emphasis for research in database security from mandatory to discretionary controls.

Several models of security in object-oriented databases have been discussed in the literature [1, 2, 3, 4, 5, 7, 9]. Most of these secure object-oriented models are concerned with multilevel object models providing mandatory controls. Models of discretionary access controls have also been proposed ([6, 10], discussed in Section 2), but none of the models address the secure interoperation between databases to allow the secure sharing of information. For example, in the health care industry two hospitals may agree to exchange patient information, but not billing or accounting data. What are the options for facilitating this exchange while retaining discretionary control of access to the data? Within a single database, a promising discretionary access control model has emerged which appears to address the needs of the finer granularity and richer data modeling capabilities of the object-oriented database model and provide a foundation for interoperating between databases: user role based access control. User role based security is based on the needs of an individual at a particular time. Thus authorization depends on the role of the user at the time access is requested. We think that role based security will be the best approach to interoperation of databases while preserving discretionary security.

The set of roles in a system usually forms a partially ordered set (which we will call a *lattice*). We have been developing a *role calculus*, a language to describe the properties of roles and their relationships to other roles. This calculus will make it easier to introduce new roles into an existing lattice, and can also be used to describe the relationships between the role lattices of two different systems. We are interested in developing such a calculus to facilitate secure interoperation between databases, so that a new role can quickly be added to the system, based on its relationships to preexisting roles. Section 3 describes our initial efforts to support dynamic role addition using a simple language, and Section 4 proposes future research.

2 User Role Based Discretionary Access Control

[6] and [10] propose models of authorization which reflect the semantics of object-oriented concepts such as the class hierarchy and methods. [6] refines and extends the notions of implicit authorization, positive and negative authorizations, and strong and weak authorizations in three domains: subjects, objects, and types. [6] also considers strong and weak authorization for authorization subjects and objects, and consistency along the authorization type domain. [10] adds a methodology for designing a user role definition hierarchy and allows the explicit specification of consistency criteria (e.g., equivalence, subsumption). In both models, users or groups of users are grouped according to their roles. An authorization object is a single object or group of objects (in the [10] model authorization objects must be methods) and an authorization type is the type of access allowed to an authorization object (e.g., read, update, create).

Both models consider positive and negative authorizations which are associated with user roles. Positive authorizations allow access to objects and negative authorizations override positive authorizations to prohibit access (in [6] this is further complicated by weak and strong authorizations which are not discussed here). The roles form a rooted directed acyclic graph called a role lattice which is a finite partially ordered set of user roles with greatest lower bound and least upper bound operators. Each node of the graph represents a role and a directed arc from role r to role r' (written $r > r'$) indicates that the positive authorizations for role r subsume the positive authorizations for role r'. A role can have multiple parent roles and all users who belong to the parents of a role also have all positive authorizations of the role. This subsumption of positive authorizations is transitive. That is, all ancestors of r, not just direct parents of r, subsume the positive authorizations of r.

As stated above, if a role has a positive authorization on an object, all roles that are higher in the role lattice receive the same authorization. Conversely, if a role is denied an authorization on an object (i.e., has a negative authorization), all roles that are lower in the role lattice are also denied the authorization. That is, positive authorizations are inherited up the lattice (from child to parent) and negative authorizations are inherited down the lattice (from parent to child).

The lattice of roles is very application dependent and often varies between databases. In the remainder of this paper we discuss a simple language to relate a new role to a pre-existing lattice of roles.

3 Interoperation via Dynamic Addition of Roles

A multidatabase system is a finite set of databases, each with its own role lattice. In order to interoperate between two databases with two different role lattices L_1 and L_2 the relationships which hold between some of the roles in the two lattices must be known. One possibility is for the administrators of the two databases to agree beforehand on an embedding of their two lattices inside a larger, shared lattice. However, in many applications, information sharing needs will not be precisely predictable beforehand, and some means of merging two lattices at run time is needed. A role calculus will provide for the dynamic merging of the role lattices and, thus, allow sharing of information without sacrificing security. For example, consider the "information highway," i.e., public access to information over the worldwide network. When a database is made accessible over the internet, one cannot predict in advance who the future users of the system will be. When a new user or program wants to access the database, we envision an authentication mechanism that will determine the appropriate privileges (roles) for the new subject. For example, the new subject may present the DBMS with a set of unforgeable certificates, which attest to roles the subject has obtained elsewhere in the network. The DBMS will verify the certificates with the help of a trusted authentication server, and then assign the new subject to roles based on the information in the certificates. In a user role based systems, this may require the dynamic creation of new roles to be merged into the existing lattice. Several techniques used to merge object-oriented class hierarchies show promise in solving role lattice merging problems.

Object-oriented class hierarchies denote the relationships between the classes in a lattice. These relationships are based on the attributes associated with each class. A class must have all of the attributes of all of the classes above it in the hierarchy. Several class insertion and class hierarchy merging algorithms have been developed, primarily to assist in the placement of new classes in class hierarchies. For example, [8] presents a methodology for supporting multiple views in object-oriented databases using a class integration algorithm. In order to apply this method to role lattices, inherited attributes must be assigned to roles describing the relationship of each role to other roles in the lattice.

Our approach is to assign properties to each role in the lattice based on their relative positions in the lattice. In our preliminary work we use the $\leq$ relationship to associate roles in different lattices. These associations are exploited by our lattice insertion algorithm to add a new role to a lattice. This translation must preserve not only the existing relationships between the roles in a single lattice but also preserve the security semantics of the roles. Adding a new role should not change relative authorizations of roles within the lattice. The lattice algorithm we have developed is a reworking of class hierarchy merging algorithms and is outlined below.

Lattice Insertion Algorithm

Input: a lattice L and a new role r with an associated set of $\leq$ relationships between r and L. Output: a new lattice L' that includes all the attributes of L and r.

1. Create a new lattice L' by copying L.

2. Create a new generator role: Let x be a role in L' and let S be the set of attributes that x and r have in common. If S is non-empty and L' does not contain a node whose set of attributes is exactly S, create a new role g and add it to L'. The location of g is determined by a depth first downward traversal of L'. The last role encountered on any branch whose attributes are a subset of S will be a direct parent of g, and the first role encountered on any branch whose attributes are a superset of S will be a direct child of g.

3. Repeat step 2 until a fixed point is reached.

4. Let the set S' be the set of attributes of r. If possible, rename a new generator role in L' to r, so that the renamed role now has S' as its attributes. Otherwise, a new role must be added to L' to represent r: determine the placement of r in L' by a depth first downward traversal of L'. The last role encountered on any branch whose attributes are a subset of S' is a direct parent of r, and the first role encountered on any branch whose attributes are a superset of S' is a direct child of r.

5. If a new leaf role was added to L', add a single new bottom role as the child of all leaf roles.

In other work (submitted for publication) we have shown that a more general version of this algorithm has two important properties: *relationship consistency* and *closeness*. The consistency property ensures that if there is any lattice that will respect all the security specifications in the input lattice as well as the input set of relationships for r, then the generalized algorithm will produce such a lattice as output. If no such lattice exists, then the generalized algorithm will suggest all of the best possible ways that the user can change the input set of relationships for r so that security can be preserved. The best possible changes are defined by a "closeness" test, which employs a metric of distance between the requested set Q of relationships for r and those subsets of Q that would preserve security. The generalized algorithm uses a metric for closeness that is generic, i.e., not specific to a particular security policy.

4 Research Agenda

Currently, a number of secure object-oriented database models emphasize security within a single database. We believe secure interoperation between these systems will become increasingly important. We have developed a Lattice Insertion Algorithm which dynamically adds new roles to existing user role lattices. The placement of a new role depends on the specification of relationships in a simple language. A role calculus will provide a more complete and flexible mechanism to establish relationships between role lattices. These relationships can then be exploited to allow more powerful flexible means of dynamic addition of roles to lattices.

In our current work we are also considering other facets of interoperation such as environments where the location and identity of potential users of the system are not known in advance, as in a database that is available for public access over networks. There are three main issues in this extension: verifying that users are who they claim to be, determining the appropriate permissions for the user, and, if necessary, creating and integrating new roles with exactly the permissions of the new user. In addition to secure interoperation, we are interested in other discretionary authorization issues including models which allow users to invoke methods which have more authority than the invoker and models which allow users to delegate tasks to other users.

References

[1] Jajodia S, Kogan B. Integrating an object-oriented data model with multilevel security. In Proceedings of the 1990 IEEE Symposium on Security and Privacy, pp 76–85, 1990.

[2] Keefe T, Tsai W, Thuraisingham B. SODA - a secure object-oriented database system. Computers and Security, 8(6), 1989.

[3] Lunt T. Multilevel security for object-oriented database systems. In Proceedings of the 3rd IFIP Workshop on Database Security, pp 199–209, 1990.

[4] Millen J, Lunt T. Security for object-oriented database systems. In Proceedings of the 1992 IEEE Symposium on Security and Privacy, pp 260–272, 1992.

[5] Morgenstern M. A security model for multilevel objects with bidirectional relationships. In Proceedings of the 4th IFIP Workshop on Database Security, pp 53–71, 1991.

[6] Rabitti F, Bertino E, Kim W, Woelk D. A model of authorization for next-generation database systems. ACM Transactions on Database Systems, 16(1), 1991.

[7] Rosenthal A, Herndon W, Thuraisingham B, Graubart R. Multilevel security for object-oriented database management systems. Working Paper WP-92B0000375, The MITRE Corporation, 1993.

234

[8] Rundensteiner E. Multiview: A methodology for supporting multiple views in object-oriented databases. In Proceedings of the 18th VLDB Conference, pp 187–198, 1992.

[9] Thuraisingham B. Multilevel secure object-oriented data model: Issues on noncomposite objects, composite objects, and versioning. Journal of Object-oriented Programming, 4, 1990.

[10] Ting T, Demurjian S, Hu M. A specification methodology for user-role based security in an object-oriented design model: Experience with a health care application. In Proceedings of the 6th IFIP Workshop on Database Security, 1992.

Author Index

Published in 1990–92

AI and Cognitive Science '89, Dublin City University, Eire, 14–15 September 1989
Alan F. Smeaton and Gabriel McDermott (Eds.)

Specification and Verification of Concurrent Systems, University of Stirling, Scotland, 6–8 July 1988
C. Rattray (Ed.)

Semantics for Concurrency, Proceedings of the International BCS-FACS Workshop, Sponsored by Logic for IT (S.E.R.C.), University of Leicester, UK, 23–25 July 1990
M. Z. Kwiatkowska, M. W. Shields and R. M. Thomas (Eds.)

Functional Programming, Glasgow 1989
Proceedings of the 1989 Glasgow Workshop, Fraserburgh, Scotland, 21–23 August 1989
Kei Davis and John Hughes (Eds.)

Persistent Object Systems, Proceedings of the Third International Workshop, Newcastle, Australia, 10–13 January 1989
John Rosenberg and David Koch (Eds.)

Z User Workshop, Oxford 1989, Proceedings of the Fourth Annual Z User Meeting, Oxford, 15 December 1989
J. E. Nicholls (Ed.)

Formal Methods for Trustworthy Computer Systems (FM89), Halifax, Canada, 23–27 July 1989
Dan Craigen (Editor) and Karen Summerskill (Assistant Editor)

Security and Persistence, Proceedings of the International Workshop on Computer Architectures to Support Security and Persistence of Information, Bremen, West Germany, 8–11 May 1990
John Rosenberg and J. Leslie Keedy (Eds.)

Women into Computing: Selected Papers 1988–1990
Gillian Lovegrove and Barbara Segal (Eds.)

3rd Refinement Workshop (organised by BCS-FACS, and sponsored by IBM UK Laboratories, Hursley Park and the Programming Research Group, University of Oxford), Hursley Park, 9–11 January 1990
Carroll Morgan and J. C. P. Woodcock (Eds.)

Designing Correct Circuits, Workshop jointly organised by the Universities of Oxford and Glasgow, Oxford, 26–28 September 1990
Geraint Jones and Mary Sheeran (Eds.)

Functional Programming, Glasgow 1990
Proceedings of the 1990 Glasgow Workshop on Functional Programming, Ullapool, Scotland, 13–15 August 1990
Simon L. Peyton Jones, Graham Hutton and Carsten Kehler Holst (Eds.)

4th Refinement Workshop, Proceedings of the 4th Refinement Workshop, organised by BCS-FACS, Cambridge, 9–11 January 1991
Joseph M. Morris and Roger C. Shaw (Eds.)

AI and Cognitive Science '90, University of Ulster at Jordanstown, 20–21 September 1990
Michael F. McTear and Norman Creaney (Eds.)

Software Re-use, Utrecht 1989, Proceedings of the Software Re-use Workshop, Utrecht, The Netherlands, 23–24 November 1989
Liesbeth Dusink and Patrick Hall (Eds.)

Z User Workshop, 1990, Proceedings of the Fifth Annual Z User Meeting, Oxford, 17–18 December 1990
J.E. Nicholls (Ed.)

IV Higher Order Workshop, Banff 1990
Proceedings of the IV Higher Order Workshop, Banff, Alberta, Canada, 10–14 September 1990
Graham Birtwistle (Ed.)

ALPUK91, Proceedings of the 3rd UK Annual Conference on Logic Programming, Edinburgh, 10–12 April 1991
Geraint A.Wiggins, Chris Mellish and Tim Duncan (Eds.)

Specifications of Database Systems
International Workshop on Specifications of Database Systems, Glasgow, 3–5 July 1991
David J. Harper and Moira C. Norrie (Eds.)

7th UK Computer and Telecommunications Performance Engineering Workshop
Edinburgh, 22–23 July 1991
J. Hillston, P.J.B. King and R.J. Pooley (Eds.)

Logic Program Synthesis and Transformation
Proceedings of LOPSTR 91, International Workshop on Logic Program Synthesis and Transformation, University of Manchester, 4–5 July 1991
T.P. Clement and K.-K. Lau (Eds.)

Declarative Programming, Sasbachwalden 1991
PHOENIX Seminar and Workshop on Declarative Programming, Sasbachwalden, Black Forest, Germany, 18–22 November 1991
John Darlington and Roland Dietrich (Eds.)

Building Interactive Systems:
Architectures and Tools
Philip Gray and Roger Took (Eds.)

Functional Programming, Glasgow 1991
Proceedings of the 1991 Glasgow Workshop on
Functional Programming, Portree, Isle of Skye,
12–14 August 1991
Rogardt Heldal, Carsten Kehler Holst and
Philip Wadler (Eds.)

Object Orientation in Z
Susan Stepney, Rosalind Barden and
David Cooper (Eds.)

Code Generation – Concepts, Tools, Techniques
Proceedings of the International Workshop on Code
Generation, Dagstuhl, Germany, 20–24 May 1991
Robert Giegerich and Susan L. Graham (Eds.)

Z User Workshop, York 1991, Proceedings of the
Sixth Annual Z User Meeting, York,
16–17 December 1991
J.E. Nicholls (Ed.)

Formal Aspects of Measurement
Proceedings of the BCS-FACS Workshop on
Formal Aspects of Measurement, South Bank
University, London, 5 May 1991
Tim Denvir, Ros Herman and R.W. Whitty (Eds.)

AI and Cognitive Science '91
University College, Cork, 19–20 September 1991
Humphrey Sorensen (Ed.)

5th Refinement Workshop, Proceedings of the 5th
Refinement Workshop, organised by BCS-FACS,
London, 8–10 January 1992
Cliff B. Jones, Roger C. Shaw and
Tim Denvir (Eds.)

Algebraic Methodology and Software
Technology (AMAST'91)
Proceedings of the Second International Conference
on Algebraic Methodology and Software
Technology, Iowa City, USA, 22–25 May 1991
M. Nivat, C. Rattray, T. Rus and G. Scollo (Eds.)

ALPUK92, Proceedings of the 4th UK
Conference on Logic Programming,
London, 30 March–1 April 1992
Krysia Broda (Ed.)

Logic Program Synthesis and Transformation
Proceedings of LOPSTR 92, International
Workshop on Logic Program Synthesis and
Transformation, University of Manchester,
2–3 July 1992
Kung-Kiu Lau and Tim Clement (Eds.)